D0849666

Yale University Press

New Haven and London

Valerie Hansen

Negotiating
Daily Life
in Traditional
China

How Ordinary
People
Used Contracts
600–1400

Published with the assistance of the Frederick W. Hilles
Publication Fund of Yale University and the Chiang
Ching-Kuo Foundation for International Scholarly
Exchange (USA).

Set in Trump type by Best-set Typesetter Ltd., Hong Kong.
Printed in the United States of America by Book Crafters,
Inc., Chelsea, Michigan.

Library of Congress Cataloging-in-Publication Data

Hansen, Valerie, 1958–
    Negotiating daily life in traditional China : how
  ordinary people used contracts, 600–1400 / Valerie
  Hansen.
    p. cm
  Includes bibliographical references and index.
  ISBN 0-300-06063-7 (cloth : acid-free paper)
    1. Contracts—China—History. 2. China—
  Economic conditions—To 1644. 3. China—
  Social conditions—221 B.C.–A.D. 960 4. China—
  Social conditions—960- 1644. I. Title.
  KNN858.H36   1995
  346.51'02—dc20
  [345.1062]   94-49177

A catalogue record for this book is available from the
British Library.

The paper in this book meets the guidelines for permanence
and durability of the Committee on Production Guidelines
for Book Longevity of the Council on Library Resources.

10 9 8 7 6 5 4 3 2 1

In memory of Marston Anderson and Anna Seidel

Contents

List of Illustrations   viii

Acknowledgments   ix

Note on Conventions   xi

Table of Equivalent Measures   xiii

1. Why Study Contracts?   1

Part I Contracting with People

2. The State's Reluctance to Recognize
   Private Contracts   17

3. Government Recognition of Contracts   47

4. The Age of Governmental Taxation   78

5. Contracts under Mongol Rule and
   Afterward   113

Part II Contracting with the Gods

6. Tomb Contracts   149

7. The Courts of the Underworld   189

8. The Courts of the Living and the Courts
   of the Dead   222

Appendix A Known Tomb Contracts   231

Appendix B Deities Named as Sellers
in Tomb Contracts   239

Glossary   243

Bibliography   251

Index   277

Frontispiece: Detail of Fig. 1

Illustrations

Figures

1. *Daily life in Turfan* 21

2. *Recycled paper as a historical source* 22

3. *Moneylender Zuo lends twenty silver coins* 37

4. *Widow Along goes to court (and wins)* 70

5. *How the illiterate signed documents* 72

6. *This-world money and underworld money* 169

7. *The most common tomb contract* 170

8. *The right way to bury tomb contracts* 177

9. *A contract in duplicate—one copy for the gods, one copy for the deceased* 186

10. *Protecting the dead from summonses* 201

Maps

1. *The borders of Tang China, 618–907* 18

2. *The borders of Song China, 960–1260* 79

3. *China under Mongol rule, 1260–1368* 114

4. *Distribution of tomb contracts written as in Earth Patterns* 160

5. *Jiangxi province* 197

Acknowledgments

I began this book in the spring of 1989, under a grant from the Committee on Scholarly Communication with the People's Republic of China, funded by the United States Information Agency, to work on rubbings held in the Beijing Library. The Center for Middle-Period History at Beijing University provided an academic base, and Zhang Guangda, Qu Chaoli, and Deng Xiaonan did their best to make me feel at home during that initially exhilarating but ultimately tragic spring. I drafted most of the book during a one-year leave on a Morse Fellowship from Yale University. The Centre for Asian Studies at Hong Kong University provided me with library facilities and a much-needed affiliation. The director, Edward Chien, and his able lieutenant, Coonor Kripalani-Thadani, were the most gracious of hosts. During that year I was able to read through Niida Noboru's pioneering works on contracts, discussed in chapter 1. Alison Conner, of the Law Department at Hong Kong University, provided stimulating companionship at lunch, a lawyer's point of view, and an apartment with a wonderful view of the harbor.

Other Yale funds made short research trips possible. The Griswold Fund enabled me to go to the Beijing Library, and later to the Jimbun Library in Kyoto. The Cheng and Lee Fund financed a visit to the Dunhuang collection at the Bibliothèque Nationale in Paris, a return trip to the Beijing Library, and preparation of the illustrations and maps. The librarians at these and other institutions, notably Ji Yaping in Beijing, Monique Cohen in Paris, and Rose Kerr at the British Museum all did their best to help me find the materials I needed.

The library staff at Yale, especially Kung Wen-k'ai, have been unfailingly helpful. And a generous subvention from Yale's Hilles Fund made publication possible.

Barend ter Haar wrote a long and thorough critique of the entire manuscript, as well as copious notes on each page. By the time I had studied his generous comments, I felt as if we had shared a month-long phone call between New Haven and Leiden. Bao Weimin deserves special thanks for checking all the translations. Chikusa Masaaki, Victor Mair, and Sugiyama Masaaki helped me make sense of several of the most difficult texts. Cynthia Brokaw read and commented on the entire manuscript, while experts in their fields reviewed individual chapters: chapter 2 (Wallace Johnson and Victor Mair), chapter 3 (Victor Mair), chapters 4 and 5 (Paul Smith). The book benefited from the participation of audiences at talks given at the Law Department and the Centre for Asian Studies at Hong Kong University, at Connecticut College, at Wesleyan University, and at the Traditional China seminar at Columbia University. An earlier version of chapter 6 was presented at the Second International Conference of Song Studies, held in August 1991 in Beijing, and has subsequently been published in Chinese. Su Zheng worked as my research assistant and found many tomb contracts in archeological journals. Donna Perry drew the maps, and Jan Murray and Richard Solaski made helpful design suggestions. Valuable references or ideas were provided by Richard Barnhart, John Chaffee, Emily Honig, Thomas Lee, Liu Heping, Joseph McDermott, Jan Murray, Jonathan Spence, Ellen Widmer, and Judith Zeitlin.

Any time the mother of two young daughters finishes a book, she has an enormous debt to those who helped with childcare. When there was only Lydia, her regular babysitters were unfailingly reliable. Others pitched in at crucial times. My beloved in-laws, Joe and Toni Stepanek, came all the way from Boulder to Hong Kong so that I could visit Dunhuang and Turfan the first time, and they are about to stay with Lydia and Claire so that I can go a second time. My greatest debt is to my husband, Jim, whose enthusiasm for this project, so far removed in time from his own interests, never flagged.

Note on Conventions

In the footnotes, primary sources are cited in italics and secondary sources in roman type.

If the citation is to a secondary work, the reference will read: (author, date of publication: page), with full publication information given in the bibliography.

References to primary sources, all in classical Chinese, read: (*title*, chapter or volume: page). In the case of texts that are divided not into numerically ordered sections but into named sections, the Chinese name of the relevant section (bieji, fulu, and the like) appears. Again, full publication information is in the bibliography. Because Chinese archeological journals give cumbersome titles to brief entries, often by unnamed scholars, I give the reference simply as: *name of journal* (most often, *Kaogu* and *Wenwu*), year, number, and page. When several photographs or figures appear on the same page, as they do in many Chinese books and archeological journals, I cite the page followed by the figure number.

To help readers unfamiliar with Asian languages, I cite previously published translations of passages in English, having checked the primary sources. When I have done my own translation, I cite the primary source first, followed by references to other translations. In the few instances when, after consulting the original text, I have retained much of someone else's translation, I cite that translation first, then the original passage.

Many of the contracts cited in chapters 2 and 3 have been reprinted in Yamamoto Tatsuro and Ikeda On's extraordinarily helpful two-part work *Tun-huang and Turfan Documents Concerning Social and Economic History*, volume 3, *Contracts*, parts A and B. Part B, published in 1986, consists of photographs of some of the contracts transcribed in part A and published in 1987. I cite by contract number, so a typical reference reads Yamamoto and Ikeda 1987:#260. The 1987 volume lists 499 contracts in the body of the text, 25 in the supplement (*bu*), and 12 for comparison (*Cankao*). On occasion, when I cite the photograph as well, the reference includes both parts and reads Yamamoto and Ikeda 1986:47; 1987:#260.

Personal names pose a dilemma. Should one simply romanize the Chinese? Or translate? In the interest of those who do not read Chinese and who will find the English equivalent easier to remember, I have translated personal names. Many are the numerical names in common use throughout the period; for instance, Zhu Ten-Thousand Seven, rather than Zhu Wanqi.

Because translations of official titles are according to Charles O. Hucker's *Dictionary of Official Titles in Imperial China*, interested readers will be able to look up the original Chinese titles in his English index. The Chinese titles in parentheses follow my own translation of any titles that do not appear in Hucker, and the characters appear in the glossary.

Table of Equivalent Measures

Length

Chinese inch (*cun*) = 2.8–3.1 centimeters

Chinese foot (*chi*) = 10 Chinese inches
= 28–31 centimeters

Step (*bu*) = 5 Chinese feet = 1.5 meters

Decafoot (*zhang*) = 10 Chinese feet
= 2.8–3.1 meters

Third-mile (*li*) = 300 or 360 steps = 440–556 meters

Volume

Pint (*sheng*) = 1.6–1.9 liters

Peck (*dou*) = 10 pints = 6–9 liters

Picul (*dan* or *hu*) = 10 pecks = 60–90 liters

Area

Sixth-acre (*mu*) = 450–600 square meters

Weight

Ounce (*liang*) = 37 grams

Catty (*jin*) = 16 ounces = 597 grams

Picul (*dan*) = 120 catties = 72 kilograms

Money

Cash = 1 bronze coin

String = 700–1,000 cash

Because all units of measure have varied across time and space, the modern equivalents can be only approximate.

Sources: Fan (1994):626–627; Jun and Hargett (1989):30; Ogawa (1985:1223–24).

1

Why Study

Contracts?

To most modern readers contracts suggest dry, multipage documents divorced from everyday existence. Happily, traditional Chinese contracts pulsate with life. They were used by people at all social levels, who paid scribes to draft contracts and then read them aloud. If literate, those who commissioned the contracts signed them. If not, they sketched their finger joints or drew their personal marks. People who used contracts were sufficiently familiar with legal language to alter stock texts to fit their own circumstances, and the details they inserted afford wonderfully informative glimpses of their concerns.

Most of the contracts in this book are about straightforward, sometimes poignant, transactions—the purchase, sale, or rental of a house, a plot of land, a draft animal, a slave, a concubine, even a child. Because of their widespread use, contracts illuminate how ordinary people experienced the massive changes spanning the years from 600 to 1400, the centuries of China's medieval transformation. This book tracks the process by which the legal standing of contracts was completely reversed. In 600, officials did not recognize contracts and used government registers to record land ownership. By 1400, the registers had fallen into disuse, and contracts had become the only proof of ownership.

At the beginning of the period covered by this book, the central government enjoyed an unprecedented level of control over both the countryside and the cities. Most peasants grew their foodstuffs and bought little, except perhaps salt, at local markets. Officials set prices every ten days and supervised weights and measures at the strictly regulated markets. Books were copied by hand and rare, and only the sons of powerful aristocratic families took the newly established civil service examinations. Under the equal-field system,

described in chapter 2, all land belonged to the emperor. Local officials conducted periodic surveys of land and households, reported their findings to
their superiors, and redistributed land every three years. Official land registers were the only basis of legal title. Contracts between individuals had no
legal status. The government recognized only those transactions that had
been registered with it, and the sale of land was illegal. As the system of
land registration and taxation broke down after 755, the emperor's claim to
ownership weakened. The central government simply did not have the
necessary manpower to draw up an annual census or the authority to force
people to give up their land. Increasingly, people started to buy and sell
land, as discussed in chapter 3, and contracts began to be the only reliable
record of changes of ownership.

Starting in the eleventh century, during the Song dynasty (960–1276),
Chinese society became more pluralistic, and its economy more market
driven and diversified. The economy developed so rapidly that some have
called the process a commercial revolution (Elvin 1973). Rich merchants conducted trade on a national scale. Many cultivators produced goods for local
markets, and many used money to purchase the foodstuffs they needed.
The emperor ruled with the assistance of a bureaucracy recruited through
civil service examinations, while a locally powerful gentry retained control
of the countryside and resisted any increases in the land tax. Instead, the
central government depended on indirect taxes from the salt, wine, and tea
monopolies to raise revenue. It also sought to increase the stamp tax on
contracts. As chapter 4 shows, the populace continued to use contracts but
failed to register them, and people resisted paying a sales tax on contracts
that had inched its way up to 15 percent by the end of the dynasty.

After centuries of fighting northern peoples, the Song dynasty was conquered by the Mongols in 1276. Among historians the Mongol regime is
known for its inefficiency and corruption (Li Gan 1985). Still, because the
Mongols linked the contract tax to the purchase of land, they seem to have
been far more successful than their predecessors in collecting it, as is
argued in chapter 5. The use of contracts continued under alien rule, and
the considerable number of foreigners resident in China at the time also
utilized contracts to record their purchases of livestock and land. By 1400,
officials were forced to depend on contracts as proof of ownership.

The sources for this study straddle the chasm between the years of
scarce, hand-copied manuscripts and the period, after the tenth century, of
more plentiful woodblock-printed books. The limited sources for the earlier
period overwhelmingly reflect the point of view of high bureaucrats

resident in the capital. Fortunately two enormously important, and very different, repositories of primary documents in northwest China provide a powerful antidote to the official record. Two hundred and fifty contracts from the seventh and eighth centuries survive from Turfan in the province of Xinjiang, with about the same number from the ninth and tenth centuries, from Dunhuang, Gansu. The five hundred contracts from Turfan and Dunhuang provide a convenient starting point for this book; other sources, often literary, from central China supplement these isolated contracts by illustrating how they were used.

After the tenth century, the number of extant contracts drops, with only about thirty surviving from the next four centuries. Most of these are for the purchase of land from one place—Huizhou, in modern Anhui province. Because there are so few contracts, noncontractual sources become even more important. Bureaucrats obsessed with collecting the stamp tax on contracts wrote about the population's attempts to evade the tax. They also compiled books of advice for new magistrates and recorded diverting, sometimes supernatural, tales about contracts in their miscellaneous notes. Rare legal sources provide further information: individuals giving depositions tell why they drew up contracts, and a casebook documents the populace's constant attempts to forge and twist contracts to suit its own purposes. Plays first performed under the Mongols have plots hinging on unusual contracts, and two Chinese-language textbooks for foreigners visiting China are crammed full of tips about contracts.

A different type of contract, those that were buried in tombs, provides an instructive comparison. More than two hundred are extant, from all over China, spanning the first to the twentieth centuries (see appendix A). These tomb contracts, the subject of chapter 6, clearly reflect the influence of real-world contracts and testify to the pervasive use of contractual thinking among the Chinese. Clauses in them address many of the same problems that real-world contracts do, including the resolution of prior claims, usually by earlier occupants of the same grave plot. Because these contracts were meant to enable the bearer (the deceased) to establish title in the afterlife, they shed light on the darkened courts of the underworld, discussed in chapter 7. These courts had the power to punish those who had gone unpunished during their lifetimes. While many of the penalties the courts administered to the spirits were the same as those in earthly law codes, crimes were defined differently. Some, like murder, were also criminal offenses in the real world. Others, like preventing someone's engagement, were not.

This study ends in the year 1400, for it would be impossible to give adequate coverage to the large number of contracts from different provinces in the Ming (1368–1644) and Qing (1644–1911) dynasties. Scholars who have recently begun to examine these contracts describe important regional differences, in both contractual phrasing and in land tenure, that are only suggested in the contracts from earlier periods.

Previous Approaches to the Study of Contracts

The following pages should make obvious my debt to Niida Noboru, whose pioneering study of Tang and Song documents ([1937] 1983) and subsequent work (1960a, 1962, 1964) opened up the study of Chinese law. Much of Niida's work consisted of locating and transcribing contracts, or records of them, in a wide range of sources including the standard histories, miscellaneous notes, epigraphical compendia, encyclopedias, and Dunhuang documents. He also looked at literary sources (1937) and tomb contracts (1938), all potential sources on China's legal tradition. In his voluminous studies he classifies contracts by type and analyzes their different clauses, but rarely translates them. Niida's many examples convince the reader of the ubiquity of contracts, yet his argument remains largely implicit. His work has been continued by other Japanese scholars, most notably Ikeda On, who has tried to analyze what contracts reveal about landlord-tenant relations (1973b, 1975, 1986), but whose overarching accomplishment has been, with Yamamoto Tatsuro, to publish all the contracts known to Niida as well as those subsequently discovered at Turfan and Dunhuang. The first volume of their study (Yamamoto and Ikeda 1986) consists of photographs of a selection of the contracts; the second (1987) gives indispensable transcriptions accompanied by a valuable English-language introduction. These two volumes have greatly facilitated my research. They also provide references to the considerable body of secondary literature, most of it in Chinese and Japanese.

Much of this literature engages in what I feel is the sterile exercise of trying to gauge, on the basis of isolated contracts, just how exploitative tenant-landlord relations were. Japanese historians writing in the years after World War II drew attention to the issue of land tenure in the centuries after the government no longer redistributed land. They posited the existence of manors analogous to the feudal estates of medieval Europe. One school, led by Sudō Yoshiyuki, saw all laborers as bound to the land, whereas the other side, led by Miyazaki Ichisada, argued that the existence of contracts implied that peasants were free agents. Neither side examined surviving contracts closely, and most Western scholars today question the very existence of those manors (Golas 1980, McDermott 1984). More recently, scholars interested in the nature of tenancy have turned their attention to contracts, but as one Chinese scholar has perceptively shown, different scholars have classed the identical contract as favoring the land-lord, favoring the tenant, or treating both equally (Kong 1983: 265). One simply cannot tell, on the basis of an out-of-context contract, what the relationship between two people was.

While some scholars have tried to read too much into a single contract, others have studiously ignored contracts that contradicted their vision of a harmonious, conflict-free society. In doing so, they were following the teachings of Confucius, who believed that man's innate goodness would emerge in ritual, that the sage ruler should govern by example, and that only the lesser ruler would stoop to governing by punishment. Although later Confucian thinkers came to acknowledge the role of law in punishing those whom ritual had failed to educate, Confucius's real legacy was a prejudice against law in favor of ritual and custom. It expressed itself in the conviction that gentlemen should fulfill their obligations simply because they were gentlemen. This vision of Chinese society is belied by the strong propensity to use contracts to define relationships with others, even with family members.

Still, because all educated men studied the classics first in learning to read and then in preparing for the civil service examinations, Confucius's highly idealistic view shaped legal thinking throughout the medieval period—and even today influences scholarship on Chinese legal history. If each person behaved as he should, it was thought, men of good character would have no reason to go to court because no conflicts would occur. Of course, the Chinese did go to court, and they went often. Throughout the years 600 to 1400 the judicial system at the local level consisted of the district magistrate, who heard cases in addition to his duties of governing the district, collecting taxes, and maintaining order. Depending on the severity of punishment, his superiors sometimes had to review his decision. Death sentences went all the way to the capital. Disputes about contracts and other civil matters stayed at the local level, with few instances of appeals to higher courts and many instances of repeated appeals as the parties vainly sought a settlement more to their liking (Miyazaki 1980:62, 66).

Although the Chinese did have occasion to go to court, their ideal remained for individuals to draft a private agreement without depending on the judicial system to enforce it. In this respect their understanding of contracts differed from the modern Western view, which sees a contract as "an agreement between two or more parties which the law makes enforceable, provided certain conditions are met" (MacCormack 1990:235). Modern lawyers use the concept of consideration to distinguish between contracts that the government will enforce, and deeds and promises that it will not. The distinction is a fine one. In the words of one authority on modern contract law, "In the normal course of events, the promisee will prove that the consideration conferred some benefit on the promisor, or that it imposed some detriment on the promisee himself" (Atiyah 1971:64). Hugh Scogin (1994:32–36) has ably described the analytic pitfalls of using the definition of contract, itself the product of the last two centuries, as a standard against which to measure traditional Chinese contracts.

A Working Definition

Traditional Chinese contracts had both an oral and a written component. They had to be written, but because so many people could not read or write, they were also read aloud at the time of signing. The contents of written contracts were fixed in a way that no oral agreement could be. Even illiterate people needed the certainty of written agreements: many contracts from Dunhuang end with the line, "For fear that there will be no proof later on, we draw up this contract." Variations of this sentence continue to appear in contracts as late as the nineteenth and twentieth centuries (Myers and Chen 1976:7).

Yet traditional Chinese contracts were also oral. A short story, "The Tale of Li Wa," set before 790, describes the reading of a contract. The author, Bai Xingzhen (d. 824), tells of two rival funeral houses that agree to stage a competition to see which shop has better mourners and musical instruments. One of the owners proposes these terms to the other: " 'The loser will be fined 50,000 coins to pay for wine and food; is that acceptable?' The two sides agreed and then summoned someone to draw up the contract, who took the signatures of the guarantors and then read the contract out loud" (*Tangren xiaoshuo* 1978:103; reference courtesy of Judith Zeitlin).

The story provides crucial documentation of a little-discussed practice: reaching an oral agreement before drafting a contract. The speed with which the two men are able to have the contract drafted indicates that writing contracts was an everyday occurrence in eighth-century Changan. It is merely an incidental detail in the story, but inasmuch as the contract does not figure in the subsequent development of the plot, the author would have no reason to distort the process of contract writing.

This book includes several other contract signings in which a contract is read aloud. Most occur in plays in which the audience needs to know the contents of a contract, but the novel *The Water Margin* tells of a bill of divorce that is read out, and the Chinese-language textbook *Old China Hand* contains a lesson in which a broker reads a contract to the merchants who commissioned it. The reading took place at the time of signing so that all present would be familiar with the terms of the agreement.

Chinese contracts were read aloud because they derived from the blood covenants (*meng*) of the seventh and sixth centuries B.C. These agreements between two equal parties, usually states, were not binding until a pre-scribed ritual had been performed and the gods had witnessed the agree-ment (Lewis 1990:43–50). Upon completion of the sacrifice, the spirits were summoned and the agreement was read out. The participants called on dif-ferent gods—those of the Yellow River, of the hills, even the sun—to witness their oath. The sacrificed animal and one copy of the text were placed in the earth, while another copy was placed in an archive specifically for such agreements (Chen 1966:271–273; Dobson 1968:271). When the founder of the Han dynasty (202 B.C.–A.D. 220), Emperor Gaozu, made a pact with his followers, they modified the ancient practice by sacrificing a white horse, which symbolized heaven. They then wrote the text of the agreement in red on iron tallies, which they kept safe in a golden box within a stone chest (Seidel 1983:311; *Han shu* 1B:8a).

The very long history of Chinese contracts challenges Sir Henry Maine's assertion that the most important development in human society was the shift from "status to contract" (1861:170). Like other nineteenth-century theorists, he saw all societies developing along the same path, with primitive societies treating individuals on the basis of family and social ties and more advanced societies replacing those ties with contractual ones. Given that the earliest written records mention contracts, one has to ques-tion whether a society based on status ever existed in China. Evidence testifying to the use of contracts shows clearly that, as early as the Han dynasty and perhaps before, people went to court over disputes, a finding confirmed by archeological materials (Hu and Feng 1983; Scogin 1990). The earliest surviving dated land contracts go back to the first century A.D., and scholars agree that private sales of land occurred even earlier, perhaps in the fifth or fourth centuries B.C. (Hulsewé 1978:13).

One of the earliest sources on law, the Confucian classic *The Rites of Zhou*, links contracts with suing in the courts. Traditional scholars dated the text to the ancient Zhou dynasty (1027?–256 B.C.), whereas most modern scholars see it as a text from the fourth or third century B.C. (Loewe 1993:24–29). *The Rites of Zhou* states that "one uses the *zhi*-type and the *ji*-type of contract to make a binding agreement and to prevent lawsuits" (*Shisanjing* 14:734b; Niida [1937] 1983:38; Scogin 1990:1400). Scholars have puzzled over the meaning of zhi and ji in this passage. Are they a compound? Or do they denote two types of contracts? The passage suggests that increased use of contracts would result in fewer suits, an unlikely outcome from a modern perspective. Elsewhere the text says that zhi-type contracts were used in the big markets, ji-type in the small (*Shisanjing* 15:737b); but the difference between the two is not explained.

In trying to clarify this point, later analysts have revealed something of the use of contracts in their own times. The Han-dynasty commentator Zheng Xuan (127–200) took zhiji as a compound and said "zhiji is a term for two copies of the same text, which are separated, like the lower-the-hand (*xiashoushu*) contracts of today." "Lower-the-hand" referred to a type of contract that gave the text of the agreement twice and was torn in the middle, so that each party retained a copy. Discussing the same passage in the mid-seventh century, the Tang commentator Jia Gongyan (fl. 650) said "lower-the-hand contracts in the Han are similar to today's finger-joint contracts, which are the same as the ancient zhiji contracts" (*Shisanjing* 14:734b; Niida [1937] 1983:38). Such contracts, with each person drawing three lines to represent his joints, have been found at Turfan in northwest China; an example is shown in figure 3 (see chapter 2). And in the Song dynasty, Huang Tingjian (1045–1105) added his own explanation: "How is it that today even the poorest people cast off their wives and trace their hands on contracts? If they do not trace their hands, then today when people make a contract to hire a maidservant, they draw their joints if they cannot write. This practice is so common that in the lower Yangzi valley, contracts for land and houses also use the tracing of hands" (*Huang Shangu*, bieji 11:16b). All these writers bear witness to the use of contracts in their own time, be it the second century, the seventh, or the eleventh; and their comments are borne out by foreign visitors.

One of the most detailed descriptions of a Chinese contract comes from an anonymous Arab merchant known as Sulaiman, who visited China in 851 and whose notes were published in about 916: "If a man lends a sum of money to someone, he writes a note to him; the borrower in turn writes a note, which he marks with two of his fingers together, the middle and the index fingers. The two notes are placed and folded together, and several characters are written in the place where they join. They are then unfolded and the note by which the borrower acknowledges his debt is returned to the lender" (Reinaud 1845:42–44; Sauvaget 1948:19–20; Niida [1937] 1983:76n45).

This comment shows how the process of drawing up a contract looked to someone who could not read Chinese. The observer does not realize that the characters drawn on the seam of the two contracts were those meaning "contract," *hetong*. He implies that the borrower inked two fingers and printed them on the contract, when the usual custom was to draw lines at the joints. Occasionally a person would make an impression of a finger, a hand, or even feet and hands (Zhang Chuanxi 1982:30). Some of the details are not quite accurate, but Sulaiman's account shows that use of and respect for contracts distinguished the Chinese from their neighbors, even in the ninth century.[1]

Another Chinese practice that drew the attention of foreign visitors was the inking of finger joints. Although the spacing of finger joints varies only slightly from person to person, the Chinese believed that three lines drawn at the joints could prove anyone's participation in a disputed agreement. When the Persian chronicler Rashīd al-Dīn visited China in 1304, he commented: "It is usual in Cathay, when any contract is entered into, for the outline of the fingers of the parties to be traced upon the document. For experience shows that no two individuals have fingers precisely alike. The hand of the contracting party is set upon the back of the paper containing the deed, and lines are then traced round his fingers up to the knuckles, in order that if ever one of them should deny his obligation this tracing may be compared with his fingers and he may thus be convicted" (Yule [1914] 1966, 3:123).

One case is always cited in connection with this practice. A magistrate in the fourteenth century was able to detect a forged contract by carefully

1. The Chinese were not the only people to use contracts at this time. Starting in about the ninth century, the English wrote duplicate copies of agreement. They cut them apart at the seam, where they often wrote the word "cyrographum," meaning handwritten. In one such agreement a widow agreed to plow fields, perform other duties, and pay money rent to Gloucester Abbey in 1230 (Clanchy 1979:35, 65n17, plate VII).

examining the lines of the finger joints. He reasoned that the joints of a thirteen-year-old boy should be much closer together than those of an adult (*Muan ji* 22:15a). The case showed only that a child's finger joints are spaced more closely than an adult's—not that the finger joints of two adults can be differentiated.

Drawing one's finger joints was much like the practice of drawing an X on contracts in the West: the mark itself did not constitute sufficient evidence to prove participation. Much more convincing would have been the testimony of the guarantors and the witnesses, who could vouch whose mark it was. Witnesses offered an independent check on the contents of any contract; they could be consulted if anyone suspected that the contract had been tampered with. To give but one example: when a judge in Zhejiang in the mid-thirteenth century was presented with a contract he suspected was forged, he summoned the cultivator, the guarantor, and the witnesses to testify (*Qingmingji* 9:302–303).

The guarantors had good reason to be accurate witnesses because they were personally liable for any of the debt the borrower or his immediate family failed to repay. In modern contracts guarantors are paid for their services; they may also have been in the past, although no records of payment survive. One fourteenth-century source tells of a man who buys a young boy to be his servant and needs to hurry home because his guarantor will serve for only one hundred days.

Chinese contracts, then, were written agreements between two or more parties to buy, sell, rent, or borrow a given commodity. The Chinese had a variety of terms for them (*hetong, quan, qi, qiyue*). These agreements gave the name of the weaker party, often omitting that of the stronger. After being read out, they were signed by witnesses and guarantors.

What Contracts Show

This book uses contracts to highlight the medieval transformation. Anyone reading about the redistribution of land under the equal-field system has to question whether the government of the Tang dynasty enjoyed the control described by our largely bureaucratic sources. The government may have forbidden the sale of land except under exceptional circumstances, but contracts from Turfan show that people did buy and sell land. They also violated the government's strict regulations about the sale of livestock and slaves. Contracts from Dunhuang make it possible to see how people adjusted to the decline of the equal-field system in subsequent centuries.

The economy of the Tang was largely a barter economy, with trade strictly regulated by the government. Many of the recorded transactions describe the use of cloth, grain, and some silver coins. The use of money continued to expand in succeeding centuries. Four times as many copper coins were issued in the eleventh century as in the eighth, although the population stayed constant at sixty million (Hartwell 1978). Paper money was introduced, for the first time in world history, in the eleventh century (Elvin 1973:156–59). Government officials realized that even with more coins and paper money, not enough money was in circulation, and in 1141 an edict permitted gold, silver, and silk to be used to buy land, as long as each commodity was converted into money at its fair market value (*Qingmingji* 4:122). As the increasingly desperate government printed more money, inflation resulted and further complicated exchange rates. Prices in contracts from the twelfth and thirteenth centuries are given in paper money, but because contracts always specify the year in which the money was issued, it is evident that the value of paper money varied depending on the year it was printed. The simultaneous use of these different media of exchange must have been very inconvenient. Prices after the fall of the Mongols are given in ounces of silver, not in coins, betraying the collapse of both paper money and government coinage. Contracts make it possible to trace a complete cycle in the use of money, from silver to paper money and back to silver again.

Contracts also illuminate the educational levels in Chinese society. The same contract records the names of people at very different levels of literacy: some write their names easily, some can draw personal marks only with difficulty, and some can do neither. Examination candidates and officials who studied the literary language for years could express themselves easily in writing. Merchants and the affluent could read and write simple letters, while most peasants could not read at all.

Scholars have long suspected that the increased use of woodblock printing in the tenth and eleventh centuries led to increased literacy as well, and evidence about contracts confirms their hunch. A houseboy caught stealing money from his master offered as compensation a servant girl, with a simple contract on her arm saying that she belonged to the master forever. He was not alone in his ability to draft such a contract. Judges writing court decisions in the thirteenth century confronted a host of forgeries and a populace skilled in the use of documents. Still, knowledge of contractual language was not limited to those who could read and write. An illiterate milknurse appearing in a play was able to dictate a contract to a peddler who recorded it.

The women who appear in contracts owned land and had the power to sell it. Like men, they drew their mark or sketched their joints, but they drew the middle finger of their right hand, not their left, as shown in figure 5 (see chapter 3). Dependent as women were on their fathers and husbands, their economic standing could suddenly plunge. One widow was forced to sell some of her land after her son was sent to a neighboring town for breaking the law. She was not completely defenseless, though, for she successfully brought suit against a squatter and got her land back.

The women in the contracts are not just purchasers or sellers but also the commodity sold. The sale of one eleven-year-old girl in 731 fit Tang regulations perfectly; she could only be purchased after five guarantors vouched that she was not a commoner sold to pay off a debt. Dramatic economic growth increased family size as men took concubines, and the size of the market in women grew correspondingly (Ebrey 1993). Starving women could sell themselves to brokers, who resold them as concubines without inquiring into their family background. Twelfth-century sources report the kidnapping of women for the same purpose. People debated whose claim to a woman was stronger—her original husband's or her purchaser's.

The families in this book differ sharply from the stereotype of the unchanging Chinese nuclear family. The complicated products of remarriages, adoptions, and divorces, they remind us of the difficulty of producing a surviving male heir in an age of extremely low life expectancy. As in our own time, divorce sometimes benefited women and sometimes hurt them. One angry woman, who was able to obtain a divorce and custody of her last unmarried daughter, went on to found a successful business. Another wept on discovering that her husband had divorced her without consulting her. People involved in divorce disputes remarried quickly, often within a year, suggesting that Chinese families were far more fluid at this time than previously thought. These were the centuries when women's lives became more constricted. Foot binding, introduced in the tenth century, was widespread by the fourteenth, and remarriage of divorced and widowed women was increasingly frowned on.

Daily life from 600 to 1400 consisted of a series of transactions to buy, sell, or rent land, animals, people, or money. Once ordinary people made the decision to sell something, often because they were short of money, they had to find a buyer and arrange for a contract to be drafted. They used a text that anticipated the subsequent claims that could and did arise. After the contract was read to them, they signed it or drew their marks. People were so familiar with contracts that they conceived of death in much the same terms as they understood life. They armed their dead with contracts asserting ownership of their grave plots, to be used in a full-fledged subterranean court system. The pages that follow explain how ordinary people living between 600 and 1400 used contracts to negotiate daily life—and to reduce death's perils.

Part One

*Contracting
with
People*

2

The State's

Reluctance

to Recognize

Private

Contracts

In 618, after overthrowing the Sui dynasty, the first Tang emperor established a dynasty that was to rule China for the next three centuries (map 1). The Tang was a time of extensive contact with the foreign peoples who traveled along the Silk Road from India and Central Asia. It came to stand as an ideal for later dynasties, including its successor, the Song, and is now thought by many to mark the peak of China's cultural development.

The Tang Code

One of the lasting accomplishments of the Tang was *The Tang Code*, promulgated in 653 and surviving today in its 737 reissue. *The Tang Code* does not devote a separate unit to contracts, but relegates the few provisions about them to a section containing miscellaneous articles, suggesting that they may have been a later addition (Twitchett 1966; MacCormack 1985, 1990). Those few provisions, though, capture the state's unwillingness to intervene in private transactions, just at a time when contracts were used increasingly to record those same transactions.

The Tang Code is a clear statement of how things should be, according to Confucian principles. Superiors may beat inferiors; husbands, their wives; and fathers, their sons—but not vice versa. A reading of the code gives the strong impression that those who drafted it sought to cover all possible, and some impossible, contingencies. For example, the code bars illicit sexual intercourse not just with one's close relatives but also with female first cousins once removed on one's father's side, with one's father's and grandfather's concubines, and even with one's paternal great aunts (*Tanglü shuyi* 26:493–495 [articles 411–413];

Map 1. The Borders of Tang China, 618–907, superimposed on modern provincial boundaries. At the height of Tang power (640–755), cities as far west as Turfan and Dunhuang were under direct central government rule. (Drawn by Donna Perry.)

Johnson 1979:288). Because of its goal of inclusiveness, the code is a convenient starting place to look at laws governing the use of contracts. Yet *The Tang Code* was not the only law of the Tang. Statutes (*ling*), regulations (*ge*), and ordinances (*shi*) could all supplement and supersede the code (Twitchett 1957–58:23–36; Ikeda, Yamamoto, and Okano 1980:8–15). The statutes of the Tang have been collected by the famous Japanese legal scholar Niida Noboru, but only a small portion of the regulations and ordinances survive. So while it is possible to examine the original legislation of the Tang, one rarely knows how it was amended in the course of the dynasty (Johnson 1979:5).

One of the first acts of the Song, in 963, was to reissue *The Tang Code* under a new title, *The Penal Code of the Song* (*Song xingtong*). The two codes are largely the same (Langlois 1981). The Song version does include a few more provisions about contracts passed in the course of the Tang. The new title captures the thrust of the original code: penal law took up far more of the code's contents than did civil law. Even though regular redistribution of land had not taken place since 755, and would not take place under Song rule either, the Song compilers retained all the provisions in the code about land redistribution. As it assumes the continuing existence of the Tang land system, so too does it assume the continuing existence of the tightly regulated markets, divided into sections, in which officials set prices every ten days. Like the land system, this system of market regulation assuredly died out after the eighth century; if it ever existed, it did so only in the seventh century.

Why would the Song adopt a code that was so obviously out of date? The goal of the rulers must not have been to write a new code to fit the changed social and economic conditions of the tenth century. They certainly knew the empire was not the same as it had been in the seventh century, when *The Tang Code* was promulgated. They reissued the code because they wanted their new dynasty to be just as glorious as the Tang. They also knew that they could amend the code and that the code did not constitute the law that officials consulted on a day-to-day basis (McKnight 1987). In short, they adopted *The Tang Code* for its symbolic value, not for its content. The same must have been true of the Japanese, who adopted the code in the eighth century; of the Koreans, who did so in the tenth century; and of the Vietnamese, who did so in the fifteenth century (Johnson 1979:9).

The Turfan Documents

Since the beginning of the century, historians have wondered if the system described in *The Tang Code* existed anywhere but on paper. Did the Tang really have the resources to carry out triannual population and land surveys? to supervise markets? to prevent the enslavement of commoners? The only data available to answer these questions lie in the Turfan depression, in what is now Xinjiang province, along what were the very fringes of the Tang empire (map 1).

Turfan is so remote that it is the farthest point on earth from any ocean. Its lowest point, Lake Aiding, lies 156 meters below sea level. Surrounded by high mountains on all sides, the depression receives few breezes, and with the Taklamahan Desert to the southwest, it has little rainfall. It is a hot, dry place with temperatures averaging 38°C (100°F) in the three months of the summer, sometimes reaching 47°C (117°F). In the thirteenth and fourteenth centuries some Chinese gave Turfan the name Huozhou (prefecture of fire), a wordplay on the region's name under the Mongols, Hezhou (Hu 1987:2–9). Because the sand has been recorded at temperatures of 82°C (180°F), people nowadays bury themselves in it to enjoy its therapeutic powers. Turfan's wonderfully dry climate is ideal for preserving textiles, wood, leather, paper, food, and even fragile silk artificial flowers.

The region may be hot, but it is not desolate. The word *turfan* originally probably denoted a "fortified [tax-collecting station]" and in Uighur Turkic has come to mean "fertile and flourishing" (Mair 1990:36–37). Its underground waterways allow the cultivation of melons, grapes, and mulberries. In 1959 an irrigation channel was redirected through the Astana graveyard of what had once been the medieval city of Gaochang, whose ruins survive today. Salvage excavations began. Between 1959 and 1975 in two graveyards, Astana and Karakhoja, 456 tombs were excavated, of which all but one had been opened earlier—either by local plunderers or by foreign marauders at the beginning of the century. Many of the artifacts that Sir Aurel Stein took from Astana are now on view in the Delhi Museum, and the several thousand fragments of documents that Count Ōtani collected have recently been published (Oda 1984, 1990). The visitor to Turfan can still view a few of the artless wall paintings in the tombs of commoners buried there (fig. 1).

Among the artifacts left behind by the various grave robbers were ten thousand fragments of documents, spanning the years 273–778. Five percent of the documents date to the period before the establishment of the Gaochang kingdom in 502; 30 percent, from the Gaochang kingdom; and 65 percent, from after 640, when the Tang took control (Hu 1987:104). In one of the great labors of the century, Chinese historians based at Wuhan University painstakingly pieced these fragments together to form sixteen hundred documents, including two hundred fifty contracts, which have been subsequently published (*Tulufan chutu wenshu*). Even these reconstructed documents are incomplete, as the scarcity of paper in northwest China dictated that scrap paper be cut up and used again, often to make soles for shoes for the dead (fig. 2). One figurine of a dancer has arms made of thirty-three twisted pawn tickets from Changan, which include receipts

Fig. 1. Daily Life in Turfan. This portrait, from tomb 13 at Astana, shows a prosperous householder with his wife, alongside his possessions and servants. Prepared on six separate sheets pasted together, the artwork dates to the fourth or fifth century and is one of the earliest surviving Chinese paintings on paper.

The deceased, in the center, sits on a raised platform under an elaborate canopy, holding a fan. Just under the fan is his writing brush and inkstone. A shade tree, with a bird perched on a branch, grows over his head. His wife stands nearby. To her left, an almost identical, but smaller, female cooks over a bed of coals, in a kitchen equipped with a foot-driven pounding tool, two clay ovens for bread, and two water cisterns. Behind her are stacked plates and jugs, and in the background is a field with a fruit tree; rakes lie unused on the ground. The sun is in the upper right corner, and in the opposite corner is the moon. The Big Dipper appears in two positions to the left and right of the tree, showing different times of day. Beneath the moon a male servant tends a horse pulling a small chariot. The lack of artistry in this mural and others from Astana suggests that most of those buried at Turfan were ordinary people.

Surviving documents reveal that this couple's contemporaries would have used contracts to buy, sell, or rent any of the pictured items, whether land, orchard, house, draft animal, or slave. (Xinjiang Uighur Autonomous District Museum 1987, plate 142.)

for pawned pieces of cloth ranging in value from twenty to eighteen hundred coins (Chen 1983a). Still other fragments were pasted together to make papier-mâché coffins. Because these documents were not selected with any particular bias, they provide a genuinely random sample of written materials circulating at the time.

Anyone using the Turfan materials must confront the issue of typicality. Is it possible to judge the use of contracts in the Tang on the basis of evidence from such a remote outpost of the Tang empire? The most compelling reason to try is that the Turfan materials constitute the only body of primary, randomly preserved documents from the seventh and eighth centuries. A few of the documents unearthed at Turfan, like the pawn tickets of the doll's arm, come from central China, but the vast majority are local. They provide a grassroots view of Tang rule during its first one hundred fifty years, when the dynasty enjoyed its greatest power and had not yet been weakened by the An Lushan rebellion of 755.

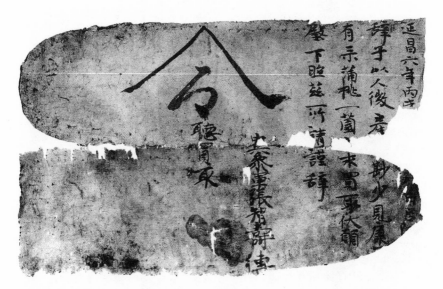

Fig. 2. Recycled Paper as a Historical Source. Unlike the official chronicles and bureaucratic records underlying most histories of China, the contract pictured here was preserved by accident, as were other documents cited throughout this book. The soles of these paper shoes for the dead were cut from a discarded contract to buy a grape orchard. Clearly visible are the stitching holes along the edge of the two shoe linings, which measure 40 by 24 centimeters. The soles were excavated in 1972 from the Turfan tomb of Lu Aqing. (Reprinted from Xinjiang Museum 1975a:42, fig. 69.)

On a present-day visit to Turfan, the most striking evidence that one is
not in central China is the presence of Muslims: veiled women sell ice
cream and work in the fields. Because Islam did not come to northwest
China until the tenth and eleventh centuries, the ancestors of these
Muslims who lived in the Tang dynasty were Buddhists, Zoroastrians,
believers in local cults, or most likely a mixture of all three. The Astana
tombs provide a variety of evidence indicating that Turfan was a culturally
mixed city in the Tang. Faces on tomb figurines show the same variations
that are evident today. The Astana tombs also bear witness to the coexist-
ence of northern Chinese and Central Asian cuisines. Chinese wonton and
meat dumplings cooked for the dead have been found there, as has the
brittle, pinpricked bread of the Middle East that one still sees for sale in the
streets of Turfan.

The high proportion of contracts at Turfan, two hundred fifty from
among sixteen hundred documents, speaks to the importance of contracts
to peoples who did not necessarily know Chinese. Because the non-Chinese
adopted Chinese names, it is impossible to decide which names on contracts are foreign, but some reveal the signatories to be merchants from
Sogdia, now Samarkand (Yamamoto and Ikeda 1987:#29, #32; Hu 1987:63).
Turfan today is home to many Chinese, but since the last thousand years
have been a time of continuous Chinese expansion into outlying regions, it
probably felt much more diverse during the Tang dynasty. Many of the
Chinese who settled in Turfan had been exiled or deported there. Two
contracts surviving from central China (to be discussed below) match up
with the Turfan contracts so closely that they suggest a surprising degree of
uniformity of contractual language, even at a time when China was not
united. Although contracts in languages other than Chinese do not survive
and so cannot be compared, the close resemblance between the Turfan and
central Chinese contracts suggests little foreign influence on the wording of
the Turfan contracts.

Turfan first came under Chinese rule in 48 B.C. during the Han dynasty.
In the centuries that followed, different polities formed and collapsed in
the Turfan depression, some influenced by the Turkic (Tujue) peoples to the
west, some by the Chinese to the southeast. Even in this early period, the
people of Turfan used contracts. One of the earliest, dated 367, says: "Wang
Nian sells Camel Ci to Zhu Yue and receives Camel Jia. Neither side
profits. If either camel absconds, the two owners will each resolve the
problem. If someone changes his mind about the transaction, he will be

fined ten carpets to contribute to the other party" (Yamamoto and Ikeda 1987:#2; Hou 1982). The names of a witness and the person who wrote the contract follow, although the rest of the contract is missing. This contract is almost a snapshot of life in Turfan: one can picture the two men agreeing to exchange their camels, one of whom is named Superior, and the other Ci, for his origins in Kucha (called Qiuci at the time).[1] The penalty for breaking the agreement is not money, which was not extensively used at such an early period, but rugs, which continue to be valued highly even today. This contract hints at a legal sophistication that historians know must have existed in China since the Han dynasty (Lin 1989; Scogin 1990), if not earlier, but about which little information survives.

In 502 the Qu family, who lived near the modern city of Lanzhou in Gansu province (see map 1), united the region, established their capital at Gaochang, and named their city gates after those at the capital city of Luoyang. In line with this Turkic family's policy of encouraging cultural contacts with the Chinese, the first Qu ruler requested texts of the classics and the histories, as well as Chinese teachers from the Northern Wei dynasty (386–534). Fragments of *The Book of Songs* (*Shijing*), *The Classic of Filial Piety* (*Xiaojing*), and *The Analects* (*Lunyu*) have all been found at Astana, testifying to the knowledge of Chinese among the people of Gaochang, or at least among their scribes (Hu 1987:39–42).

Land Contracts

Providing even more eloquent testimony of Chinese influence at Gaochang are the Chinese-language contracts that survive from the period of rule by the Qu family. Contracts for the purchase of land, houses, and slaves, for loans of grain, cloth, and money, for the renting of land, and for the hiring of labor all survive. One of the earliest surviving land contracts dates to 541. Much of it is missing, but the number of recurring standard phrases makes it possible to reconstruct most of the original text:

1. If one takes the character *ci* to mean "this," then the sentence reads, "Wang Nian sells this camel to Zhu Yue and receives a good camel."

In the eleventh year of the Zhanghe reign era, someone [name missing] buys 5 sixth-acres of unfertile land by Kong Jing's ditch from Zuo Fode. The northern border extends to the ditch, the east shares the same border as Fan Si's land, the south . . . and the west borders on Cao Lingsi's land. [The sentence fixing the price in rugs is incomplete.] Within these four borders, anything extra will not be returned and anything short will not be made up for. The buyer and the seller first reached an agreement and then drew up a contract. Once the contract is drawn up, neither party can cancel the agreement. Should one party cancel the contract, he must pay a fine in rugs to the party who does not cancel. Commoners have private agreements they are obliged to fulfill. The buyer and seller each sign their name to show good faith, and they divide the cost of the wine.

Scribe [   ]
Witness A Shun
[hole] Shun [hole]
[contract torn here]

(Yamamoto and Ikeda 1987:#4)

This is a straightforward contract marking the sale of a plot of land, for which the boundaries are given, for a price in rugs. The stock phrase about reaching an oral agreement (*he*) and then drawing up a written contract (*quan*) refers to the making of an offer and its acceptance. The contract provides for only one contingency: the possibility that either party will back out of the agreement. The next clause emphasizes this is a private agreement that commoners are obliged to uphold, and so distinguishes it from a transaction involving officials. The sharing of wine upon completion of the deal is a standard practice that goes back to ancient China and continues to this day in the form of a banquet after the contract is signed.

Land contracts were also in use in northern China at this time. The unscrupulous brother of one regional ruler, Xiao Hong (473–526), lent money for a fixed term to people who put up their fields, houses, and stores as collateral. When they failed to make the necessary payments, he seized their property (*Nanshi* 51:1278; Balazs 1954:122n121). The texts of these contracts are not extant; but two contracts, one from Lingtai county, Gansu, and one from Zhuoxian, Hebei, provide a rare opportunity to compare a Turfan contract with its Chinese counterparts. After the date, 477, the contract from Gansu reads:

Guo Mengji of Chungu buys 35 sixth-acres of land from his older
brother, Yizong, to be his family's land forever, and pays 40 pecks of
grain. The land is not stolen. If someone claims the land,
compensation should be found for this plot. The price of grain at the
time is 1 picul 5 pecks, equaling 50 catties and worth 40 Chinese
feet of cloth. To the south of the land is a big road, south of which
is Guo Qi's land. To the west is Guo Fengqi's land. To the east is
Luo Hou's and Guo Qin's land. The north faces the Baonan
mountains.

    Once the contract tally is broken, neither side may change its
mind.

Witness Guo Yuanzhi
Text according to Guo Qi, Guo Seng, Guo Qin, and Seng Ren

(Yamamoto and Ikeda 1987:cankao #10; Liu Qingzhu 1983:94)

In addition to giving the borders of the plot and the procedure to be followed
should someone else claim the plot, this contract records the price of the
plot in grain, in units of volume and weight, and in value in cloth. Written
on a brick, the contract contains the unique clause specifying that it takes
effect at the time the tally is broken, that is, the two halves of the brick are
separated. Although this text does not name a scribe, the last line indicates
that four men, two of whom owned adjacent plots, dictated its contents.
Written in misshapen characters of uneven size in crooked lines, it testifies
to the use of contracts among common people—and even among brothers,
who, according to Confucian teachings, should have trusted each other and
so not have needed a contract.

    The 477 contract is from Gansu, just to the west of Xi'an. The 507
contract comes from a tomb in Zhuo county, Hebei, just southwest of
modern Beijing. After giving the date, it says:

Zhang Shenluo of the northern quarter buys 3 sixth-acres of tomb
land from his fellow county-dweller Lu Adou. To the south is the
tomb of Qi Wang, the northern border is 265 Chinese feet long. To
the east is the tomb of Qi Tu, and the western border is 60 Chinese
feet long. Lu Adou obtains nine bolts of silk for the land. The land is
guaranteed not to be stolen. If someone claims ownership, depending
on the amount of land calculated, it is up to Dou to find good land as
compensation. Officials have government, while the people have
their own ways. Once this contract is drawn up, both parties should

not change their minds. The party that does so first must pay five bolts. We draw our fingers as a token of our sincerity.

Person who wrote this contract Pan Mao
Witness Lu Shanwang
Witness Lu Rongsun

(Yamamoto and Ikeda 1986:2, 1987:cankao #11; *Taozhai cangshiji* 6:11a–b; Gernet 1957:387–389)

This contract shares many features with the Turfan contract of 541 and the Lingtai contract of 477. It starts with the names of the buyer and seller, neither of whom—strangely—signs the contract (Gernet 1957:388). Could both parties already be dead? Two sons of the seller serve as witnesses. Surrounded by tombs on all sides, the plot is referred to as tomb land. Then the contract gives the length of the north-south and east-west borders, a different way of giving dimensions than at Turfan or Lingtai. It penalizes the party that cancels the transaction, and it provides for subsequent claims of ownership as well. The Turfan contract says, "Commoners have private agreements they are obliged to fulfill," while the contract from Hebei offers, "Officials have government, while the people have their own ways"; but the intent is the same. People used contracts for their own transactions, and they drew them up without consulting officials. Given the early dates of these contracts and the fact that China was not unified in the first half of the sixth century, one can only conclude the three contracts show surprising similarities—and, more important, that the Turfan contracts do not vary significantly from their counterparts in other parts of China.

Other contracts from Turfan testify to the great variety of contracts in use. Some were lengthy. A contract from 616 for renting land contains many more clauses than the document from 541. After the date, it reads:

Zhang Xiangxi rents one sixth-acre of millet land from Zuo Youzi. When, in the tenth month, the millet is ready to harvest, it will be measured by the official measure for a picul. The millet should be clean. If dirty, it should be winnowed before being measured. The tax and corvée obligations of the land are the landlord's responsibility. If the irrigation dikes break or a fine for misuse of water is incurred,[2] that is the tenant's responsibility. (Yamamoto and Ikeda 1987:#114)

2. Kong (1983:244) discusses variant interpretations of the word "*zhe*" (to punish, to blame) and cites a contract in which it clearly means "to fine" (*Tulufan chutu wenshu* 5:76).

Then come the same clauses about penalizing the party that cancels the agreement, the obligation of commoners to carry out private agreements, and the role of signatures as proof of good faith. The contract concludes with a force majeur clause: should destructive winds or drought occur, the landlord should take the usual measures when a great change occurs.[3] At the end are the signatures of the scribe and one witness, Feng Zhongde. Feng's name occurs a second time as a witness on an addendum to this contract, in which a different scribe simply referred to the earlier contract and altered a few names to make another rental agreement. Surely this was a cost-saving measure.

The same awareness of what can go wrong marks a contract written in 638 by a monk named Asheli, the Chinese transcription of the Sanskrit word for teacher. It was subsequently cut into four different shoe patterns, possibly because it was not valid after the Tang conquest in 640. Brilliantly reconstructed by Oda Yoshihisa, this contract allows us to see how sophisticated Gaochang contracts had become on the eve of the Tang conquest. After giving the date, it says:

> Shi [   ] buys one piece of land that can be cultivated annually from Wen Yang, the official in charge of digging canals (*sikong*). It carries with it a corvée obligation of 5.5 sixth-acres and 200 feet. The price is hereby set at 390 silver coins. When the money is all paid up, ownership of the field will change hands. The corvée obligations of the land go with ownership of the land. To the east, the land reaches the ditch; to the south, the road. To the west, it shares the border with Guo Qinghuai's fields. The north reaches the ditch. Within these four borders, anything extra will not be returned and anything short will not be made up for. The paths for carts and the water channels will remain as before.
>
> If, afterward, someone falsely makes claim to the land, it is up to the original owner to resolve the matter. The cart path through the fields starts in the main road and goes through the middle of the field. The buyer and seller reached this agreement and drew up a

3. This reading follows Ikeda's (1973a:12–13) emendation of *mie* to *hua*. A similar clause occurs in contracts from Dunhuang: "Follow the precedent for big change" (*yikan dali*) (Yamamoto and Ikeda 1987:#414).

contract. Once the contract is drawn up, neither party can cancel the agreement. Should one party cancel the contract, he must pay double to the party who does not cancel. Commoners have private agreements they wish to fulfill. To show good faith, the buyer and seller each sign their name.

Scribe Asheli
Witness You [   ]
Second Witness Yan [   ]

(Yamamoto and Ikeda 1987:#13)

This contract and the rental agreement above retain much of the language of the earlier contracts, but the new provisions about corvée, right of way, access from the main road, and subsequent claims to the piece of land all show an increasing legal sophistication. The contract does not come out and say so, but the implication of the last clause about private agreements among commoners is that the buyer and seller are making this sale without the knowledge of government officials. Because the buyer assumes the corvée obligations of the seller, the state has no reason to know that the sale has taken place.

Starting in 502, the Qu family was able to rule the Turfan area alternately by playing the Chinese off against the Turks and by paying tribute to the Turks, but in 640 the Tang finally defeated the Turks and took Turfan. There they immediately established the same administrative structure that governed the rest of the empire and applied the same tax system (Zhang Guangda 1988:70). Gaochang was named prefectural seat, with four counties under its jurisdiction. Turfan was the prefecture most distant from the capital, but it had the exactly same type of local government as the rest of China. Gaochang was subject to the same equal-field system as the entire empire.

The newly established Tang dynasty had adopted the fiscal system of its predecessors, the Northern Wei and the Sui (589–618), which presupposed an unchanging, self-sufficient, agrarian economy with a chronic shortage of labor and a resulting surplus of land. This fiscal system, the equal-field system, postulated that the emperor owned all the land in the empire and was obliged to distribute it among his subjects. After carrying out land and population surveys, the government ranked households by wealth and then divided all land into two categories: personal shares

(*koufen*) and permanent holdings (*yongye*). Every year families made declarations, officials updated tax registers, and every three years, officials
updated household registers and redistributed land (Ikeda 1973b). Personal
shares were to be reallotted every three years until the recipient reached
age sixty, when the land reverted to the state. Permanent holdings were
to be held in perpetuity, an inducement to invest in the land, usually
in the form of mulberry trees for feeding silk worms. In theory the
government, not private individuals, initiated and recorded all transfers
of land.

Historians differ on whether or not the Gaochang rulers implemented
the equal-field system before 640, but they agree that household registers
were maintained and that land was periodically redistributed, at least in the
initial years of Tang rule. In the land-short oasis towns of the Silk Road, the
registers record both the amount allocated and the amount not yet allocated. According to Tang law, each able-bodied male was awarded 100
sixth-acres of land (80 of personal share land, 20 of perpetual holdings), with
a smaller allotment in areas where land was scarce (40 of personal share
land, 20 of perpetual holdings) (*Tongdian* 2:15). Even though there was a
chronic shortage of irrigated land in the oases of the Silk Road, each resident
of Turfan was theoretically entitled to the same allotment as his counterparts who lived in the land-scarce regions of China proper, namely 60 sixth-
acres. In fact, most of the people in Turfan received about 10 sixth-acres of
land, or only one-sixth of what they were entitled to (Han 1986:19–23). The
Turfan contracts for the rental or purchase of land usually involved small
amounts of land, often just a few sixth-acres (Kong 1983:275). With the
exception of several big landlords, the people of Turfan did not receive the
amount of land they were supposed to under the equal-field system, but
they do seem to have been allotted equally small parcels.

The Tang Code explicitly forbade the sale of personal share land, specifying different types of beatings depending on how much land had been sold.
The law held that people who sold personal share land were supposed to
inform the authorities, so that the household registers could be adjusted. If
they failed to do so, the personal share land would revert to its original
owner, and any payment was confiscated by the state (Twitchett [1963]
1970:129; MacCormack 1985:31; 1990:237). Yet even from the beginning
the law included an exemption clause: "This clause does not apply to those
who are entitled to sell the land" (*Tanglü shuyi* 12:242 [article 163]). The
commentary to this article of the code, issued sometime after 737, implies

that the sale of permanent holding land was also illegal. For it specifies the circumstances under which it is legal to sell either category of land, whether personal share or permanent holding:

> "In cases in which one is entitled to sell land" refers to instances in which a family is poor and permanent holding land is sold to defray funeral expenses, or in which personal share land is sold to pay for a house, a mill, a store, or something similar, or in which one is moving from a land-short locality to a land-rich locality, and according to the statutes, one is permitted to sell it. (*Tanglü shuyi* 12:242 [article 163]; MacCormack 1990:238; Twitchett [1963] 1970:136; Niida [1937] 1983:90–91)

The New History of Tang confirms that the ban on the sale of land, issued between 650 and 655, applied to both personal share and permanent holdings. It adds: "Afterward, the powerful and rich annexed the land and the poor lost the land. Accordingly the emperor ordered the buyers to return the land and penalized them" (*Xin Tangshu* 51:1345). According to the law, families could sell their permanent holdings only for the most Confucian of reasons: to meet their filial obligations to bury their parents properly. And they could sell personal share land only to acquire other fixed property or if they were moving. The inclusion of so many exceptions suggests that the ban on selling land was very difficult to enforce, even from its inception.

In 640, when the Tang armies conquered Turfan, the local residents became subject to Tang law. Because the equal-field system, as it was presented in *The Tang Code*, forbade the sale of personal share and perpetual holding land, the populace should have stopped buying and selling land. In fact, it continued to buy and sell land. In an agrarian society such as that of Tang China, people had to use contracts to record transfers of land. Land determined a family's well-being. With enough of it, a family could prosper; with too little, a family would be doomed to struggle for its existence. Accordingly, families could not be cavalier about recording the purchase, sale, rent, or exchange of land, even if they were breaking the law by doing so. Because the people of Turfan did change the wording of their contracts in the years immediately following the Tang conquest, we can conclude they—or their scribes—were familiar with the provisions of the code affecting contracts. The people of Turfan adopted the provisions of Tang law that strengthened the hand of those renting land: landlords discovered they could charge interest on overdue rent, and they could hold guarantors responsible if tenants absconded.

A tenancy contract from 643, three years after the Tang conquest, combines elements of both Gaochang and Tang contracts. After the date it says:

> Zhao Huaiman rents [   ] from Zhang Huanren and 2 sixth-acres from Zhang Yuanfu. For each sixth-acre of land, a rent of 2 piculs and 2 pecks of wheat [   ]. It will be measured according to the Gaochang standard measure. The wheat should be clean. If dirty, it should be winnowed before being measured. The tax and corvée obligations of the land are the landlord's responsibility. If the irrigation dikes break or a fine for misuse of water is incurred, those are the tenant's responsibility. If destructive winds or drought occur, the usual practice in time of great change will be followed. When the sixth month arrives, the wheat should be completely paid. If it is not paid in the sixth month, each month one peck will be paid for each picul still owed. If this rent is not paid, then the property of the renter equaling the value of the wheat will be seized. If the debtor absconds, then whose names appear afterward are liable. The three people [rest of contract cut off].

> Landlord Zhang Huanren
> Landlord Zhang Yuanfu
> Tiller Zhao Huaiman
> Scribe Fan Yanshou
> Witness [   ]
> (Yamamoto and Ikeda 1987:#137)

The first half is identical to the 616 rental contract cited above and, like it, does not give the exact location of the land to be rented. Three years into Tang rule, Gaochang measures and standard contracts are still being used. Yet some clauses are new. Now the tenant is obliged to pay 10 percent interest on any late rent, and the landlord can confiscate the debtor's property should he fail to pay. The final clause, holding the guarantors liable, is also an adaptation from Tang contracts.

The shift from Gaochang to Tang contracts was complete by 659, the date of a rental agreement (Yamamoto and Ikeda 1987:#148) that is almost identical to that of 643 except that Chinese, not Gaochang, measures are used. The provisions about interest, corvée and taxes, winnowing, destructive winds, and drought are all retained. The contract ends with a clause penalizing the party who withdraws from the agreement. It uses the Tang terms for guarantor (*baoren*) and witness (*zhijianren*) and drops the Gaochang practice of naming the scribe (*qianshu*), the chief witness (*shijian*), and the other witnesses (*linzuo*). It is the right half of one piece of paper; a duplicate version is written on the left half. The signatories took up the Chinese practice of writing the characters for contract (*hetong*) on the back of the document and then tearing the contract in two.

Some changes in contracts occurred after the imposition of Tang rule. In the Gaochang contracts the parties have the scribe write their names; in the Tang, they draw their finger joints. The Gaochang contracts use the term *quan* for contract, while those from the Tang use *qi*. Also, as Zhang Guangda (1986:80) notes, unlike the Gaochang contracts, the Tang contracts give the counties in which the participants reside, a sure indication of the new administrative system of the Tang.[4] Overall, the changes between the Gaochang and Tang contracts were incremental, suggesting that the change from the legal system of the Qu family to that of the Tang was a gradual one.

Moneylender Zuo's Tomb

The contracts from one tomb at Astana provide an ideal testcase for assessing the impact of Tang rule. In 673 a soldier and moneylender named Zuo Chongxi was buried at the age of fifty-seven with fifteen contracts, dating from 660 to 670. Fourteen are legible. Rolled up together, they look as if they were deliberately placed in the tomb (*Tulufan chutu wenshu* 6:401–442). Moneylender Zuo used a contract to buy a fifteen-year-old slave, and he used one to purchase ninety bundles of hay, presumably for his herds of sheep and camels. He used eight contracts to lend money or silk cloth, which served as an alternate currency. And he used four more to rent land from the poor. Presumably only a fraction of the contracts he held during his lifetime, the fifteen include examples of the major types of contracts in use in Turfan under the Tang: those for buying or renting land, for acquiring

4. See Ikeda (1986:19) for a discussion of other differences between Gaochang and Tang contracts.

or exchanging goods, and for incorporating new sources of labor into the household, either as slaves or as family members.

The surviving contracts in Zuo's tomb are in different handwriting, which shows that Moneylender Zuo hired more than one person to draft contracts. If frequency of use is any indication, having contracts drafted was not expensive. The cost of drawing up a contract was only a fraction of the value of the goods involved. People in Turfan lived in a largely subsistence economy, in which many of their transactions were barter. Still, they had contracts drawn up for even the lowliest of transactions—the loan of a gown, the exchange of camels, the purchase of a shirt.

The contracts are similar in format: they begin with the date, name the parties and goods involved, specify when ownership will change hands, and spell out the consequences should either party break the agreement. The following contract is slightly longer than the other contracts in Money-lender Zuo's tomb, but the others duplicate long passages, testifying to the prevalence of legal boilerplate in the seventh century. The repetition of wording in all the Turfan contracts points to the existence of a class of scribes who drew on a limited number of phrases (perhaps from models, perhaps from memory) to draw up contracts. For all we know, Moneylender Zuo may have been illiterate.

Here is an example in which all the stock phrases have been italicized:

On the twenty-sixth day of the fourth month of the first year of the Qianfeng reign (666), Zheng Haishi of Chonghua district borrowed 10 silver coins from Zuo Chongxi. In addition, he will pay interest of 1.5 silver coins every month. The day when Zuo wants the money back, Zheng will promptly return it. If Zheng keeps Zuo's money for a prolonged period, then Zuo is authorized to take over Zheng's family assets and various possessions, and his personal share land and his gardens, to make up the original amount. The family can make no excuses preventing him from taking their goods.

In the event that public and private debts cease to be collected, this agreement will not fall within the bounds of what is suspended. *If Zheng absconds, his wife and children will pay first, and then his guarantors will make up the debt for him. Officials have government law, and common people follow private contracts.*

The two sides agree to make this contract, and they draw their finger joints as a sign of good faith.

Lender Zuo
Borrower Zheng Haishi
Guarantor Zhang Haihuan of Ningda district
Guarantor Zhang Huanxiang of Chonghua district
Witness Zhang Huande

(Yamamoto and Ikeda 1986:21; 1987:#76;
Tulufan chutu wenshu 6:417–418; Ikeda 1975:53–54)

According to this agreement, Moneylender Zuo lent Zheng Haishi 10 silver coins and charged him 15 percent interest each month, and as collateral Zheng put up his household possessions and his personal allotment of land (given him by the government during the periodic redistribution of land). At the end of Moneylender Zuo's contract come the names of the parties involved, the guarantors, and the witnesses. The scribe's name is not given. Because he was lending money and in the superior position, Zuo did not draw his finger joints, but the borrower and his guarantors did.

The instructions in this contract, should Zheng fail to pay off his debt on schedule, match the terms of *The Tang Code*. Article 398 of the code specifies punishments (different severities of beatings) for those who fail to pay their debts according to the schedule given in contracts, but the article does not explain either the procedure for registering a complaint or the circumstances that would make the courts intervene in such a dispute (*Tanglü shuyi* 26:485). The language in Moneylender Zuo's contract follows article 399: "In those cases in which a debt is owed and no suit is brought, and the creditor seizes money and goods worth more than the contract specifies, then the creditor is liable for the possession of illicit goods" (*Tanglü shuyi* 26:485–486 [article 399]). This clause implicitly allows the creditor to inform the authorities that someone owes him or her money, but it also allows the creditor to take possession of goods equaling the disputed amount without informing the authorities. Other parts of this contract stray dramatically from the code. The contract's rejection of an imperial amnesty on debts directly challenges the emperor's authority, and the interest rate of 10 percent a month is higher than the 6 percent allowed by the code.

Moneylender Zuo did not always charge interest. In 665 he lent woven silk interest-free to a fellow moneylender so that he could go to Gaochang for ten days. The contract specifies that he was liable for interest according to the prevailing rate in the district, probably 10 percent per month, only should he fail to return the cloth within the allotted time (Chen Guocan

1983a:230). The frequency of contracts at Turfan setting the monthly rate of interest at 10, sometimes 15, percent interest indicates that the government lacked the means—or the will—to enforce an interest rate of 6 percent a month.

Ten of the contracts in Moneylender Zuo's tomb are one-time agreements with different individuals, but three are with the same farmer, Zhang Shanxi (Yamamoto and Ikeda 1987:#77, #78, #161; Chen 1983b:252–257; Hori 1980:34–64; 1983:81–83; Ikeda 1975:55–56). In 668 Moneylender Zuo and Farmer Zhang signed a contract in which Zuo lent Zhang 20 silver coins, at a monthly interest of 2 coins, or 10 percent (fig. 3). They signed the contract in the third month, just at the time of the first planting, when many cultivators were short of money. Zhang promised to pay the money back whenever Zuo asked for it, and he put up his household possessions and one vegetable field as security. Two years later, in 670, in the second month, Moneylender Zuo agreed to rent a different vegetable field from Zhang, for which he would pay rent twice a year, in the sixth and ninth months, for three years. In the fourth year he was to make a cash payment of 30 silver coins. He made no payment at the time of signing.

Contrary to prevailing stereotypes, the person renting the land, Moneylender Zuo, was demonstrably better off than the owner of the land. Only one month later, Moneylender Zuo lent Zhang 40 silver coins, at a monthly interest of 4 coins, again 10 percent. Although we do not know whether Zhang paid Zuo back, Zhang seems to have been getting deeper and deeper into debt. Moneylender Zuo may have lent money to Zhang and rented his land with the hope of ultimately taking it over. His tomb includes one document in which he petitions the county magistrate for the right of ownership to a grape orchard owned by a Mr. Zhao (*Tulufan chutu wenshu* 6:426). Possibly Mr. Zhao, like Farmer Zhang, may have begun by borrowing money from Moneylender Zuo; ultimately he fell so deep in debt to Zuo that he had no choice but to sign his land over to him. Surviving contracts show that people generally tried to rent plots close to each other (Kong 1983:273). Moneylender Zuo rented two fields bordering on Zhang ditch; the orchard he claimed had once belonged to his ancestors also abutted Zhang ditch.

These contracts show that Moneylender Zuo was involved in a wide variety of transactions, but reveal little about him as a person. His tomb contains several objects and documents that supplement the information gleaned from the contracts. Zuo was buried with a crude figure of a woman labeled "Wife Heduan" (*qi Heduan shen*). Heduan was the Chinese tran-

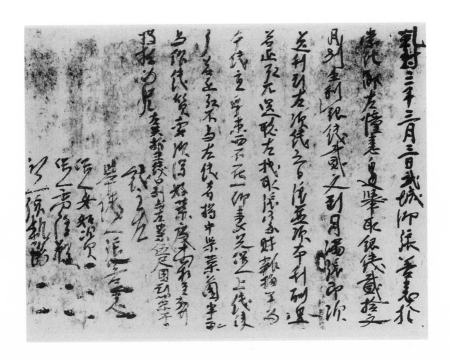

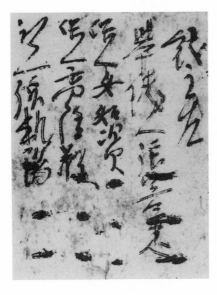

Detail

Fig. 3. Moneylender Zuo Lends Twenty Silver Coins. When Moneylender Zuo Chongxi died in 673, he took to his grave this contract and fourteen others—perhaps because he was hoping to collect on them in the netherworld. Signed by four parties in 668, this contract charges Farmer Zhang 10 percent interest per month on a loan of 20 silver coins to cover the costs of buying seed for spring planting. Moneylender Zuo, as the more powerful party to the contract, did not sign, nor did he draw his finger joints. The weaker party, Farmer Zhang—and his three guarantors—all had to sign once the contract had been read aloud by the person who drew it up. The three lines marking their finger joints are shown in the detail. (Reprinted from Xinjiang Museum 1975a:57, fig. 87.)

scription of the Turkish word for queen, *kutoun* (Li Zheng 1973:11, 20n7).
Was Moneylender Zuo married to a Turkish woman? Could he have been
Turkish himself? We cannot be sure.

One of the documents in the tomb is an inventory listing the goods
accompanying Zuo to the netherworld: 6 slaves, 30 pecks of silver, 50,000
piculs of grain, and 10,000 pieces of white silk (*Tulufan chutu wenshu*
6:402–403). Because a full description of the contents of the tomb has
not yet been published, we do not know the relationship of this list to the
actual goods in the tomb. These inflated figures probably refer to paper
facsimiles of the goods in question, which were burned at the funeral.

The inventory begins by summarizing Moneylender Zuo's good deeds:
he built a statue of the Buddha and two attendants, and he sponsored the
writing or recitation of *The Yulanpen Sutra*. This depiction of Moneylender
Zuo as a devout Buddhist makes sense, given the extent to which religious
and mercantile activities overlapped on the Silk Road (Liu Xinru 1988). One
other document in the tomb is also intended for Zuo's use after his death:
it is a letter from a relative denying any responsibility for the theft of 500
silver coins, which occurred five years before Moneylender Zuo's death
(*Tulufan chutu wenshu* 6:441–442, plate 2). Five hundred coins was a
considerable sum for any individual to have and meshes nicely with the
image of the rich moneylender that the contracts impart.

The tomb also contains an epitaph of Moneylender Zuo:

> His name was Chongxi. He attained the high rank of Martial Guard.
> His glory reflected back to the Lu dynasty. His virtuous behavior and
> great honesty set an example for others. His wealth was as vast as
> that of Duke Jing of Qi, and he was not at all arrogant or
> extravagant. His spirit rose above the clouds and his reputation
> spread to different places. He humbled and lowered himself and
> gained a name by acting righteously. He was completely loyal and
> genuinely filial, and his understanding of ritual far surpassed the
> usual. He died on the twenty-second day of the fifth month of the
> fourth year of the Xianheng era (673) in his own home, at the age of
> fifty-seven. He was buried in the western plain of the city. What a
> great loss! And so we place him in this tomb. (Zhang Yincai 1973:73)

This epitaph is filled with references to the Confucian classics. By
mentioning the Lu dynasty, the author of the epitaph indirectly suggests
that Moneylender Zuo was a descendant of the author of *The Zuo Commen-*

tary on the Spring and Autumn Annals (*Zuozhuan*), Zuo Qiuming, who served the Lu. The writer repeats many cliches in the hope of making his subject sound like a paragon of Confucian virtue, but he makes mistakes, too. Duke Jing of Qi is mentioned in *The Analects*, the record of Confucius's conversations with his disciples: "Duke Jing of Qi had a thousand teams of horses, but on the day of his death the people could think of no good deed for which to praise him. Bo Yi and Shu Qi starved at the foot of Mount Shouyang, yet the people sing their praises to this very day" (Waley 1938:207; *Shisanjing* 16:2522). Duke Jing of Qi may have been a wealthy man, but because he never did any good deeds, he suffers from comparison with the two poor men. Surely this is not the image of Moneylender Zuo the author is trying to convey! The author of the epitaph was sufficiently literate to be able to write up a text, but not so well educated that he understood the nuances of the Confucian classics. He might have been a scribe qualified to draw up contracts.

The documents in Moneylender Zuo's tomb are invaluable because they allow us to see different facets of the same individual, facets that the official Chinese record rarely presents. His epitaph resembles others from the Tang in its conventional use of Confucian language, but it differs in that it is from the tomb of a very low ranking soldier. Moneylender Zuo may have been a rich man, especially compared to his neighbors, but he was not a prominent man. Nothing would be known of him if his tomb had not been excavated. The fifteen contracts in his tomb are unusual. They were buried whole, and any damage has occurred since the time of burial. Other tombs from Turfan have two or three contracts, even eight on occasion, but none has so many intact. Why Moneylender Zuo buried so many contracts with him is a question best left to the second half of this book, which concerns the use of contracts in the underworld.

Commercial Contracts

As *The Tang Code* regulated land contracts, so too did it attempt to regulate contracts for the sale of livestock and slaves. The Turfan documents provide valuable evidence for gauging the extent of compliance with these regulations. As part of its close supervision of markets, the code required anyone selling male or female slaves, cows, horses, camels, mules, or donkeys to have the market supervisor draw up a market certificate (*shiquan*) within three days of the sale. "After the market certificate is drawn up, if the sold item has a pre-existing illness, then the item can be returned." The law called for the punishment of anyone attempting to cheat by falsely claiming the purchased slave or animal was ill, and for the punishment of any market official who failed to draw up such a market certificate on time (*Tanglü shuyi* 26:500–501 [article 422]; *Tang liudian* 20:8b–9a; Twitchett 1966: 246).

The Tang Code does not say so, but it is very likely that the drawing up of such a contract involved an ad valorem tax on the goods involved. The official history of the preceding dynasty, the Sui, mentions such a law in existence as early as 311, when the Jin established its capital at Nanjing. *The Tang Code* was based on the Sui code, and although that code does not survive in its entirety, the text of this particular article does:

> From the time that the Jin dynasty crossed the Yangzi, a tax of 4
> percent was levied on all sales of male and female slaves, horses,
> cows, land, and houses for which there was a contract. The seller
> paid 3 percent, the buyer 1 percent. In instances where there was no
> contract, the tax was fixed based on the worth of the goods involved.
> It was also 4 percent (*Sui shu* 24:689).

On the face of it, this tax seems unenforceable, even in an age in which oral agreements were common. Why would anyone pay a tax on such sales, especially when no contract had been signed and there was no documentary proof of the sale? The Tang revision makes more sense. The tax no longer applied to houses and land, but was limited to those agreements governing the purchase of livestock and slaves, both movable goods.

Six of the seven surviving Turfan contracts documenting the sale of livestock, dated 649, 649, 650, 695, 733, and 741, are contracts between individuals, not the market certificates specified by *The Tang Code* (Yamamoto and Ikeda 1987:#20,#21,#22,#30,#32,#33). The seventh private contract in the group, dated 673, declares the intent to register the sale of a camel and so shows an awareness of the provisions of the code (Yamamoto and Ikeda 1987:#29; *Tulufan chutu wenshu* 7:389–390). After the date, we read:

> Du [   ], a unit leader in Qianting, Xizhou [Turfan], uses fourteen
> bolts of silk to buy a yellow camel, ten years of age, from a Sogdian,
> Kangwu Poyan. Once the camel and the cloth are exchanged, the
> transaction shall be complete. If someone makes a wrongful claim to
> the camel, it is up to the original owner and guarantors to provide
> compensation, and Du knows nothing of this. If the camel does not

drink water or eat grass for three days, then it can be returned to the original owner. The awaited guarantors have not yet gathered, so we draw up this private contract. When they have gathered, we will get a market certificate. The two sides harmoniously establish this contract and draw their joints as proof. (Yamamoto and Ikeda 1987:#29)

This contract explains that the sale will be complete when the cloth and camel change hands, not when the official market certificate is drawn up. The buyer may have followed the letter of the law exactly because he needed a market certificate in order to pass through government checks at the border passes, where the papers of draft animals were scrutinized carefully because of their potential role in battle.

The Tang Code regulated the sale of slaves even more strictly than that of livestock. The commentary to one article even says, "Male and female slaves, like money and goods, are for their owner to dispose of" (*Tanglü shuyi* 14:270 [article 192]). The code divided society into three rigidly separated groups: the privileged, commoners, and inferior classes (*jianmin*) who included slaves (Johnson 1979:28–29). Slaves and commoners were forbidden to intermarry, with the penalty for doing so being one and one-half years of penal servitude (*Tanglü shuyi* 14:269–270 [article 191]).

Two surviving documents that record the sale of slaves are actually the market certificates called for by *The Tang Code*. One certificate, dated 731, stipulates that the sale of a eleven-year-old girl to a man from Changan for forty bolts of silk will take place once the cloth and the girl have changed hands. The government official who wrote up the document interrogated the seller to ascertain that the slave was indeed from the inferior classes, and the five guarantors verified that she was not a commoner who was being sold into slavery because of poverty. The names of the seller, the buyer, the five guarantors, and the slave herself come at the end of the contract. The 732 contract follows this format, adding a clause that the official saw the original contract (from the prior sale of the slave in question) and that the guarantors will be liable should the slave turn out not to be a member of the inferior classes (Yamamoto and Ikeda 1987:#31, bu #13).

These two market certificates for slaves from Turfan have been found attached to permissions issued by an official to go through the pass (Zhu Lei 1983:511; *Tulufan chutu wenshu* 9:26–39). A third market certificate, probably from sometime between 744 and 756, has been found at Dunhuang

(Yamamoto and Ikeda 1987:#256). At least in northwest China, where caravans went in and out of border passes, and through official checks, owners of slaves and livestock needed documentary proof of ownership. If the slave had been born into the master's family, then the owner's word would suffice, as one document allowing a man to go through the passes with his slaves reveals: he simply stated that his slaves were born in his household (*Tulufan chutu wenshu* 9:135–136; Dong 1990:144; Zhu Lei 1983:512).

Not everyone complied with the complex regulations for selling slaves. In 661, when Moneylender Zuo bought a slave from a fellow moneylender, he drew up a private contract, as did the two purchasers of slaves in the mid-seventh century (Yamamoto and Ikeda 1987:#23,#25,#26; *Tulufan chutu wenshu* 6:410–411). The prevalence of interest rates higher than those specified in *The Tang Code* and the failure of many to register the purchase of livestock or slaves with the authorities suggest people conducted their daily transactions independent of the local authorities. It was only when they wished to go through the passes that they had to submit the correct documentation to demonstrate legal ownership of livestock and slaves.

Because the compilers of *The Tang Code* were especially concerned that a commoner might pledge the labor of his child to pay off a debt, fail to redeem the child, and so enslave the child, the code allowed creditors to take possession of goods or slaves, but it denied them the right to enslave commoners in order to pay off a debt (*Tanglü shuyi* 26:486 [article 400]). To judge from one official's comment, this provision was as difficult to enforce as that requiring the drawing up of a market certificate for the purchase of a slave. When Han Yü (768–824) was an official in Yuanzhou (now Jiangxi, Yichun county), he investigated the extent of debt within the prefecture and found 731 slaves who were in bondage, either because they had been impoverished by floods and droughts or because they could not meet their debts to the government and private individuals (*Changli xiansheng* 40:4b–5a). The problem of commoners being sold into slavery persisted. One of the last Tang emperors, Shaozong (r. 889–903), called for a slave's previous contract to be checked at the time of sale so that his or her origins could be verified. He bemoaned the large numbers of people sold into slavery to pay off debts (*Tang dazhao lingji* 5:25a–26b; Zhu Lei 1983:509).

Government Intervention in Private Disputes

Generally, the compilers of *The Tang Code* agreed that government intervention in private contracts was best avoided. An edict appended to the article concerning failure to repay debts explains when the government will interfere and when it will not:

> In all instances when public officials and private individuals lend money or goods, the transactions will be according to the private contract, and officials will not intervene, as long as the monthly interest charged does not exceed 6 percent, and as long as the accumulated interest shall not exceed the value of the principal, even if much time has passed. . . .[5]
>
> In cases in which the contract violates the law concerning accumulated interest, in which the creditor seizes more than the goods specified in the contract, or in which the debt is not the product of accumulated interest on the given loan, officials will intervene.
>
> Anyone holding property as security for a loan cannot sell it to anyone but the owner. If the accumulated interest has surpassed the value of the principal and the debtor cannot redeem the goods, then the supervisor of the market should be informed. He will arrange for the sale of the goods. Any surplus, after the debt has been repaid, will be given to the debtor. If the debtor absconds, then the guarantors will pay in his or her stead. (*Song xingtong* 26:412–413; MacCormack 1985:46–47; 1990:246–247; Gernet 1957:299–300)

Subsequent edicts set different rates, variously 5 percent, or 4 percent for private loans and 5 percent for government loans, sometimes allowing the addition of the accumulated interest to the principal, sometimes forbidding it (*Tang liudian* 6:20a-b; *Song xingtong* 26:414). The compilers of *The Tang Code* may have claimed the right of the government to intervene when the monthly interest was above 6 percent, but their phrasing suggests that they were of two minds: on the one hand, they wanted to let individuals draw up contracts without the state's interference, but on the other hand, the state reserved the right to interfere if certain conditions were not met. The Chinese state was not alone in its reluctance to interfere. Writing at the end

5. Compare with *Tang liudian* 6:20a–b, which sets rates at 5 percent and says that officials will not interfere when the accumulated interest is added to the principal.

of the twelfth century, the English legal theorist Glanvill noted the unwillingness of the royal court to intervene in private agreements; parties in
such disputes could, however, sue in local courts (Simpson 1987:4; Baker
1990:362).

The people drawing up contracts did not anticipate going to court. All
of the Turfan contracts describe ideal scenarios in which purchasers are able
to come up with the money to buy the plot of land they want, in which
tenants can make the rent, and in which debts will be repaid. Some of the
contracts include provisions for different problems, but none spell out the
enforcement mechanisms. Who was going to seize someone's property if he
did not make the rent? Was his guarantor really going to make good on his
debt to Moneylender Zuo if he absconded? Who was going to decide what
constituted a drought? What if the buyer did not perform his new corvée
obligations? What if someone else made a claim to the land? The clauses in
these contracts about the obligations of private citizens suggest that people
were signing the agreements among themselves and did not expect to go to
court.

Yet the Turfan documents reveal these very people took their debtors
to court for what *The Tang Code* allowed them to: failure to pay according
to the time limits set in a contract. One of the few documents buried in
Turfan but originally from the city of Luoyang in central China is dated 648.
Because it was buried intact, not cut up into shoe linings, it was presumably
carried to Turfan by those lending the money who wanted to keep a record
of the transaction. It is a contract drawn up after the parties had already
gone to court for nonpayment of a debt. In borrowing money from Mr.
Zhang and Mr. Suo, Mr. Heng put up his house as security. After three
months in which he failed to make monthly payments, Zhang and Suo went
to their district head, who passed the case onto the county court. The court
ruled that all interest had to be paid by the end of the month and that the
loan had to be fully repaid by the end of the following month. If debtor Heng
failed to make the payments, then his house was to be put up for sale. Once
the lenders received their money back, the rest of the money was to go to
debtor Heng, who signed his name to the judgment (*Tulufan chutu wenshu*
4:269–270; Yamamoto and Ikeda 1987:#66; Chen Guocan 1983a:245–246).

This decision follows the provisions of *The Tang Code* exactly and
shows the willingness of the court to intervene when an individual fails to
fulfill the terms of a contract. Because it is from Luoyang, not Turfan, it
reveals that the courts intervened in contract disputes in China proper, not
just in the northwest. It reveals less about popular access to the courts, for

Mr. Zhang was probably a member of the powerful Zhang clan who regularly intermarried with the deposed ruling family from Turfan, and who had been resettled in Changan and Luoyang after their defeat by the Tang in 640 (Hu 1987:54; Wechsler 1979:223).

A Tang tale about a very wealthy merchant, Dou Yi, provides further evidence that contracts were used in the capital for real estate transactions. Merchant Dou made his fortune by giving a series of loans to an impoverished foreign merchant, probably from east of Samarkand, who repaid him by recommending the purchase of a house for 200 strings of cash (Niida [1937] 1983:467n5). Merchant Dou made the purchase with money that he withdrew from a countinghouse. On the day the contract for the sale of the house was drawn up, the foreigner informed Merchant Dou that the house contained valuable Khotanese jade. Even though Dou did not believe him, he summoned a jade carver, who confirmed the worth of the stones. Merchant Dou rewarded his Sogdian adviser by giving him both the house and the contract he had used to buy it. In another deal, Dou proved ownership of a house by showing the contract to his neighbor, again attesting to the use of contracts in the capital for real estate transactions (*Taiping guangji* 243:1874–78).

Conclusion

Few Turfan documents date to the period after 755, when a rebellion led by the Sogdian general An Lushan almost succeeded in toppling the Tang empire (Twitchett 1979:453–461). The Tang emperor was forced to summon his armies back from the frontiers, and from Turfan, to meet the threat in the capital. The Tibetans, who had displaced the Turks as the main enemy to the north, took advantage of the dynasty's weakness to attack its northwestern frontier and took Turfan in 792. They held it only briefly, for Turfan came under Uighur rule in 794, and remained under non-Chinese rule until 1756 (Hu 1987:67–68, 85).

The loss of Turfan was only one of many the Tang endured after 755. In order to suppress the rebellion, the emperor had to relinquish his rights to collect the land revenue to his regional commanders, who paid only an annual quota to the central government. Because individual household registers were no longer updated, contracts took on an increasingly important role as the sole records of ownership, a change to be documented in the chapters that follow.

The people of Turfan managed to conduct their daily transactions and use contracts without consulting local officials. They distinguished between private contracts—for use among themselves—and government contracts—drawn up under the supervision of officials. This distinction did not prevent them from going to those same officials if they had a dispute involving a private contract, but they do not seem to have anticipated the problems that were bound to arise when they signed their private contracts. The wording of the surviving contracts suggests that the people shared the lawmakers' ambivalence about government intervention in contract disputes. After all, as they wrote in so many of their contracts, "Officials have government law, and common people follow private contracts."

3

Government

Recognition

of Contracts

The second cache of original contracts from the Tang dynasty was found at the end of the nineteenth century in a cave in Dunhuang, Gansu province (see map 1). Dating to the ninth and tenth centuries, the Dunhuang discovery makes it possible to track the changing role of contracts in the years following the collapse of central government power in 755. Dunhuang was remote but, like other more centrally located areas, was governed by a regional ruler.

Those signing the Dunhuang contracts shared the wariness of those at Turfan about state intervention in private agreements. Until the middle of the ninth century they still referred to household registers, but with increasing uncertainty. If the registers were updated, they said, then a given transaction should be recorded. Eventually those drawing up contracts stopped mentioning the registers. Instead, they cited the contracts as proof of land ownership. And the rulers at Dunhuang, like the military governors elsewhere in a divided China, started to accept contracts as proof of ownership.

Only some 600 kilometers and one century separate the contracts at Dunhuang from those at Turfan, but the differences are striking. Contracts to lease or buy land constitute 4 percent of those from Dunhuang, versus 40 percent of the contracts from Turfan (Yamamoto and Ikeda 1987:11). Many of the Dunhuang contracts record loans of grain and silk or set the terms for hiring. Aware of the possibility that a dispute will occur, the drafters incorporate clauses limiting the circumstances under which two parties can bring suit. As a result, some of the contracts from Dunhuang are longer than those from Turfan and show much greater legal sophistication. Others are much shorter, and written in very unsure hands.

The many dated examples and the surviving literature underline the ubiquity of contracts in Dunhuang daily life.

Some of the differences between the two caches stem from the reasons for their preservation. The Turfan documents were cut up from paper present in an average household. The Dunhuang documents, in contrast, all came from one repository for waste paper discovered by the resident caretaker.[1] When Daoist Wang noticed the plaster jutting out, he tapped on the hollow wall and discovered another cave lay behind the wall paintings. In cave 17, the famous library cave of Dunhuang, were stored more than fifty thousand different documents, dating from the third century to the eleventh. The library cave was sealed off sometime in the first half of the eleventh century, with the latest Chinese documents dated 1006 (but documents in other languages may have been later). Was the cave sealed off to protect it from the Xixia conquerors who took Dunhuang in 1036? No one knows for sure.[2]

Because the cave contained many scraps of paper, including writing exercises with the mistakes crossed out and corrected, most scholars today agree that it was a repository for paper that could no longer be used. A poem in one popular narrative suggests that Buddhist teachings held that paper with writing on it was not to be thrown away. The monk Huiyuan (344–416) drafted this poem when he discovered that the people of the palace used paper with writing on it in their lavatories:

> Students of Confucianism study the five classics,
> Students of Buddhism study the three schools,
> They observe ritual and carry out loyalty and filiality,
> So they can be named as officials.
> The answers to the examination questions
> Are written in the same characters as Buddhist sutras.

1. Since then, the Dunhuang documents have been dispersed to different libraries around the world. Here I provide the number assigned by Yamamoto and Ikeda (1987) to a given contract as well as the standard Dunhuang document number denoting which library holds it ("P" for the Pelliot collection in Paris, "S" for the Stein collection in London, "*Beitu*" for the Beijing Library). The reader may wish to consult *Dunhuang shehui jingji* for alternative transcriptions and photographic plates, but since the transcriptions are generally less reliable than those of Yamamoto and Ikeda, I do not give the citation to the Beijing collection unless I have found it useful.

2. Ma (1978) presents a careful discussion of the unresolved issues concerning the library cave.

Yet some do not reflect on this and value them,
But dirty them in the toilet.
To erase their sins, as numerous as the sands of the Ganges,
Many lives of repentance would not be sufficient.
Their bodies will sink for five hundred ages
They will always be insects living in a toilet.

(Dunhuang bianwenji 1957:192; Waley 1960:122)

Arthur Waley is surely right to suggest that this kind of thinking must have underlain the creation of the repository for waste paper.

Although cave 17's mysteries remain unsolved, it is clear that the Dunhuang documents provide a sample of the types of documents circulating at a monastery—not those from ordinary households as at Turfan. Most of the Dunhuang documents are copies of Buddhist texts, or sutras, which were copied to generate merit. Once copied, they were of no use, so they were placed in the repository. The relegation of the manuscript copies to the library cave is almost surely related to the appearance of woodblock-printed editions of the Buddhist canon at this time.

Paper was so valuable that the backs of the sutras and even the margins were used for writing exercises by the many lay students who studied reading and writing at the monasteries (Mair 1981:90–91). Written with a stylus on silk or on paper, the documents show handwriting ranging from the misshapen, crooked characters of those just learning to write Chinese to the balanced, clear hand of the highly literate. The Dunhuang documents afford a glimpse of a whole range of scribes acquiring their trade, which included learning how to draft a contract. Among the many different types of exercises performed by the future scribes was the writing of contracts; accordingly, many of the Dunhuang contracts are contracts copied by the students for practice. Many of the actual contracts record loans of grain and silk, either made by a monastery or witnessed by monks or nuns. Given the low literacy levels throughout the society, a group of scribes must have existed who drew up contracts for a small fee, although they did not identify themselves.

The Dunhuang documents pose the same problems of typicality as those from Turfan. Also in the far northwest, Dunhuang lay at the western end of the strategically important Gansu corridor, at the intersection of the northern and southern silk routes, and was under Chinese rule for longer periods of time than Turfan. Today one sees the same mix of faces—some covered, some not, as at Turfan—but the Chinese seem to be in the

majority, and most people speak Chinese. Present-day Dunhuang seems
more Chinese than Turfan. Dunhuang is a prosperous oasis with tall, green
trees and gushing channels of irrigated water. In the 1930s it felt prosperous
to the missionary Mildred Cable, and its greenery must have provided
welcome relief to the weary travelers of the Silk Road. Dunhuang's location
and fertility brought many visitors, who supported the construction of the
Dunhuang caves, a massive complex of more than five hundred caves, lying
25 kilometers to the southeast of the town. The cave walls were covered
with plaster; the paintings on them, still bright after all these centuries,
depict both the Chinese and the non-Chinese who ruled Dunhuang in
different periods.

Dunhuang first came under Chinese rule in the Han dynasty, was lost
when the Han fell at the end of the second century, and was reconquered by
the Sui, who reunited China in 589. When the Tang took over from the Sui,
the dynasty gained control of Dunhuang, but the Tang lost the oasis in 781
to the same Tibetans who later conquered Turfan.

The only surviving contract from the period of direct Tang rule is a
market certificate for the sale of a slave, dating to between 744 and 758. It
records a merchant's sale of a thirteen-year-old non-Chinese slave. At the
bottom are the names and ages of the slave's former master, the slave, and
the five guarantors. All vouch that the slave "is a member of the inferior
classes, and they are not lying." As is characteristic of Turfan contracts too,
the name of the buyer, here the owner of the cloth, is not given, as he is in
a superior position and is not liable should anything about the sale prove
illegal. As required by Tang law, the certificate was issued by the director of
the market, and it carries the stamp of the prefect. Since it lacks the marks
or finger joints of those whose names appear at the end, this must have been
the copy kept in the government offices, not the copy given to the slave's
purchaser (Shi 1972:70; Ikeda and Yamamoto 1987:#256).

Although this certificate conforms exactly with the provisions of *The
Tang Code*, it is impossible to generalize about the degree of compliance
with the code at Dunhuang on the basis of this one example. Unlike most,
this certificate was not found in the library cave. Of unknown provenance,
it strongly resembles seven official passes dated 748 that give permission to
go through the gates excavated in front of cave 122. So this market certificate, like the two from Turfan, may well have been attached to an official
pass.

Contracts in Literature

One story from the Tang, *The Tale of Lord Yuan of Mount Lu*, provides tantalizing clues about the use of contracts and the procedures for selling slaves. It tells of the famous monk Huiyuan, who is studying *The Nirvana Sutra* at a monastery on Mount Lu (*Dunhuang bianwenji* 1957:167–195; Zhu Lei 1983; Waley 1960:97–123; S2073). After the local earth god warns of an impending raid, all the other monks leave Huiyuan and flee with the monastery's treasures. The bandits find the monk meditating outside one of the halls. The leader of the gang, Bai Zhuang, is especially taken with Huiyuan, who "had the face of a bodhisattva, whose body gave off a silvery aura, who was seven feet tall, whose hair looked lacquered, and whose lips seemed to be painted red." He asks the monk to accompany him. Huiyuan agrees, provided he can continue to recite sutras.

The monk travels far and near with the gang, until one night a Buddha appears to him in a dream and instructs him to sell himself as a slave to Prime Minister Cui for 500 strings, money he can then use to repay the gang leader for his room and board in this life. He will also be paying off a debt from a previous life, in which he had acted as a guarantor. Once the debt is repaid, he is to return to Mount Lu. The story's emphasis on repaying the debt, and the weight on the monk's heart until he does, bespeak a well-developed commercial ethic. The monk awakes from his dream and starts to recite *The Nirvana Sutra*, which annoys the leader, and he and the monk have a quarrel. The monk proposes that he be sold, with the proceeds to be given to the leader to cover his food and drink. The brigands' leader laughs aloud at the suggestion and says: "You are very mistaken. If I had bought you, then I could show the old contract and be able to sell you. But since I captured you, how can I sell you?"

Here the leader demonstrates knowledge of the Tang law; he needs the contract to prove that the monk was a member of the inferior classes and not a commoner illegally sold into slavery. His objection is revealing: nothing in the law prevents a commoner from becoming a slave, as many did on failure to pay their debts. The law intervenes only when the enslaved debtor is up for sale to a third party, and when he or she comes into contact with the market supervisors who issue market certificates. In the narrative the gang leader does not fear that the authorities will seize his ill-gotten slave—he fears only that should he want to sell his slave, he will be unable to.

Then the monk Huiyuan reminds him of another way to prove

someone is a slave: "If you want to sell me, just pretend that I am a slave born into your household, and you can sell me even if you don't have the earlier contract." In an interesting twist, the monk who does nothing but recite *The Nirvana Sutra* demonstrates a surprising familiarity with the laws regarding the disposal of stolen goods.

The bandit leader subsequently follows Huiyuan's suggested course of action. When they go to visit a broker in slaves and horses in Nanjing, the broker accepts the putative master's word that the slave was born into his household and agrees to help find a buyer. They proceed to the prime minister's mansion. The prime minister, who dreamed of the monk the night before, asks if he was born to his present master or if he was purchased. The broker replies that he was born into his current household, and the prime minister agrees to buy him. In an act so unusual that the author is forced to say "This was not the normal practice," the monk proceeds to read aloud the contract he himself has drafted.

> ✱✱✱ year.[3] ✱✱✱ month. I sell myself to be the slave of Lord Xiang, to whom I will give completely loyal service for his entire life. If I abandon the job in midcourse, for all my coming lives I must die and go to the subterranean prison (*diyu*). Once I have finished serving my sentence, I will be reborn as an animal. Carrying a saddle, with stirrups hanging at my side, with an iron bit in my mouth, I will carry my obligation on my back.
>
> If I serve my lord for a full lifetime, then in all coming lives I will be rewarded by going through the ten stages of bodhisattvahood and joining the Buddha's assembly. (*Dunhuang bianwenji* 1957:177)

This very Buddhist document shares important elements with standard contracts. Like all the Dunhuang contracts, it leaves space for the date to be filled in later, states Huiyuan's obligations, and gives the penalty for failing to observe the agreement. It diverges from other Dunhuang contracts in its failure to name the price, which he and the prime minister have already agreed on, and in its statement of the benefits accruing to Huiyuan should he adhere to the agreement. The Dunhuang contracts frequently name a penalty for failure to meet the terms, but they do not reward those who meet their terms. This contract would not have made sense to an audience

---

3. Huiyuan uses the Chinese word *mou* (usually translated as "certain" or "so-and-so") before the year and month to signify that they are to be filled in later. The character *mou* will be indicated throughout this book with three asterisks, as here.

totally ignorant of either Buddhism or contracts; its interest lies in the monk's artful melding of Buddhist doctrine with contractual language. Huiyuan joins the prime minister's household and is freed six years later when he begins his career of preaching.

Like the author of the tale about Huiyuan, the author of another popular narrative from Dunhuang assumes an audience familiar with contracts. The historical Buddha lived in the sixth century B.C. in northern India, but this narrative from the middle of the eighth century tells of a Buddha who lives in a very Chinese-seeming southern Indian kingdom, whose prime minister, Sudatta, goes on a trip to find a wife for his son and then decides to become a follower of the Buddha (Mair 1983:10–11). He wants to buy a park to give to the Buddha, but the only suitable park (where no animals have previously been killed) is owned by the crown prince, who does not want to sell it. An Indian god assumes the guise of an old man, who advises the crown prince to set the price high: covering the ground with gold and putting silver on all the tree limbs.

> If he [Sudatta] is made to empty his storehouses and exhaust his
>   coffers,
> There is no expectation that he will be willing to buy it;
> Thus the terms of the agreement will not be met,
> And the park will remain in your hands.

We glimpse here how an agreement is reached. One side, here the crown prince, makes an offer that the other side, Sudatta, must accept or reject. The crown prince does as advised, and Sudatta immediately agrees to the very high price.

> On the very spot and facing each other, they discussed the terms,
> Then proceeded to draw up a contract at once;
> Many guarantees were attached,
> And heavy fines were fixed for breach of contract.

(Mair 1983:52–53; *Dunhuang bianwenji* 1957:370)

Only after the buyer and seller have reached an oral agreement do they draw up a contract. This may be a story about Sudatta, it may be set in a putative India, and the people in the tale may have Sanskrit names (transliterated into Chinese), but what they do—and how they do it—is what the Chinese of the Tang dynasty did when they sold land. The listeners of this narrative were sufficiently experienced to expect any contract to include guarantees and penalties for breach of contract. Anything less would defy belief.

Dunhuang under Tibetan Rule

With the exception of the one market certificate to buy a slave from the mid-eighth century, all other contracts date to after 781, when Dunhuang fell to the same Tibetans who would take Turfan five years later. It is not clear what kind of legal system, if any, the Tibetans imposed, although one unusual plaint, dated 833, suggests that the Tibetans did have a court system for adjudicating disputes. In it a widow sues her neighbors for encroaching on her property twenty years earlier and mentions that previous Tibetan officials banned appeals (Fujieda 1961:212–218; S5182). The Tibetans divided the residents of Dunhuang into settlements, monastic households, and commoners (*buluo, sihu, baixing*). Chinese-language contracts continued to be used. Many of the surviving contracts are very short requests for loans of grain from a monastery to a monastic dependent, or from one individual to another.

Some, like the following contract from 822, show the influence of Tang law.[4]

One dark brown bull, six years old, with no brand marks.

On the twentieth day of the first month of the year of the tiger, because Linghu Pangpang lacks food and seeds, he now takes the above bull and sells it to Wu Guanghui of the same settlement for a final price of 19 piculs of wheat, according to Chinese measure. The bull and the wheat are to be exchanged on the same day, with nothing left hanging. If afterward someone claims the bull as his own or says that it is stolen, it is up to the seller to resolve the problem. It is not the concern of the buyer. If within three days after the contract is drawn up, the bull should turn out to have a pre-existing illness, or not eat grass or drink water, he is to be returned to the original owner. After three days, according to the terms of this contract, neither party will be permitted to change its mind. The party that first changes its mind will be penalized 5 piculs to be given to the party that does not. For fear that no one will believe this, we draw up this private contract. The two parties stamp the contract, drawing their finger joints for the record.

4. Because many of these documents do not give a fixed date but merely cite the year of a given animal or the place of the year in a sixty-year cycle, dating the Dunhuang documents poses many problems. I follow the dating given by Yamamoto and Ikeda (1987).

Of the 19 piculs, 3 are millet.

Accepted.

(Yamamoto and Ikeda 1987:#259 [S1475])

The names and ages of the owner of the bull, the owner's brother, and the three guarantors follow. The three-day trial period is the same as that stipulated in *The Tang Code* for livestock and slaves.

Like Turfan contracts, this contract gives the names of the buyer and seller, cites the price, and specifies what subsequent problems the original owner is obliged to resolve and which are the new owner's responsibility. It records the ages of the two brothers and the guarantors under their finger joints, which would have made identifying them much easier. The new owner, who is the stronger party, does not draw his joints at the end of the contract or give his age.

This contract differs from those at Turfan in two important, and characteristic, ways. It does not name the scribe. And it gives the reason for the sale. Not all Dunhuang contracts fit the provisions of Tang law so neatly. One contract from 803, also for the sale of a cow, does not include the three-day grace period (Yamamoto and Ikeda 1987:#257; Gernet 1957:350 [S5820, S5826]).

Only one contract from the Tibetan period, dating to 815 or 827, is for the sale of land. In a confident, legible hand, the contract says:

In the Western Stem area of the tenth district of Yiqiu is one plot of land in seven parcels totaling 10 sixth-acres. To the east is the road; to the west, the irrigation ditch; to the south, Suo Sheng's land; to the north, Wu Zaizai's land. On the third day of the tenth month of the year of the sheep, An Huanqing, a commoner in the Upper Settlement, today sells the above piece of land to his fellow settlement dweller Wu Guozi, because suddenly he has so many debts that he cannot pay his taxes. This land has a final sale price of 160 Chinese pecks, here totaling 150 pecks of wheat and 10 of millet, both according to Chinese measure. Once the sale is complete, Wu Guozi assumes responsibility for the upkeep and cultivation of the land. If, later on, people encroach on the land or claim it is theirs, An Huanqing must divide off the above land and give it to Guozi. The land and the wheat must be exchanged and paid for on the same day, with nothing left hanging. Once the sale is complete, the party who first changes its mind about the sale will be penalized 50 pecks of wheat, to be paid to the party that does not.

If there is an imperial amnesty afterward, An Huanqing will be penalized 5 taels of gold, to be paid to the officials. Officials have government law, and commoners have private contracts. The two sides use stamps and draw their finger joints as a record.

Owner of the land An Huanqing, age 21
An's mother, age 52
Uncle Zheng Deng
Witness Zhang Liangyou
Brother-in-Law An Hengzi

(Yamamoto and Ikeda 1986:47; 1987:#260 [S1475]; Niida 1960:280–282)

As is typical of contracts from Dunhuang, the buyer, Wu Guozi, does not sign the agreement. His failure to sign, and the explanation that An Huanqing cannot pay his taxes, show that the buyer is the superior party in the transaction. The seller, the mother, and the brother-in-law all draw their joints, and the uncle draws a seal version of the character meaning to sign, *ya*, showing his agreement, suggesting that he is literate whereas they are not. The identification of An as a commoner in the Upper Settlement marks this contract as one from the period of Tibetan rule.

The clause denying the applicability of the imperial amnesty sets an extraordinarily high penalty of 5 taels (approximately 200 ounces) of gold for the seller, should an amnesty be issued, although it does not explain what would have constituted an imperial amnesty during the period of Tibetan rule. Such an amnesty on private debts would presumably negate all sales, such as this one, resulting from a person's being in debt. An Huanqing would have been able to claim back his land on the grounds that he sold it to pay off a debt. Yet the penalty is set high enough to ensure that An Huanqing would never try to reclaim his land in the case of an amnesty (Niida 1960:682).

This contract shares many clauses, though not the exact phrasing, with earlier contracts from Turfan: the clauses giving the four borders of the land and its price, granting the buyer responsibility for maintaining irrigation works, charging the seller with resolving any future claims to ownership, and penalizing the party who cancels the agreement. The same clauses occur in other Dunhuang contracts, but the frequent Turfan clause distinguishing private agreements from government law appears only in this contract. Seemingly the residents of Dunhuang do not share the conviction of those in Turfan that private agreements are completely separate from government affairs.

Because the language in the contracts from Dunhuang is as uniform as in those from Turfan, the Dunhuang scribes must have referred to model contracts. While the gist of many clauses is the same, the actual wording differs from Turfan contracts, suggesting that the Dunhuang documents are not later versions of the Turfan contracts but developed independently.

Land Contracts outside Dunhuang

Other sources testify to the use of contracts for land sales elsewhere in China in the years after the 755 An Lushan rebellion. Yuan Zhen (779–831) included an incident in the biography of a friend who, sometime before 806, had an argument with the prefect of Tangzhou (now Biyang, Henan; see map 1), who wanted him to marry his daughter. The friend summoned the local elders and asked them, "So the prefect says my fields are enough to keep me here?" He then threw all their rental contracts into a fire and gave them his land (*Yuanshi Changqing ji* 56:1b).

Liu Zongyuan, the famous philosopher of the Tang, tells of someone else exasperated by contracts, but for a different reason. When he traveled to Yongzhou (now Lingling, Hunan; see map 1), a neighbor knocked on his door one morning and said, "I was unable to meet the obligations of paying taxes and private contracts, so I cleared the land and came here to live" (*Liu Zongyuan ji* 29:764). Liu does not say where the man was originally from.

Two funerary texts shed further light on land contracts. One, dated 835 from Jiangdu, Jiangsu, is for a prefect who died at the age of eighty-four and was buried in a tomb with his wife, who had died earlier. The text begins with a brief family tree giving the first names of his great-grandfather, grandfather, and father and the maiden names of their wives. Prefect Xu and his wife had five sons and two daughters. Of the five sons, two died early, one died without gaining office, one worked in the palace in the imperial wardrobe, and one served in a garrison. Of the daughters, one died young after marrying and the other was widowed young. This is a sad catalogue, especially because none of the seven had children. The eighty-four-year-old man died knowing his family line had died out with him and no one would worship him as an ancestor. The end of the funerary text gives the length of each of the four borders of the tomb plot, the names of the neighbors on four sides, the date, and the price (3,800 coins). The contract ends with names of the mother of the sellers, the younger brother, and three guarantors (Ikeda 1981:234–35; *Jiangsu jinshizhi* 5:33a–34b; Tao [1937] 1982:242).

This format must have been copied from land contracts of the time, as was the end of a tomb text on a funeral vase dated 900 from Lake Shanglin, Zhejiang. After giving a flowery biography of the deceased sixty-three-year-old, it concludes Wang willingly sells "the area within the above four borders, and this is not the concern of any of his kin, or anyone else" (*Wenwu* 1988.12:90–91). This disclaimer was designed to preclude any challenges the seller's family might make after the sale and provides evidence that families were exercising the right to veto land sales by their relatives. The emperor granted them this right in an 811 edict: "In the cases of mortgaging or selling land, or borrowing money with the land as collateral, one must first give relatives on the father's side right of refusal. If they do not want the land, then ask the neighbors on four sides. If the neighbors on four sides do not want it, then others are entitled to buy it" (*Song xingtong* 13:207; Qu Chaoli n.d.). In subsequent centuries this procedure would prove too cumbersome to be workable. These contracts for the purchase of tomb land contain only short sections detailing the purchase of the plot, but the clauses resemble those from Turfan and Dunhuang. Quite possibly every locality in China had its own contracts marked by regionally specific set phrases.

Immunity from Imperial Amnesties

The single land contract from the period of Tibetan rule set a very high penalty in order to discourage the original owner from seeking relief under an amnesty. Many later Dunhuang contracts also include a line claiming immunity from such amnesties. One such claim occurs in the most frequent type of contract, of which forty-one examples survive, for the loan of seed or grain to tide the borrower over until the harvest (Yamamoto and Ikeda 1987:#291–#332).[5]

> On the first day of the third month of the year of the tiger, Cao
> Maosheng, a commoner from the Lower Settlement, borrows 18

5. Eric Trombert, of the Dunhuang manuscripts research team of the Centre National de la Recherche Scientifique, is exploring why there are so many of these loan contracts under Tibetan rule and so few afterward.

pecks of beans from monk Haiqing because he has no seed to plant. The beans are to be repaid by the thirtieth day of the autumn month. REPAID IN THE EIGHTH MONTH.

If the deadline is not met and the beans not returned, twice the amount of beans will be due, and the borrower's household goods and other possessions can be seized to make up the value of the beans. If he absconds, the guarantors will pay the debt. If there is an imperial amnesty before the deadline, it is not grounds for forgiving the debt. For fear that people will not believe, we accordingly draw up this notice. The two sides stamp it and draw their joints as a record.

Owner of the beans
Borrower of the beans Cao Maosheng, 50 years old
Guarantor: his son, Buddhist novice Fagui, 18 years old
Witness
Witness monk Cideng

(Yamamoto and Ikeda 1987:#301 [S1473])

This is an interest-free loan from a monk to the father of a novice monk, provided it is paid back on time—which a later notation, here given in capital letters, indicates it was. If the father had been unable to repay the borrowed beans, he would have been liable for twice the amount of beans he originally borrowed. The contract authorizes the lending monk to sell the borrower's household goods should he fail to make good on the debt, just as *The Tang Code* allows. The guarantor, his son, is to pay the debt back should his father disappear. This is standard for Tang contracts, as is the lender's failure to sign the contract.

The contract diverges sharply from Tang law in denying the applicability of an imperial amnesty to the transaction. The father's debt to the monk will continue to stand even if the emperor orders all debts forgiven. Two other contracts from the Tibetan period contain the same provision (Yamamoto and Ikeda 1987:#312, #313). Read most simply, these denials are simply a statement of fact. The parties concerned are under Tibetan, not Chinese, jurisdiction, and amnesties issued by the Chinese emperor do not apply to them. But such denials continue even after 848, when Dunhuang again came under Chinese rule (Niida 1960:756–757).

The clause disavowing amnesty is an important one, for it shows that the ordinary people participating in these low-level transactions recognized the arbitrary nature of imperial rule and sought to protect themselves from it. As great as the emperor's power was, the people drawing up these contracts did not think it right that he should cancel their private agreements at will. Surely those making the loans were in a position to dictate the terms to those borrowing the grain and cloth. It was they who denied the benefits of an amnesty to those who were chronically in debt and to those whom the emperor sought to aid.

In 848, when an independent military governor reconquered Dunhuang and pledged loyalty to the Tang emperor, the Tang nominally regained Dunhuang (Beckwith 1987:149, 170–171). Dunhuang was not alone in being ruled by an independent governor, who led a unit called the Returning-to-Righteousness Army (*Guiyijun*). After the 755 An Lushan rebellion, China broke into many such regions whose rulers collected their own taxes and remitted only a small portion to the central government. In 907, when one of these military governors overthrew the last Tang emperor, the fiction of the Tang empire finally was exposed and China separated into several regional kingdoms. Dunhuang may have been farther from the Tang capital of Changan (Xian) than the other kingdoms, but once it came under the rule of the Returning-to-Righteousness Army, it experienced exactly the same type of self-rule as regions closer to the capital.

Although many of the Dunhuang contracts claim immunity from imperial amnesty, most of the documented Tang amnesties actually forgive only debts to the government, usually for back taxes, and say nothing about private debts (Katō 1953:622; Niida 1960:752–753). In 819 the emperor issued an amnesty in which he discussed the problems of private debt. Some residents of the capital were in debt because rich families had taken advantage of their need for a short-term loan. The debtors then fled, died, or caused unrest, all to the disadvantage of the public. Accordingly, the emperor called for debts to be forgiven in cases in which "the debt is more than ten years old, the original debtor and his guarantor are dead, or the debtor has no property" (*Wenyuan yinghua* 422:11a; Chen Guocan 1983b:267).

A subsequent regulation of 824 called for forgiveness of private debts by ordering the courts not to hear plaints involving disputes of thirty or more years earlier, in which the creditor or the guarantor had absconded or died without any proof, and in which only the contract survived. The regulation was issued in response to the number of suits in the courts about ambiguous, often very old contracts (*Song xingtong* 26:414; MacCormack 1990: 248–249).

The Tang did not regularly issue such amnesties, assuming private debt not to be within its jurisdiction, but some of the Five Dynasties rulers did issue moratoriums on public and private debts. In 906 the founding emperor of the Latter Jin ordered that all private debts be forgiven once the debtor had paid back 100 percent of the loan in interest (*Rongzhai suibi* 3:9: 515–516; Niida 1960:753). Still, the residents of Turfan and Dunhuang clearly believed that the emperor could declare such a moratorium on debt at any time, and they wanted to protect themselves from that possibility.

A set of five contracts, used by lay students as copying exercises, illustrate what contracts were like after the 848 restoration of Chinese rule.[6] They include the clause denying the applicability of imperial amnesties. The contracts dated between 878 and 909 were found on a scroll, with a list of lucky and unlucky grave sites (Yamamoto and Ikeda 1986:77–78; 1987:#264, #265, #266, #269, #270, #382, #383 [S3877]). Pasted on upside down, the contracts have no relation to the grave-siting text. They are in two hands, both of students learning how to write, and contain corrections in a third hand, probably that of a teacher. The phrasing of the five contracts is significant because students were copying specifically these texts as they learned to write.

One contract for the sale of land begins with the borders of four plots totaling 7 sixth-acres and the date, 909.

> Commoner An Lizi and his son Geheng, of Hongrun canton, because they are short of means, take their family's personal share land and sell it to a commoner of the same canton, Linghu Jintong. The price of the final sale is one bolt of raw silk 40 Chinese feet long. The land and the price have been exchanged today, with nothing left hanging.
>
> Once the sale is complete, Jintong, his sons and grandsons, and his nephews will always have the land as their own. If the household registers are subsequently updated, then Jintong's name should be entered as the householder. The corvée obligations, taxes, and responsibility to keep up the waterworks are to be resolved by those who own the land. If kinsmen or in-laws, siblings, or others subsequently fight and claim the above land, then it is up to the guarantor, Geheng, and his siblings, to resolve this. It is not the

6. Actually there are seven contracts in the set, but two are the same and one is incomplete.

buyer's affair. If an imperial amnesty is issued, it will not be grounds
for challenging this transaction.

The two parties meet face to face and stamp the contract.
According to the law, changing one's mind is not allowed. If
someone first changes his mind, he will pay a superior plowing cow
to the party who does not.

For fear that no one will believe this, we accordingly draw up
this private contract, to be used as proof later on.

Landowner An Lizi
[rest of contract torn]

(Yamamoto and Ikeda 1987:#269)

This contract calls for the new householder's name to be entered in the
household registers only if the government happens to update them. The
wording suggests that the Returning-to-Righteousness government, like
other regional governments, had allowed the household registers to lapse
because it did not have the manpower to keep them current. This percep-
tion was sufficiently widespread to have entered into the monastic school
curriculum. The contract discusses a range of problems and the solutions to
them should a dispute break out subsequent to the signing. If others claim
the land as their own, or if a dispute over the payment of taxes occurs, it is
the seller's obligation to resolve them.

Five surviving contracts for the rental of camels, studied by Jacques
Gernet (1966) provide an interesting comparison. They, too, only take effect
when the rent, given in bolts of cloth, is paid to the camel's owner. The
camels were used for long trips—900 kilometers to Turfan, 1,700 to
Changan—and many disasters could occur. The camel could die en route,
return unable to work, be stolen by thieves, or run away with its renters. All
contingencies were the responsibility of the renter, say these contracts, not
the concern of the camel owner.

The camel rental contracts do not mention an imperial amnesty, but
the 909 contract for the sale of land specifies that such an amnesty will not
apply to the sale. Would the court uphold such a clause directly challenging
imperial authority? It seems unlikely, but the court might choose to accept
the rest of the contract and ignore that one clause.

The proviso against imperial amnesties appears in three more of the
five contracts copied in the margins of this grave-siting text: one for selling
a house, one for the exchange of land and houses, and one for the sale of a

seven-year-old son. Interestingly, these copied contracts closely follow the format of the few actual land contracts that survive. A 936 contract for the sale of a house includes the clause denying the applicability of imperial amnesties. It also ends with the statement, "Fearing that others might not believe this contract, we draw up this text to use as proof later." The lines list slightly to the left, and the names at the end of the contract are not evenly aligned, both signs of an inexperienced writer. The seller and his mother draw their finger joints. Two neighbors (*tongyuanren*), four witnesses (*jianren*), and three secondary witnesses (*linjianren*) make simple, tentative marks. Only one of the secondary witnesses was sufficiently literate to write the Chinese character for understood, *zhi* (Yamamoto and Ikeda 1986:94; 1987:#273 [S1285]). In a more accomplished hand is a contract for the purchase of a house dated 956. The lines are vertical, the characters perfectly spaced and well formed. The clause denying the force of an imperial amnesty is again included, and the end of the contract is missing (Yamamoto and Ikeda 1987:#277 [P3331]). An exercise contract dated 957, in a skilled hand, also includes the proviso about amnesties (Yamamoto and Ikeda 1986:105; 1987:#280 [P3649]). The range of handwriting in these exercises points to varying levels of literacy among those copying the contracts. It also suggests that they were in use among a wide variety of social strata.

Another exercise contract dating to 976, sixteen years after the founding of the Song, shows total mastery of the writing stylus (Yamamoto and Ikeda 1986:109; 1987:#282 [Beijing Sheng 25]). It continues the pattern of the contracts analyzed above and retains the clause about amnesties. A contract for the sale of a slave girl, dated 991, phrases that clause a little differently: "If an imperial amnesty is issued, it will not be grounds for returning to challenge the sale" (Yamamoto and Ikeda 1987:#286 [S1946]). These contracts show no sign of any changes instituted by the new dynasty, except for the adoption of the Song calendar. This fact is not surprising. After appointing the Returning-to-Righteousness Army its representative in Dunhuang, the Song allowed it continued autonomy (Tohi 1980).

Bills of Divorce

Bills of divorce differed from other contracts because they marked the end of a relationship between husband and wife rather than initiating one between buyer and seller, mortgager and mortgagee, owner and lender. The bill of divorce allowed either spouse to remarry without fear of being prosecuted for the crime of taking a second husband or wife (as opposed to a concubine), an offense under Tang law. Strikingly, no marriage contracts survive.

The Tang Code allowed a man to cast off his wife should she disobey his parents, fail to bear children, commit adultery, be jealous, have an incurable disease, talk too much, or steal. These "seven outs" (*qichu*) were not rigid rules. If a wife had no family to take her in, or if she had mourned her parents-in-law for three years, or if her husband's family abandoned her simply because they had become rich, the law specified that she could only be divorced if she was incurably ill or had committed adultery, the two greatest offenses of the seven (*Tanglü shuyi* 14:267–268 [article 189]; Johnson 1979:108n76; MacCormack 1990:278–282). *The Tang Code* also allowed divorce in cases where husband and wife agreed they were incompatible and both sought a divorce (*Tanglü shuyi* 14:268–269 [article 190]). This is the provision the Dunhuang bills of divorce cite.

How frequent was divorce at Dunhuang? It was certainly a course of action open to the people of Dunhuang, but we do not know how often they pursued it. Only one actual bill of divorce, from the period after Song unification, has been found (Yamamoto and Ikeda 1987:#442); the rest are all writing exercises, three of which are very similar (Yamamoto and Ikeda 1987:#441, #487–#489, #491–#493, #497). The writing exercises and the actual bill all begin with a description of what marriage should be like:

> Marriage should last one hundred years, with mutual affection like
> that between water and fish. Man and wife should have ten sons, all
> to be high officials, and they should have daughters who are
> beautiful and gentle, both to their relatives and to others.

But the texts go on to record what happens when the ideal is not met:

> The union of cream and milk will eventually separate into two
> streams. How can a cat and a mouse live for long in the same nest?
> Today, after consulting with our fathers and their children, with our
> elder brothers and younger brothers, with their wives and children,
> we are no longer to be called husband and wife. (Yamamoto and
> Ikeda 1987:#441, #488, #497)

The flowery language of these bills of divorce makes one doubt they were used often.

Contracts in Small Booklets

The simplicity of language used in a group of contracts copied into small booklets points to much more frequent use. I have seen three of these tiny booklets in the Stein collection in London; one more is in Paris (Yamamoto and Ikeda 1987:#495 [S5647]; #496 [S5700]; #498 [P4017]; #499 [S5583]).[7] The poorly drawn characters conjure up unschooled people who practiced writing their first Chinese characters in these cheap, rough brown-paper booklets that are glued, not sewn, together at the seam. Dating to the tenth century, the booklets contain writing exercises for wills, dividing property, adoption, selling a house, freeing slaves, and hiring labor. One booklet includes the torn-off end of a contract for the sale of land, which carries the clause about amnesties. It is in an uneven hand with some misshapen but no mistaken characters, suggesting a moderate command of the language (Yamamoto and Ikeda 1986:137; 1987:#498 [P4017]). Another booklet, measuring 11.0 by 7.5 centimeters, gives texts for contracts to buy a house, free slaves, and adopt a son. Three different types of handwriting appear, suggesting three students shared this one booklet.

The very short, very badly written contract for the sale of the house provides a fascinating glimpse of the rudimentary contracts that circulated alongside the longer versions discussed above. Of a total of 105 characters, 12 are mistaken—and some of the mistakes are basic indeed. The writer confuses characters that look alike, such as *mai* (to buy) for *mai* (to sell), and characters that sound alike, such as *zhi* (to know) for *zhi* (possessive particle). Such errors occur frequently in the work of those learning to write. The errors may be those of the copyist, whose characters are big, misshapen, and clumsy, or they may have been in his original.

The beginning of this contract is missing but must have included the four dimensions of the plot on which the house rested. The contract continues:

> To be sold to commoner Yao Wenqing of [   ] canton in a final sale
> at a price of 2 piculs per foot, for a total of 16 piculs for the house
> and other goods. The other goods and the house must be exchanged⁻
> on this day with nothing left hanging and the grain paid to the
> bushel. Once the sale is complete, the sons and grandsons will
> continue forever and the men and women will be owners. The Li

7. In most cases I have had to content myself with examining photographs and transcriptions of the contracts discussed.

family [the sellers] cannot abscond. If subsequently relatives, siblings, or in-laws come and dispute the claim, the neighbors must find a good house as compensation. If afterward an imperial amnesty is issued, it will not be grounds for disputing this agreement. The two parties face each other and stamp this as final. (Yamamoto and Ikeda 1986:134; 1987:#496 [S5700])

The wording is terse. Still, it manages to convey the same sense as other contracts in many fewer characters. The price is set (probably at the customary local rate), subsequent claims on the house are to be compensated, and imperial amnesties will have no effect. The survival of this poorly written, truncated contract testifies to the use of contracts at even the lowest educational level—and to the richness of the Dunhuang materials.

Contracts and Local Courts

The large number of clauses in the Dunhuang contracts points to increasing awareness of the likelihood that the two parties signing a contract will end up in court sometime in the future. Some of the most revealing contracts are those drafted by judicial officials in order to resolve a dispute. The first of these is dated 852, four years after the imposition of rule by the Returning-to-Righteousness Army in 848.

A lay monk and his brother used a contract to record the exchange of 25 sixth-acres of land for 11 sixth-acres of another monk's land (Yamamoto and Ikeda 1986:71; 1987:#262 [P3394]).[8] This long contract, much of it taken up with the borders of the different plots to be exchanged, contains several clauses indicating that it was written under the supervision of local officials. It gives the date of a decision in a court case permitting this exchange of land because each desired it. In fact, the contract specifies, "once the land is exchanged, each will take possession of his own land, and it will be entered into the official record as fixed, and it will be the owner's property forever." The contract gives a price to be paid by Monk Lu for the trees, walls, and road to the well on the Zhangs' land. If the Zhangs are unable to prevent someone from subsequently making a claim to the land, they must compensate Monk Lu and the new plot must be entered into the official record. The monks signing this contract are carrying out a legal exchange

8. Gernet (1957:382–387) provides a translation and analysis of the contract, and Niida ([1937] 1983:194–199) transcribes and discusses it.

under Tang law, under official supervision, and they want everything to be recorded on the land registers. In 852, four years after the reestablishment of Chinese rule, the land registers still have meaning.

The penalties for abrogating the contract are also much stronger than in private contracts: he who cancels must pay twenty loads of wheat into a military storehouse, not to the other party, and receive thirty beatings with the heavy stick as well. Everything suggests a court-ordered exchange to compensate Lu for a debt Zhang could not pay.

This is not an exchange among equals, as Gernet (1957:386–387) points out. The original owner of the land indicates his agreement, but the name of the new owner, Monk Lu, does not appear. Zhang guarantees compensation should someone make a claim to his former land, but Monk Lu does not. Zhang's two sons, his nephew, his younger brother and son all act as guarantors, who are liable should he abscond. No less than seven witnesses are present.

Here, too, we see a range of marks and signatures pointing to very different levels of literacy within the society, and within individual families. Zhang stamps his fingerprint after his name, as do two sons who act as guarantors and a third who is not a guarantor. All are presumably illiterate. Zhang's younger brother, who also acts as a guarantor, writes his name in Tibetan. Of the seven witnesses, only one monk can sign his name, Fayuan, in ill-formed characters. The other six make no mark at all.

In another case fifty years later, a monk rented his land to a commoner:

> This contract is drawn up on the seventeenth day of the eighth
> month of the fourth year of the Tianfu reign (904). Linghu Faxing, a
> commoner monk from Shensha Canton, has two parcels of personal
> share land totaling 8 sixth-acres, which are by Meng Shou's land (and
> Yangyuan ditch). Because he needs more revenue, he has consulted
> with his neighbor in the same canton, commoner Jia Yuanzi, and
> agreed to take (as rent) one bolt of good raw silk, 8 long, and one bolt
> of brown felt, 25 Chinese feet long, of Yuanzi's. The above plots of
> land are to be rented to Yuanzi for twenty-two years to plant as a
> tenant. Twenty-two years from this year the land will be returned to
> the original owner.
>
> With the exception of the land tax, all the other obligations of
> the land, including corvée tasks, are the responsibility of the owner
> of the land. The land tax, which is paid annually to the government,

will be presented by Yuanzi. The upkeep of the irrigation channels is
to be divided equally between the two.

   If, from now on, an imperial amnesty is issued, it will not be
grounds for further dispute. Furthermore, should relatives or others
claim ownership, it is up to the guarantor to resolve the claims and
to find a good piece of land nearby to make up the loss. Once
agreement is reached and the two sides meet face-to-face and stamp
the contract, neither party is allowed to change its mind. If one does,
that party must pay a penalty to the government. For fear that there
will be no proof later on, we draw up this contract. (Yamamoto and
Ikeda 1986:80; 1987:#371 [P3155])

This contract too bears all the hallmarks of a court-ordered settlement.
With a number of additions in the margins (given in parentheses in the
translation) and with the measure word for the eight unnamed units of silk
still missing, it is a draft, which will be recopied in the final version to be
signed by the two parties. The five witnesses include two deciding officials
from the office manager's office (*dusi panguan*), a clerk (*yaya*), and, finally,
the inspector-in-chief (*duyuhou*). If either party reneges on the agreement,
the penalty is to be paid to government officials, not to the other party. The
new tenant appears to be the stronger party, for his name does not appear at
the end of the contract. The renter pays rent to the monk only once, at the
beginning of the twenty-two years, and never again. He obtains use of the
land and is obliged to pay only the land tax, while the monk is liable for all
other obligations that accompany the land.

   The clause denying the applicability of imperial amnesties appears
here, but for a different reason than in the other Dunhuang contracts. The
drafters of the agreement are distinguishing a typical rental agreement from
this one. The renting monk is not to be given any of the benefits accruing
to those in debt, because this is not a typical rental contract. Whatever the
monk has done, it is not so heinous that his land has been confiscated and
sold. But he is leaving the site of his land for twenty-two years. Otherwise
he could resolve subsequent claims to his land, as is usually the obligation
of the owner, not his guarantors. It seems that the court has sentenced him
to hard labor or exile for twenty-two years and devised this scheme as a way
for him to keep his land, should he live long enough to serve out his
sentence.

   Much more documentation survives from a dispute in 945, when a
widow named Along sued a squatter, Suo Fonu, for encroaching on her

family's land. The available documents include the presiding judge's decision, a contract her son used to entrust the land to his father's elder brother, and depositions taken by clerk from the widow, her brother-in-law, and the squatter (Yamamoto and Ikeda 1987:#374 [P3257]).[9] The widow submitted one piece of written evidence, a contract, as proof of her claim to the land:

> On the nineteenth day of the second month of the *jiawu* year [934], Suo Yicheng will go to Guazhou. He entrusts his father's elder brother, Suo Huaiyi, with cultivating as a tenant 32 sixth-acres of the personal share land of his father and ancestors. Until Yicheng obtains his return to Shazhou, his uncle Huaiyi will be responsible for all various beacon duties, for supplying officials with firewood and grass, and for small and large taxes and corvée obligations. Once his uncle begins to farm the land, if he harvests wheat or millet, it goes without saying that his uncle obtains the harvest and the sowing seed. If Yicheng obtains his return to Shazhou, then he will get this land back. The maintenance of irrigation channels, taxes, and corvée are not his uncle's affair. The two sides meet face-to-face and stamp the contract, and are not permitted to change their minds. He who changes his mind first will be penalized one sheep. For fear that others will not believe, this contract is accordingly drawn up to be used as proof later.

> Cultivator and uncle, Suo Huaiyi (mark)
> Cultivator, son of Suo Fu (mark)
> Witness Suo Liuzhu (mark)
> Witness, scribe, and judge Zhang Nai
> [two illegible characters]

The text entrusts the uncle with performing his absent nephew's beacon duties and paying his taxes as long as he is absent. The contract bears the marks of three signatories: the uncle, Suo Huaiyi; the nephew, Suo Yicheng, who in the contract is called the son of Suo Fu; and one witness (fig. 4).

This contract describes an unusual situation: a nephew lends his land to his uncle for an undetermined length of time, and no money changes hands. As Niida ([1937] 1983:396) points out, this is not a rental, sale, or mortgage agreement. The fourth name on the contract, Zhang Nai, indicates that a judge is acting as both witness and scribe.

9. These documents are transcribed in Liu Fu ([1934] 1957:245–49) and Ikeda (1979:652–654), and are summarized in Niida ([1937] 1093:392–396).

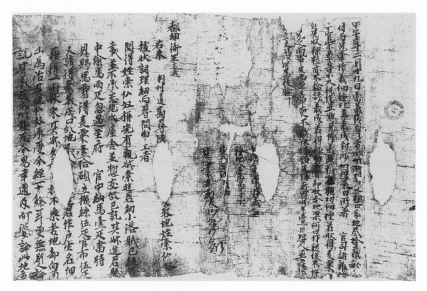

Fig. 4. Widow Along Goes to Court (and Wins). Widow Along, having fallen on hard times, went to court in 945 to evict a squatter from a plot once owned by her son. As evidence, she presented the presiding judge with a contract, signed by her son and her brother-in-law. Here we see the court copyist's transcription of that contract (which has four white holes along its folds). The contract, dated eleven years earlier than the court documents, entrusts the uncle with the care of his nephew's land while the nephew goes to the next town, as ordered by a local judge. The widow's son never returns. While he is away, a second squatter comes and claims the land. Widow Along petitions the court to award her title to the land of her now-dead son. Significantly, the court rules in her favor, showing that private contracts had become more authoritative than household registers.

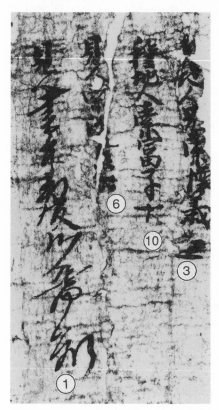

Widow Along won her case, with a contract that bore no conventional signatures. Her brother-in-law drew three horizontal lines, the number three (*san*) as his mark (3). His nephew drew the character for ten (*shi*, which looks like a plus sign) as his mark (10). One of the witnesses, who later bought some of the land from the widow, drew what looks like the Chinese word for six (*liu*) as his (6). Only the scribe, a low-level official named Zhang Nai, was capable of signing his own name, which he did with so much flourish that the last two characters cannot be made out (1). (Photograph [P3257] courtesy of Clichés Bibliothèque nationale de France © Bibliothèque nationale de France.)

Detail

The depositions make it possible to reconstruct what happened. The widow, her brother-in-law, and the squatter all dictated statements to a clerk (*duyaya*) eleven years after this contract was signed (fig. 5). They did not draw their marks after their statements. Instead, they drew the joints on their middle fingers (Niida 1939). As the nephew's mother put it in her deposition, her son had "broken the regulations and been ordered to Guazhou." Her brother-in-law's deposition was more direct: "He committed a crime and was ordered to Guazhou." Guazhou was the neighboring prefecture to Shazhou, as Dunhuang was called in the Tang. So the court not only sentenced him to go to Guazhou, but also arranged for his uncle to take over the farming of his land until his return. His mother testified that while she had 32 sixth-acres of land when her son left, she sold 12 sixth-acres to Suo Liuzhu, the witness to the agreement. The contract uses the term "personal share land of his father and ancestors" (*fuzu koufendi*). Her brother-in-law supported her from the proceeds of the remaining land. This was, of course, a kind of rent, but the family obligations between the two were so strong that it did not require spelling out in the contract. The son, Suo Yicheng, never returned, having died in Guazhou.

The uncle testified that he had to leave the land at one point to fight bandits on horseback. When he returned, an interloper named Suo Jinjun, a distant relative, had taken over the land. The uncle ended his statement saying he did not dare to sue, and the widow concurred they were frightened to go to court. The squatter Suo Fonu explained why. His name meant Buddha's slave, suggesting that he was raised in a monastery, but he said nothing of his own life. His statement began with a biography of his uncle, Suo Jinjun, who as a child fell into the hands of bandits, so long ago that he could not remember where his own house, water, and land were, and so long ago that he was not present when his family's land was divided. He escaped with two horses and went to the prefectural office, where local officials paid him for the two horses with grain and cloth. The officials also gave him the Suo family's remaining 20 sixth-acres, which he farmed for one or two harvests. When the first squatter, who "did not like the bitter land," left for the Southern Mountains just north of Lake Koko Nor, his nephew, Buddha's slave, took over farming the land and continued to do so for more than ten years before the widow sued him.

In his decision, the responsible official (*panguan*) gave a brief account of the changing ownership of the land. When the widow's husband was still alive, they owned several houses, which were then sold off, leaving her with only 20 sixth-acres of land. He acknowledged the new squatter's claim that

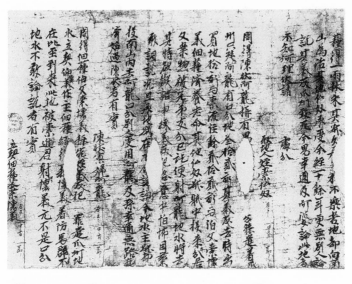

 ① ② ③

Fig. 5. How the Illiterate Signed Documents. Those who could not read and write most frequently signed documents by drawing three lines to indicate the top of the finger and the first and second joints. In these affidavits from Widow Along's 945 dispute are three sketches of fingers. That of her brother-in-law (1) and that of the squatter (3) bear the same label, "joints of the middle finger of the left hand" (*zuoshou zhongzhi jie*). The widow's finger (2) has a different label, "joints of the middle finger of the right hand" (*youshou zhongzhi jie*).

As here, men and women used the same finger but different hands. Men used the left hand, whereas the widow drew her right middle finger. Sometimes the index finger was substituted for the middle finger, but the left-right sex differentiation was retained through the twentieth century in China and in neighboring Japan, Vietnam, and Korea as well. (Photograph [P3257] courtesy of Clichés Bibliothèque nationale de France © Bibliothèque nationale de France.)

Detail 1   Detail 2

the Suo family land was not being cultivated when local officials gave the land to his uncle. But after the uncle, who had become accustomed to tribal life, left for the Southern Mountains, his nephew, the second squatter, took over the land. Although the court referred to the second squatter as the nephew of the widow, it did not explain how they were related. They do not seem to have been close kin, for the squatting nephew does not give the widow the slightest financial support, "not a needle or a blade of grass," in the judge's words. Because of the widow's difficulties in supporting herself and her grandson after her son's death, the court awarded her the land and the water so that she could live out her old age.

This case tells much about life in Dunhuang. Throughout the document, the word "land" is always paired with "water," for land without water rights could not be farmed. Farming the land was hard—so hard that the first squatter could not stand the life and fled south. The cultivators of Dunhuang had to battle a harsh environment, and they also had to contend with marauding bandits. Were the bandits the uncle left to fight the same ones who kidnapped the first squatter as a child? We cannot know.

These documents richly document the social flux of the tenth century. The widow began as the wife of a well-off rich man. She fell on hard times and had to sell property. Finally her son was arrested for an unnamed crime and was sent to a neighboring town. Her brother-in-law farmed the land, then left. A relative came. He then left. Another relative came. This tale, though from the frontier, challenges the stereotyped view that one peasant worked the same plot of land his entire life.

This case also reveals something about access to courts. The impoverished widow was not so poor that she could not pay court costs. She was not from the chronically poor of Dunhuang; she was once prosperous. She and her brother-in-law hesitated to go to court because the first squatter had an official proclamation naming him the head of the household (*huzhu*), the owner of land. The brother-in-law testified that he could not contest the squatter's claim, since it was his nephew's personal share land, not his own. After he left, his nephew had no such document, so they decided to go to court—but it is not clear why it took them eleven years to do so. Could the first official have been transferred elsewhere in the meantime?

In weighing the conflicting claims to the land, the deciding official considered the testimony of the widow, her brother-in-law, and the squatter as well as the contract her deceased son signed entrusting his uncle with the land. He did not include a copy of the family's household register or the document giving the squatter the rights to the land. No one even mentioned the government land registers. Personal share land had become entirely heritable, with the state making no claim to it after the death of the previous owner. The state did keep registers, but they were not the best guide to land ownership. Even though the official's award to the first squatter after his escape from the bandits named him head of household, the court did not consult the household register.

Even though this was just one court case, from Dunhuang, what happened in the far northwest was happening on a larger scale all over China. Once the Tang stopped regularly updating its registers, after the chaos of the 755 An Lushan rebellion, neither it nor its successors could use them to chart landowning. Because individual household registers were no longer updated and taxes were no longer reassessed, the registers were widely acknowledged to be obsolete and inaccurate.

One story from the mid–ninth century collection tells of two men who claimed ownership of the same plot in Yazhou (Yaan, Sichuan) in the far western part of Sichuan, near Mount Emei. Because neither man had a receipt for payment of land taxes, the two of them went to a local temple and asked the god to nod his head if it belonged to one of them and to open his mouth if it belonged to the other. The deity opened his mouth, and the loser gave the land to the winner (*Jianjielu* 6:6b–7a; Tao [1937] 1982:241). Surely the author included this tale because it related an extraordinary way to deal with what was becoming an increasingly ordinary problem: the lack of correct documentation to demonstrate ownership of a plot of land.

By the tenth century the Tang ban on the sale of land had been largely forgotten, as shown by the following story about one of the regional rulers of the time. The man who was to become the founder of the Latter Jin dynasty (936–946), one of the regional kingdoms in the Tang-Song interregnum, was famed for his fairness as a judge.

In 933 the official heard a case on appeal from Jiumen (now Gaocheng county, Hebei). A man had wanted to sell a plot of land to his elder brother, but they could not agree on a price, so he ended up selling it to outsiders. Under the privileges reserved for kin as specified in the edict of 811, the new owners needed the approval of the elder brother before they could draw up a contract, but the brother refused. The case went to court and was appealed to the official. He gave the following decision:

> If we are to discuss this in terms of reason, the elder brother benefits
> from the good land and the younger brother wants a good price. To
> do this is as it should be, and to prevent this is wrong. The elder

brother is extremely unrighteous and should be repeatedly beaten. Sell the land to the person paying the higher price. (*Jiu Wudai shi* 75:982)

Everyone was struck by the aptness of his pragmatic decision, which dismissed the claims of kin in favor of making a greater profit. The tale contains no vestige of the equal-field system, with its ban on the sale of land.

The Institution of Contract Tax

Regional governments began tacitly to acknowledge that their registers were not accurate and instead recognized contracts among private individuals as proof of ownership. At the same time, the regional governments stepped up their efforts to levy an indirect tax on contracts. They collected the tax through brokers, who acted as middlemen for the purchase or mortgage of a given good (Shiba 1970:165–66). Brokers, in drawing up the contract, assumed the role that scribes had played at Turfan. By the tenth century, brokers had become so common that one regional government forbade their use except in sales of land, slaves, livestock, and vehicles (*Wudai huiyao* 26:415; Shiba 1968:392; 1970:165–66). And a 939 land grant to a monastery in Xianning county, Hubei, which was inscribed on stone, gives the name of the broker as well as those of the seller and the guarantor (*Jinshi cuibian* 121:7a–9a; Niida [1937] 1983:143–144).

In 952 the prefect of Kaifeng, the city that the Song would select as their capital eight years later, petitioned the ruler of the Later Zhou kingdom about the abuses of brokers, who sold the same goods and houses several times over so they could collect repeated commissions. He suggested a reform linked to payment of the stamp tax.

> Those wishing to mortgage or pawn things or land should summon an official broker, the owner of the goods, and the neighbors on four sides to all sign the contract to vouch that the goods in question have not previously been mortgaged. When they pay the stamp tax, they should present one copy of the unstamped contract to the tax office, for the person in charge of the office to examine. He should have the official broker and the neighbors check the contract and vouch that this is not a case of remortgaging. Only then can the stamp be obtained. (*Wudai huiyao* 26:415–416)

The contract tax, then, was to be levied only after the local clerks had ascertained that a given transaction was legitimate. One of their tasks was to check with any relatives and neighbors before allowing sale to an outsider. Official brokers were those registered with the government. This memorial does not reveal how much the tax was, but it was probably near the 4 percent that it had been in the Sui and that it continued to be in the early years of the Song.

Contracts in Transition

The imposition of a contract tax marked a turning point in government policy toward contracts. *The Tang Code*, often observed only in the breach, had banned the sale of land and had taxed all transfers of commercial property such as animals and slaves. The compilers of *The Tang Code* had tried to maintain a distance from private contracts and had minimized the extent to which the state would intervene. The earliest of the Dunhuang contracts date to this period of state control. The market certificate for the sale of a thirteen-year-old slave fits the provisions of the code exactly.

Yet the taxation system designed by the compilers of *The Tang Code* was already coming apart. In the aftermath of 755, central government control declined precipitously. After Dunhuang fell to the Tibetans in 781, its residents continued to use Chinese-language contracts, often to borrow grain. The one land contract extant from this period contains a clause denying the applicability to the sale of an imperial amnesty. Many more contracts survive from after the reimposition of Chinese rule in 848. The denial of imperial amnesties persists both in actual contracts and in copyists' exercises; in long, complicated contracts and in short, booklet contracts; and in contracts written in confident hands and those written in halting strokes. All would have heard the denial of imperial amnesties read aloud at the time of signing, and all signed their names to it, whether using the joint-line marks of the illiterate, the tentative scribbles of the more literate, or the confident signatures of the fully literate.

The Dunhuang documents capture the dissolution of the equal-field system. In 852 those drawing up a contract still wrote as if the land registers were intact: the sale "will be entered into the official record as fixed." Fifty years later the situation had changed. A student exercise contract from 909 says, "If the household registers are subsequently updated, then Jintong's name should be entered as the householder." If! Updating the registers had already become so uncertain that students were including this phrase in the contracts they practiced at school. Recall the tale from Sichuan of the two men who, in the absence of household registers, went to a deity to establish ownership of a plot of land. The people of Dunhuang and elsewhere in China took the more pragmatic approach of Widow Along, who presented the contracts her two sons had signed as she sued to recover her deceased son's land.

The household registers of the equal-field system were gone. Instead, people had to use contracts to demonstrate ownership, and regional rulers of the tenth century instituted a stamp tax on those contracts. With that step they committed themselves to far more governmental involvement in the drawing up of contracts than the early Tang rulers could ever have imagined.

4

The Age of

Governmental

Taxation

In 960, fifty years after the disintegration of the Tang, the founder of the Song united China (map 2). No one could have foreseen just how difficult it would be to collect the tax on contracts. Nor could anyone have anticipated to what extent the difficulties would stem from the brokers, the agents chosen to collect the tax. Although the Song could not increase the land tax for fear of alienating powerful landowning families, it still needed money both to support its armies against the steady incursions of northern peoples on its borders and to fund its attacks against them. At first it collected the contract tax as its predecessors had, keeping it at 4 percent of the value of the item sold, but after the 1126 loss of all of northern China to the Jurchen invaders, the beleaguered Southern Song began to collect the contract tax more aggressively, raising the rate higher and higher. Throughout three centuries of Song rule, the authorities continuously raised the tax on contracts and, just as continuously, the populace evaded it.

At the time the Song was founded, the expanded use of woodblock printing prompted an explosion in the number of printed books and the number of surviving sources. Unlike the shadowy figures who drew up contracts at Turfan and Dunhuang, Song brokers increasingly became both the object of official scrutiny and the subject of bureaucratic records. Officials wrote about the activities of wily brokers in their informal notes also. Some of these collections recount anecdotes from daily life the authors found interesting; others, such as Hong Mai's *Record of the Listener* (*Yijianzhi*), focus on strange, occasionally unbelievable tales (Hansen 1990:17–22). These notes sometimes mention contracts, often for the purchase of concubines. In addition to these sources, the texts of a small number of contracts dating

Map 2. The Borders of Song China, 960–1260, superimposed on modern provincial boundaries. The Northern Song ruled north and south China until 1126, when the north fell to the invading Jin armies and the government fled Kaifeng for the new capital of Hangzhou. (Drawn by Donna Perry.)

to the Song are extant, but they are, with one exception, land contracts from Huizhou, Anhui (shown in map 2).

The Song government began its attempts to regulate contracts early. In 969 the Song emperor issued a directive requiring that all those using land contracts pay the stamp tax within two months of signing. Writing in the twelfth century, Chen Fuliang explained the rationale for the two-month waiting period: "Those who are going to mortgage or sell things should first ask their neighbors if any of them wishes to mortgage or buy the land by writing the inquiry on a placard and waiting for the reply. After two months the contract can be approved and stamped" (*Wenxian tongkao* 19:186–187). Following Tang practice, this regulation granted the right of first refusal in all land transactions to neighbors, and probably to relatives as well. By the 1070s the process for selling land had become too cumbersome, and the right of refusal was limited to kin unless the neighbors had graves on the plot (*Wenxian tongkao* 5:61). Throughout the eleventh century the rate of the contract tax stayed at the 4 percent it had been since the sixth century (*Chuijianlu* 4:116; *Yanfanlu*, xu 5:12a).

Because those who designed the tax on contracts had identified a genuinely popular phenomenon, the contract tax had the potential to increase government revenues significantly. People were using contracts continuously, and officials desperately wanted to tax all the buying and selling taking place around them. They understood the enormous revenue potential of the contract tax, but they also anticipated the costs. If they charged a tax for stamping contracts, then local people would want something in return, namely a place to take their contract disputes. But because the costs of administering a court system could have been staggering, officials sought to discourage people from going to court. If the frequency with which they extended the deadline for contract registration is any indication, government officials were never satisfied with the rate of payment of the tax. Similarly, if the frequency with which they decried excessive litigiousness is any indication, they were unconvinced that they had succeeded in reducing the number of suits brought to the courts.

The dynasty witnessed many proposals of measures designed to minimize litigation and so lessen the amount of time officials had to spend in court. One early solution, proposed in 983, was for the government to draft a contract that could serve as a model.

> The many disputes and suits over land and houses are due to the
> selfish and indiscriminate writing of contracts that give the borders
> of a plot without specifying any distances, or trick the neighbors and
> villagers without consulting them about the sale. With this kind of
> deceitful, lax behavior, the number of suits increases. Please ask the
> tax bureaus of the capital and the prefectures and counties outside to
> summon the brokers for land and houses to pick one model contract
> each for mortgages and sales and to post it as an example.
> (*Changbian* 24:542)

Like the rulers of the tenth-century regional kingdoms before them, the Song relied on private brokers to collect the contract tax for them. The official making the suggestion above assumes the magistrate will be able to persuade brokers to adopt the new models voluntarily. He proposes neither penalties for failure to comply nor financial incentives for compliance. Nothing indicates that brokers, or magistrates, followed his advice.

Only one contract from central China survives from the early years of the Song, and it is for the purchase of a tomb plot. From Anxi county (now Dingxian, Hebei, shown in map 2), it is dated 984.

> The owners of [   ] orchard in Anxi county, Ma Yin, An Qiong, with his sons An Si and An Hua, draw up a contract together. They willingly sell their own land . . . [borders incomplete]. This land runs 20-[   ] five-foot units along the east-west axis and 24 five-foot units along the north-south axis. This land Ma Yin and the others willingly sell to Shi Jin to serve as his tomb forever. Shi Jin and his descendants will be the owners. If someone makes a claim, or if someone encroaches on the land, both are the responsibility of the seller of the land, Ma Yin, and others who will personally be responsible for resolving them. They are not Shi Jin's responsibility. The price is 4 strings, 500 coins, to be paid in full at the time of the contract signing. Officials have government law and do not accept private agreements as conclusive. (Ikeda 1981:241; *Diquan zhengcun* unpaginated)

The date and the names of the four sellers follow, but the buyer, the deceased Shi Jin, is not named. Nor are any witnesses or guarantors.

This contract is strikingly similar to land contracts from Turfan and Dunhuang, with many of the same clauses. As is to be expected of a contract from a different region, the phrasing varies slightly. Shi Jin is officially the buyer, but since he is dead, a relative, probably a son, must be acting on his behalf. He receives the privileges due the buyer and is absolved of the responsibility for resolving any future claims on the land, even while dead. Perhaps the drafter of the contract wished to protect him from claims brought in the courts of the underworld, the subject of chapter 7.

Instead of the phrase which occurs so often at Turfan, "Officials have government law and commoners have private contracts," this contract reads, "Officials have government law (*zhengfa*) and do not accept private agreements as conclusive." This line distinguishes between officially recognized agreements and those drawn up among individuals. Even at the end of the tenth century people drawing up contracts say they are doing so independently of government attempts to regulate them. This contract, with its insistence on the separation of private contracts from government regulation, is a holdover from earlier times, when the government had indeed been reluctant to intervene in private contracts.

With the decline of the Tang household registers, as at Dunhuang, the only way to prove ownership of a given plot in central China was to show a contract from the time the plot had been bought. From 1056 to 1058, one Song official, Judge Bao (who later became the hero of so many plays), served as prefect of the capital city of Kaifeng. His biography in the official history tells us: "There was a big flood in the capital. Many buildings, gardens, and arbors of officials and powerful families straddled the Huimin River. As a result, the river was blocked and could not flow, so they were all torn down. Some brought land contracts to support their claims to ownership, and some had forged increased dimensions, but Judge Bao evaluated them and charged the falsifiers before the emperor." Judge Bao was also credited with encouraging people to bring their suits directly to him and so bypassing the bribe-hungry clerks (*Changbian* 184:4460; Hayden 1978:19). Although thought to have superhuman powers, Judge Bao could assess someone's claim to a plot of land only by examining the contract he or she presented.

A different tale about Judge Bao shows that even he was unable to make people fulfill unrecorded agreements. During the time he was prefect of Kaifeng, the story goes, two men went to court. One claimed that he had left two trunks filled with gold, silver, and brocades with the other man's father, who had then died; but the dead man's son denied any knowledge of the transaction and pointed out that there was no contract. Judge Bao listened to the dispute and ruled in the son's favor. The narrator of the tale comments, "Everyone agrees that people today have no conscience and are concerned only with seeking their own advantage" (*Houde lu* 2:6a; reference courtesy of Barend ter Haar). Like the narrator, the people of the Song may have thought the use of contracts was new to their age, yet all the evidence suggests that earlier officials also had to rely on written agreements when verbal accounts conflicted.

The regulation of 969 establishing the contract tax mentions only land contracts, but other sources indicate that the use of contracts to purchase concubines was widespread (Shiba 1968:394). In an incident from sometime before 1086, recorded in a set of miscellaneous notes, a man visits Kaifeng and stays at an inn, where he hears his neighbor sobbing. The neighbor explains that he has sold his daughter to a merchant for 400 strings so he can pay back money he has stolen from public funds. The man offers to buy the girl, but her father explains that, as he and the merchant have already drawn up the contract and he has received payment, he cannot get his daughter back. The visitor responds, "If you give his money back, you can obtain the contract. If he refuses, then take him to court." The father concurs, the visitor gives him the money, and they agree to meet three days later at a pier. When the man and his daughter arrive, the samaritan's boat has already sailed (*Nenggai zhai manlu* 12:350).

This tale does not quite fit with accepted practice. If the two parties had already signed the contract and money had changed hands, then the father should not have been able to redeem his daughter in order to sell her to another buyer. He was probably able to do so because the merchant feared being sued for the illegal purchase of a free woman, an offense according to *The Tang Code* and according to the penal code of the Song (*Tanglü shuyi* 26:486 [article 400]; *Song xingtong* 26:415). The advice the father was given shows the eagerness with which people went to court.

A case from Kaifeng, sometime between 1107 and 1110, contrasts the rival claims to the same woman by her husband and by a medical official who has purchased her. Her family has given her up for dead, although the corpse has disappeared from her grave. When the owner hears her say she has found her son and husband, he angrily responds: "Last year when I bought you, you had no husband. There is a contract and a broker who can prove this. How dare you?" When her husband sues in the courts of Kaifeng to get his wife back, she testifies that she sold herself, while starving, to a broker. The prefect of Kaifeng orders the husband to pay the official the sale price, but the official refuses and appeals the case to the censorate. Before they can hear the case, the woman disappears again and the case is dismissed (*Yijianzhi* 3:8:435–436).[1]

The surprised owner seems confident that his claim to the woman is stronger than her husband's. The first official to hear the case sides with the husband but still orders him to pay compensation to the buyer, and we can only wonder what the appeal judges would have thought. Hong Mai must have included the tale in *The Record* because of the woman's disappearances and because of the odd situation in which her husband found himself, suing another man for the return of his wife. Nevertheless, it seems to have been normal practice for a broker to have met a woman on the streets of Kaifeng and obtained her simply for the cost of feeding her.

1. All notes to *The Record of the Listener* give the number of the section (1 for *jia*, 2 for *yi*, and so on), followed by the chapter and then the page in the standard 1981 Zhonghua shuju edition.

An official who purchases a milknurse has a similar experience. In 1115 he buys the woman in Kaifeng from a broker, who assures him that her husband has just died. Three years later the official and his household are traveling to a new post in Anhui when a man calls to them from a bridge, saying that he is the woman's husband and demanding her return. The official tries to find the man, who has disappeared, and asks his nurse, who will not explain. That night she slips out. The next morning her corpse is seen floating on the water (*Yuzhao xinzhi* 3:44; Shiba 1968:396). The official never finds out what has happened, but it seems that one of the few courses of action open to unhappily married women was to run away from their husbands and sell themselves to brokers as slaves. It was not much of a recourse.

At the same time that ordinary people feared unscrupulous brokers might kidnap free women, officials censured those same brokers for not paying the contract tax they were supposed to collect. The anonymous author of an 1117 manual, *Self-Admonitions for Local Administrators* (*Zuoyi zizhen*), advises magistrates about the many problems they will encounter in office and recommends strict supervision of brokers dealing in different goods (Bol 1977).

> When doing business, brokers often cheat traveling merchants. You should have them call two or three reliable guarantors and provide guarantees for each other. Check their names against your register. Each is to be given a wooden sign to carry on his person. Those over seventy should not serve. Furthermore, issue placards notifying the merchants so that they fully understand. (*Zuoyi zizhen* 2:11a)

And this is what the wooden signs are supposed to say:

> *** county, *** type of broker, *** name carries on his body the sign listing the county's restrictions as below:
>   You should not trade in goods that have not been stamped upon payment of taxes.
>   You should not obstruct those transactions completed face-to-face by the buyer and seller themselves.
>   You should not raise the price or sell goods on credit, nor put off or delay traveling merchants.
>   In cases where traditionally the practice has been to deal on credit with due dates for payment, a clear contract should be drawn up and several reliable guarantors should be summoned. If you do not, you will cause lawsuits.

The above is given to ✱✱✱ name. When he meets with a traveling merchant who wishes to do business with him, the broker is first to take this sign and read it to him.

✱✱✱official   ✱✱✱mark

(*Zuoyi zizhen* 8:42b; Bol 1977:27–28)

It seems doubtful that reading these rules aloud to a potential customer would have prevented cheating, but these exhortations illuminate the problems brokers caused for magistrates. They did not pay the contract tax each time they bought or sold goods. They charged more for goods on credit, and they did not always draw up contracts specifying when payment should be made. The failure to use contracts resulted in the loss of income to the county, and no doubt to the brokers themselves. The author of this manual tries to effect a change. He wants brokers to draw up contracts to record loans for merchants who have traditionally not used them. The magistrate's complaint that brokers acted as middlemen, and charged for their services, in transactions that could have occurred without them, is one that arose when brokers were becoming active in the tenth century. As we saw in the previous chapter, the first regulations governing brokers also tried to limit the goods in which they dealt.

Self-Admonitions also gives advice to the brokers who specialized in livestock. Even though the Song adopted *The Tang Code* regulations requiring a three-day trial period after the contract was drawn up, the villagers did not follow the regulations. Instead:

In the countryside it is customary, when cattle and horses are being bought and sold that, once the deposit has been paid, the animals are given to the purchaser. An oral agreement is made that the animals should be given water and grass on a trial basis for two or three days. Only then is a contract drawn up. If the animal falls ill and the fixed number of days has already passed, and the seller does not give in, then officials have the bother of deciding who is right.

Some people pay the price and do not draw up a contract. Some people draw up a contract without paying the price. Both practices occur because they do not know the law. All provisions must be recorded to show to brokers dealing in cattle and horses and to all the country villages. This will prevent lawsuits from arising.

(*Zuoyi zizhen* 3:13a-b; Shiba 1970:167)

The author of *Self-Admonitions* wants to institute another change. He wants to make country folk draw up contracts when they first take owner-ship of a new animal—not the customary three days later, once the animal proves to be in good health. The author does not mention whether a contract tax is to be paid in the case of livestock sales, but in 1157 the contract tax on sales of bulls for plowing was canceled (*Song huiyao*, shihuo 35:10b).

For brokers arranging the sale or mortgaging of land, *Self-Admonitions* recommends even stricter supervision. These brokers were to submit a tally of all mortgages and sales of land twice a month, and to come to the magistrate's office every ten days to pay the contract tax and have the contracts stamped (*Zuoyi zizhen* 3:12a). By keeping such close watch on the brokers, local officials could presumably lower the rate of unstamped contracts. Because no such registers have been found, we do not know whether anyone followed this suggestion. The manual also urges recording the area of each plot sold—and its borders, which should be defined in reference to fixed geographical features (not a stream or a wall, which could change). Officials were urged to check the borders, presumably against their tax registers, and indicate their approval on the back of the contract (*Zuoyi zizhen* 3:13b). It seems unlikely that any of the recommendations in *Self-Admonitions* would have had much effect. The magistrate, who had a small staff and limited funds, was entirely dependent on the cooperation of the brokers to carry out these measures.

Official Efforts to Collect the Contract Tax

Self-Admonitions suggested a stepped-up level of enforcement of the con-tract tax as the dynasty's need for revenues escalated sharply after 1100. The Song needed money to fund the armies who fought first the Liao and then the Jurchen armies in the north, and it needed money to pay the 200,000 ounces of silver and 300,000 bolts of cloth stipulated in its treaty of 1123 with the Jurchen. Between 1119 and 1125 the contract tax was raised to 6 percent. Because the need to increase revenues grew even greater after the loss of northern China to the Jurchen, the tax rose to 10 percent in 1130 (*Chuijianlu* 4:166). In 1127, after the dynasty had lost the north and moved the capital south to Hangzhou, the emperor extended the time limit for paying the contract tax to 100 days after signing, and, ten years later, to 180 days (*Wenxian tongkao* 19:186–187; *Song huiyao*, shihuo 35:13b–15a).

Officials may have deplored the insufficient compliance, but the contract tax was still an important source of revenue in the Song. In 1130, when the government collected a 10 percent tax on the value of the goods sold or mortgaged, 6.75 percent went to the central government, with the remaining 3.25 percent staying in the prefecture (*Chuijianlu* 4:116). Problems with evasion persisted. In 1135 an official proposed that officials number the contracts before distributing them, so that officials could keep track of them and pressure those buying land to register the sale and pay the contract tax (*Song huiyao*, shihuo 35:6b, 14a).

During the first chaotic years of the Southern Song, the Jurchen troops continued to attack and the government was hard pressed to keep order. In the early 1130s, just after the fall of the north to the Jurchen and before peace has been restored, a native of Kaifeng brings his wife and household to the new capital of Hangzhou, where he is to take office. Because their assigned house is in the red light district, he tells his wife to pack their belongings; he will send a sedan-chair to take her to their new house in a residential district. When he comes back to get her, the landlord says that she has already left in a sedan-chair. The man's distress on losing his wife is palpable, for he can do nothing to get her back. Five years later, at an official banquet in Quxian (Zhejiang), he begins to sob during a dinner at which fresh-water turtle is served. He explains why: "When my late wife was alive, she could make this dish better than anyone else. Every time she prepared the flesh around the shell, she would dig out all the black skin until it was gone and cut the chops into perfect squares." The host sends a female servant to console him, and she turns out to be his lost wife, who has been taken away by a broker who deals in women and sold to the host for 300 strings. The husband offers to compensate his host, but the host is so embarrassed to have taken someone else's wife as a concubine that he returns her without accepting any payment (*Yijianzhi* 4:11:631–632). This unusual tale reveals yet again the dangers the infamous Kaifeng brokers posed to women's safety.

Women were even more vulnerable to the depredations of brokers when their families abandoned them. In times of disaster, men who shopped for concubines used brokers as their intermediaries, as Hong Mai mentions several times. He tells of one official who looked for a female slave among refugees who had fled their land during a famine in 1136 in Sichuan. When he spotted a woman to whom he was attracted, he asked if she had already registered with a broker, then summoned that broker to arrange the sale (*Yijianzhi* 3:2:375–376). In another famine in the 1130s, in Suixian, Henan (shown in map 2), the nephew of an official saw a refugee he liked, offered to buy her, and summoned a broker in women (*Yijianzhi* 1:13:115–116). And in one case, in Nanchang, Jiangxi, when a man sold his daughter to be the concubine of an official, they summoned a broker to draw up the contract (*Yijianzhi* 15:22:1754–55). It seems unlikely that any of these brokers paid the contract tax.

The central government was so pressed for money that it did make one attempt to increase its income from the land tax in the 1140s, when it launched a program to survey all borders (*jingjie*). It ordered local officials in selected districts to draw up maps showing land tenure and to make new land registers. According to the new program, a plot of land could be sold only after the registers had been checked against the contracts held by both buyer and seller (*Song huiyao*, shihuo 70:125b). The government's insistence on presenting a contract before granting title underlines how common contracts had become. Not everyone agreed with this policy: some warned that in the fighting of the 1120s, poor families had lost their contracts and had been forced to work the land of the rich (*Xiangshan* 22:2a–3b). The program was implemented in most of the Lower Yangzi and parts of Guangdong, Fujian, and Sichuan (Wang Deyi 1974; Qi 1987a:423–425). Court cases from Jiangxi and Fujian in the mid-thirteenth century refer to borders drawn at this time (*Qingmingji* 13:509; 4:127–128). Problems with insufficient land revenue persisted, and we are left wondering if the cumbersome requirements for land sales were ever really followed. The central government was subsequently forced to institute a variety of new taxes and to increase the contract tax.

Collecting a tax on contracts seemed easier than raising the land tax, because it was an indirect tax to be collected by brokers, not by government staff. Still, the contract tax was frequently evaded. As Zheng Gangzhong (1088–1154) explained: "Those households buying property are not poor or short of resources. It is only that once a contract is drawn up, they think the land or building is their own" (*Beishan* 1:26a). Accordingly, they had little incentive to register the contract with the government and pay a percentage of the price to local officials, solely for the purpose of getting the contract stamped. One of the dilemmas facing Song magistrates who heard cases was whether or not to admit these unstamped ("white") contracts as evidence. They realized why many people would have only white contracts, but considered them less reliable than "red" contracts, which supposedly were thoroughly checked before being stamped.[2]

The 1158 handbook for magistrates, *Suggested Policies for Local Administration* (*Zhouxian tigang*), warned its readers: "In the case of mortgaging or selling land, one can rely only on a stamped contract as proof of the exchange of goods. If the contract is not stamped, then it does not count as a transaction. Even a tax receipt is not sufficient proof. White contracts can be forged, and taxes can be secretly remitted."

The anonymous author then relates the tale of a prefect who refused to accept twenty years of accumulated tax receipts and insisted on ascertaining whether or not the original sale was valid. It turned out that he was right to be suspicious. The owner of the tax receipts had forged a contract for the purchase of the plot in question, waited for his elderly neighbor to die, then continuously for twenty years sued the young boy who inherited the land (*Zhouxian tigang* 2:14).

How did the manual's author know about this wily magistrate, who had served in Hunan more than a hundred years earlier?[3] He must have read the story in one of two anthologies of famous decisions, *The Collection of Difficult Cases* and *The Mirror for Deciding Lawsuits* (*Zheyu guijian yizhu* 6:334; *Yiyuji* 9:2a). The tale has lost an important detail in the retelling: the magistrate suspected the forger because he presented individual tax receipts for the disputed field, not just one receipt for all the land, as was the normal practice.

Just as tax receipts could not be taken at face value, *Suggested Policies for Local Administration* warns, legitimate landowners might not own stamped title to their land. In such circumstances, when the contract was not stamped or the borders were not accurate, the magistrate is advised to summon the village head, the elders, and the neighbors. Because clerks could be bribed to forge documents and because tenants and relatives could be neighbors, the magistrate had no alternative but to interrogate everyone. The author alerts magistrates to yet another danger: trustworthy people from the countryside would be terrified to go to the government office (or

2. Red, an auspicious color used in weddings, and white, an inauspicious color used in funerals, took on yet another meaning in Shanxi during the Qing dynasty (1644–1911). Red fields were those that held no family graves and could be sold, whereas white fields contained graves and could not be disposed of (Wiens 1988:4).

3. For a biography of the magistrate that includes this anecdote, see *Songshi* 285:9605. Van Gulik (1956:125–126) gives an English translation of the tale from *Parallel Cases*.

yamen) where cases were heard, because the clerks would abuse them. As a result, they would fall prey to the services of those who encouraged suits, those smooth-talking document drafters who offered their services to all comers (*Zhouxian tigang* 2:16). Small wonder that books like *Parallel Cases* put such heavy emphasis on the use of unorthodox methods to ferret out the truth: intuition, torture, paying informants, and trickery. This, then, was the dilemma faced by magistrates who heard contract disputes: they could depend neither on contracts nor on the testimony of those they summoned.

The courts that were busy with contract disputes had to hear divorce cases as well. A rich merchant from Tangzhou (now Biyang, Henan) comes home from a trip to find that his wife has decided to leave him because he is living with a prostitute. He brings his new concubine to a nearby inn and takes up residence there. His wife empties their house of all their possessions. He is so angry that he says, "You and I cannot be reconciled; we must decide this today." She replies, "If things are like this, then we must go tell the officials." They go to the yamen, where the magistrate approves the divorce, orders them to divide their property, and awards custody of the youngest (and only unmarried) daughter to the mother. The mother then moves to another village, where she sets up shop on her doorstep selling bottles and small-mouthed jars. She does so well, accumulating 100,000 strings of cash, that she is able to give her youngest daughter a substantial dowry (*Yijianzhi* 3:14:484–485; Qu Chaoli 1991:98; Ebrey 1993:10–11). This account does not mention the bill of divorce, but the husband must have drafted one in order for the magistrate to approve it.

People used contracts to record divorces, and they also used them to buy female servants. The kidnapping of free women by brokers persisted into the Southern Song. Yuan Cai (1140–1190) warned householders to check the backgrounds of wet nurses before hiring them, because brokers might have tricked them into service. "When you buy a maid or a concubine, even after the contract is drawn up, you must carefully inquire into her past. It is possible that she is the child of a free man who has been tricked (*Yuanshi shifan*, 3:13b; Ebrey 1984:299–300; Shiba 1968:395).

Li Yuangang (fl. 1170) collected stories of good deeds in his *Records of Great Virtue (Houdelu)*. He tells of one magistrate somewhere in the lower Yangzi Valley who buys a female slave to accompany his daughter to her new home after marrying. The slave starts to cry one day as she is sweeping near a depression in the floor. She explains that her father was magistrate in the district and that he used the hole in the floor as a hiding place for balls. She was sold as a slave after her father's death. The broker and the clerks confirm her story, and the magistrate arranges for her to marry into the same family as his daughter (*Houdelu* 1:7a–b).

Records of Great Virtue includes another tale of manumission. A houseboy is caught stealing 200 strings of cash from the household accounts. Before fleeing, he ties a contract he has written to the arm of a girl aged twelve or thirteen, which says, "I sell this girl to this household forever to repay my debt." The master of the house asks his wife to raise the girl until she can be married off, then burns the contract (*Houdelu* 1:7b). Contracts must have been very common if a houseboy knew how to draft one.

The magistrates may have collected the tax, but the central government claimed most of it. In 1171 it claimed a further portion of the prefecture's share of the tax collected on contracts for the sale or mortgaging of land, houses, boats, horses, and mules. The central government increased its share to 83.7 percent—roughly five-sixths—and reduced that of the prefecture to only 16.3 percent (*Song huiyao*, shihuo 35:15a–b; 70:148b–149b). Even after this, the central government continued to increase its share by small amounts (*Chuijianlu* 4:116). *The Qingyuan Code*, issued at the end of the twelfth century, included a model form for the remitting of revenues from the regions to the center: the revenues were to be split among the different budgetary categories of the central government. Various categories of contract tax were mentioned, with regions retaining 30 percent, 50 percent, or 70 percent—suggesting there was little agreement about the actual breakdown (*Qingyuan tiaofa* 30:17a–34a).

By the end of the twelfth century the contract tax was more than 10 percent, yet that figure did not include either the charge for the printed contract or the bribes for clerks (*Wenxian tongkao* 19:187; *Chuijianlu* 4:166; *Yanfanlu*, xu 5:12a). Yuan Cai, the source of so much sage advice, had detailed suggestions for those buying land. He urged them to establish that the ownership of the plot was undisputed, with no claims outstanding, and that the borders were marked clearly. He warned against buying land that had been sold conditionally, and he recommended payment in money, not in IOUs or other goods. Yuan described three stages in the process of buying a plot, once one had established that the plot was genuinely for sale: (1) to get the contract sealed, (2) to make sure the person had left the plot, and (3) to ensure that the tax registers were changed to reflect the change in ownership. He explained:

> Official articles and edicts are the most detailed about exchanging property, probably because they hope to prevent disputes. But some

people end up violating these laws about the exchange of property. They do not get stamps on deeds, or do not leave the property, or do not change the name on the tax register. When the piece of property is sold repeatedly, the lawsuits can go on for years without being resolved.

(*Yuanshi shifan* 3:21a; Ebrey 1984:322–323)

Yuan's was the voice of caution. We can be sure that many failed to carry out his recommendations, especially given the increasing cost of having a contract stamped.

Hong Mai put the actual cost at 15 or 16 percent and noted in 1191 that many people dodged the tax by secretly lowering the price of goods when drawing up a contract or by agreeing to pay on credit, practices that led to many lawsuits. He added that people were careful to pay the tax when buying houses or land, but not when buying livestock or slaves (*Rongzhai suibi*, xu 1:221–222). His suggestion that the tax be halved to encourage compliance was never implemented. These increases in the tax and the ever longer extensions for registration suggest both a government desperate for revenues and a populace skilled at evading the tax. Still, one official writing in the early thirteenth century estimated that the income from the contract tax covered the expenses of the prefectural government as well as the salaries of the county government officials, this presumably on less than one-sixth of the total revenues from the tax (*Tieanji* 20:12a).

The tax became an even more important source of revenue in the thirteenth century, as the Mongols pressed down on the Southern Song. In 1234 the Mongols conquered northern China, then under Jurchen rule, and in 1236 they attacked Sichuan. The closer the Mongols came, the more important the contract tax was to the government. Writing just after 1249, Yu Wenbao described the dramatic increases in the contract tax during the Song and the widespread attempts to evade it. Pressed by the Mongol armies, the government tried different means of enticing people to pay the tax: they tried doubling it, and they tried halving it. In 1249 the director of the revenue ministry (*Tiling hubu*) petitioned the emperor to set quotas for the contract tax: the biggest prefectures were assessed at 1,000,000 strings, middle-sized prefectures at 800,000, and the smallest at 400,000 (*Chuijianlu* 4:116). Although the prefectures probably did not make the quotas, the magnitude of these optimistic figures is telling (Jiang 1991:100).

Magistrate Huang's Struggle with Prefect Xie's Household

Although these different sources testify to the continuing use of contracts over a wide area and to the attempts of officials to tax those contracts, they do not convey how individual officials struggled from day to day to decide contractual disputes and to control powerful families in their districts. We get this sense from reading several decisions by one of Zhu Xi's disciples, Huang Gan (1151–1221), who also served as an official in Fujian and Jiangxi in the early thirteenth century. His collected papers, compiled after his death, are among the first to include the texts of decisions in court cases. In the Song, only a few officials received extensive legal training, with the vast majority having just a classical education (McKnight 1989). Because most had to acquire their knowledge of the law from their clerks or from books, collected papers often served as models for students and officials to consult when drafting the different types of documents required for government service.

One of the most informative groups of cases concerning contracts date from Huang's service around 1208 in Xingan, Jiangxi (shown in map 2). His decisions allow us to see that members of lower strata did dare to take powerful families to court for breach of contract. Magistrate Huang was not a typical judge. Armed with a strong sense of justice, he tended to do things strictly by the rules and take on issues his less righteous colleagues would have ignored. Well aware that as a judge he lacked the power to implement his decisions in the countryside (Hymes 1986:206–207), he was still prepared to challenge the household of a powerful former official, Prefect Xie, in four different cases.

One of the cases, a classic contract dispute, clearly reveals the limits on Magistrate Huang's power. The living relatives of a dead man and the Xie household had been fighting over the same plot of land, according to a deposition made in 1209. After the man died, his widow had returned to her family in 1205, in all probability leaving her son in the care of her in-laws. She sold the land to the Xies in 1207. As Huang pointed out, widows were not supposed to abandon their children, nor did they have the right to sell off their husband's property, which only their children could sell. "To cut off someone's family line, to steal his property, to pressure his wife in order to harm the children of his brother, these should not be done by someone who has human decency." Huang's implication was clear. Prefect Xie's household had done all of these things. Prefect Xie was no longer resident in Xingan, and his household refused to submit the contracts. Huang then

called for the contracts in the possession of the Xie household and petitioned the regional government to send all the earlier plaints relating to the
Xie household. Their refusal did not mean the end of the case, for officials
could proceed without such evidence, but Huang was forced to wait for the
regional government to forward the necessary documentation before he
could make a decision (*Qingmingji*, fulu 2:592–593).[4] Surviving documentation does not reveal the outcome.

This was not the only sale to the Xie household that Magistrate Huang
found dubious. He agreed with another plaintiff that the Xies had illegally
pressured his nephew into selling them a plot of land that housed four
family graves. Grave land, more than other land, was a crucial part of a
family's patrimony, and as such its sale was subject to strict rules. Magistrate Huang was especially suspicious because, when the plaintiff and the
boy's grandfather had signed a contract dividing the family property, they
had agreed never to sell the land with the graves on it. Still, in 1208 the Xie
household had purchased the land with the graves on it; the grandson, still
a minor, had signed the contract. Even though his uncle, the plaintiff, had
served as witness, he then sued. Magistrate Huang saw the plaintiff's participation in the sale as further evidence of the Xie household's power to
intimidate the rural people. Although the Xie household steadfastly refused
to submit their copies of contracts, they returned a small pond to the
plaintiff. Magistrate Huang concluded his decision with a petition to the
prefect and the regional government for copies of the documentation
(*Qingmingji*, fulu 2:590–591). Once again he was unable to proceed against
the Xie household.

In another dispute, because Magistrate Huang had copies of the contracts, he was able to rule against the Xie household; but he still was not
able to enforce his decision. Seventeen kiln workers sued the Xie household
for failing to pay them the agreed-upon price of 17 strings for thirteen
thousand large tiles. The stewards of the Xie household maintained that
they had bought small tiles and paid the correct price; the kiln workers said
they had sold large tiles and received only the food allowance due them.
This, too, was a case in which Huang's hands were tied. He had no way to
enforce the court's judgment. He ended his decision on a plaintive note: "To

4. I cite these decisions from Huang's collected papers as they were reprinted in
the 1987 Zhonghua shuju edition of the *Qingmingji*. The Beijing Library's original
Yuan-dynasty edition of Huang's papers, from which they were transcribed, was
not available to me.

order other people's tiles, to owe other people money and goods, how can this constitute innocent behavior? How can this not be forbidden? It is obvious that a private household has the power to drive people to hang themselves while officials lack the power to block the plaints of the powerful and strong" (*Qingmingji*, fulu 2:586–587).

In a fourth and final case against Prefect Xie's household, Magistrate Huang was able to reach a decision. He ordered the Xie household to stop encroaching on temple land and depriving the caretaker of his livelihood. The surviving text mentions no contracts, but Magistrate Huang must have consulted a contract before coming to a conclusion (*Qingmingji*, fulu 2:591–592).

Huang's decisions vividly depict the challenges of being a magistrate who had to rule on contract disputes at the turn of the thirteenth century. Even though a magistrate had little power to subpoena documents or to enforce his decisions, he was supposed to reach fair judgments that were based, in Huang's case, more on his sense of what was right than on the details of Song contract law.

The Collected Models of Clarity and Lucidity

With a preface dating to 1261, *The Collected Models of Clarity and Lucidity* was the first casebook to be published in China that reproduced the texts of actual decisions. Accordingly, *Clarity and Lucidity* provides unparalleled insight into how contract law was understood by local officials, and by local people, in the final decades of the Song dynasty. The signed cases are from all over southern China, from Guangdong, Fujian, Jiangsu, Jiangxi, and Zhejiang. The others simply give the title of the official who wrote the decisions; in the absence of internal evidence, we may never know who wrote them (*Qingmingji* 9:300–301; Chen Zhichao 1987:650). Many of the officials whom we can identify were associated with the increasingly influential neo-Confucian movement. Hu Ying (advanced degree 1232, died circa 1270) wrote more than any other contributor—seventy-five decisions (Chen Zhichao 1987:681). Although little is known of his life, Hu Ying tore down many popular temples when serving as an official in Hunan, subsequently building an appropriately Confucian commemorative hall to his mother (*Songshi* 416:12478–79).

Because many of the opinions were in response to appeals, the judge often summarized the case, assuming that the reader had access to the earlier decisions and relevant contracts, which must originally have been attached and now are lost. The editors of *Clarity and Lucidity* also cut the texts of the decisions themselves.[5] The decisions in contract disputes often present a brief history of the conflict, with some referring to contracts over one hundred years old (*Qingmingji* 4:108, 111; 13:511). Clearly, officials had difficulty enforcing their decisions. People went to court over widely divergent amounts of land—anywhere from several Chinese feet of land to more than 50 sixth-acres of land, or plots worth 7 strings to those worth 50 (*Qingmingji* 6:198–199; 4:100; 6:168; 4:109–110). Very occasionally a detail suggests the social class of the people involved: one family owns several thousand volumes of books, whereas another is an official family that has fallen on hard times (*Qingmingji* 10:365–366, 382–383). More often one cannot discern the litigants' social standing. Because none of the opinions quotes passages from the original contracts, none is as detailed as the case of the widow and the squatter from Dunhuang, or includes such supporting documentation. *Clarity and Lucidity* includes many more decisions, though, than survive from either Turfan or Dunhuang. Divided topically, the book was easily consulted by anyone who had to write a decision on a related issue.

Legal Knowledge among the Populace

The judges writing in *Clarity and Lucidity* realized they were dealing with a populace well schooled—almost too well schooled—in the ways of the law, and their complaints about this widespread knowledge echoed those of earlier officials. Perhaps the most famous description was that of the polymath Shen Gua (1035–1095), who commented:

> The people of Jiangxi have a reputation for their love of law suits. They have a book called *Deng Sixian* that consists entirely of forms for litigation. It starts by teaching how to alter documents. If altering does not work, the book teaches them to bring false charges. And should this method fail also, one should entrap them in order to catch them. Deng Sixian is probably the name of a person. People passed on his techniques and then named the book for him. This book is frequently used in village schools to teach people.
> (*Mengxi bitan* 25:252–253)

5. One of Liu Kezhuang's decisions survives in his collected papers in much longer form than in *Clarity and Lucidity* (*Qingmingji* 8:251–257).

Shen captures the misgivings of Confucian scholars perfectly: schoolchildren should have been studying the classics, not manuals of litigation! Jiangxi enjoyed a reputation as being more litigious than other provinces, but the existence of such a book, even in Jiangxi, was shocking to some.

Writing a century after Shen Gua, the judges in *Clarity and Lucidity* voiced their objections to a class of people whose sole means of livelihood was helping others draw up plaints and suits (Guo 1990). They were called "those who encourage suits" (*jiansong*) or, more picturesquely, "those with brushes inserted in their hats" (*erbi*), terms which vividly capture their readiness to draft documents. When Fang Yue arrived to take up his post as prefect in Yuanzhou (now Yichun county, Jiangxi), he knew of the district's reputation for litigiousness from Han Yu's writings. Yet he was hardly prepared for the following conversation with a young girl, which took place before he had even received his seal of office:

> He asked, "How old are you?"
> The reply, "Twelve."
> "Do you know how to write?"
> The reply, "No."
> "Who wrote this plaint?"
> The reply, "Gentleman Yi 104." (*Qingmingji* 12:479–480)

Official Fang was so angry that he sentenced Mr. Yi, evidently someone with a brush in his hat, to one hundred strokes with the light cane. Hu Ying also complained about this group of document drafters: "The people of Hunan all love lawsuits. Even though Shaoyang is remote and small, the craze for those with brushes inserted in their hats is considerable" (*Qingmingji* 8:280).

As the judges tried to ferret out the presence of those with brushes in their hats, they also looked for forgeries. Some were easy to detect, some not. Some forgers used old paper with new ink (*Qingmingji* 6:181–183). Or they pasted on emendations in a different handwriting (*Qingmingji* 6:176–177). Or they wrote their personal mark, usually an abbreviated character (*huaya*), on top of a stamp, when the mark should have been underneath the seal (*Qingmingji* 9:297–298). Or they paid the stamp tax on a forgery after the alleged sale had taken place and the case was already in court (*Qingmingji* 9:315–317). Or they forged the signatures of women or of the dead (*Qingmingji* 6:172–173, 170–171, 187–188; 9:306–307). It was illegal to forge official documents, and the punishment was one hundred strokes (*Qingmingji* 8:281).

A judge began one decision with a list of different ways to cheat on contracts: "Some use ink that is too heavy or too light. Some use hand-writing that is different or the same. Some disguise the amount of land. Some change the name of the plot. Some omit or alter the area or borders. All of these types are difficult to list fully" (*Qingmingji* 5:152–153). The many varieties of forgery reveal the enormous significance people attached to written contracts.

Clearly, the burden of hearing cases lay heavily on local magistrates. The relief with which the judges of *Clarity and Lucidity* decide not to hear protracted, thorny cases beyond the statute of limitations is plain. Some of the cases dismissed on these grounds show the extraordinary lengths to which people would go in order to try to win land in the courts. Remember that the Tang emperor had issued an edict in 824 declaring an amnesty on debts dating back more than ten years, if the debtor and the guarantor were dead, if the interest was too great, or if the debtor had no property. Similarly, Song law allowed judges to reject any dispute over an unclear contract in which more than twenty years had passed, or in which either the buyer or seller had died (*Qingmingji* 4:111–112, 132–133; *Song xingtong* 26:414). In cases in which the seller claimed to have only mortgaged the land while retaining the right to buy it back, the law granted him no more than three years in which to do so (*Qingmingji* 6:168–169). This kind of dispute must have been frequent because another edict applied a different test: if someone had left the land, it was a sale; if he stayed on it, it was a conditional sale and he had the right to buy it back (*Qingmingji* 6:104–105).

One judge ruled against a plaintiff in Renhe county, Hangzhou, concerning a plot that had changed hands five times since 1194, in a case brought some fifty years later. The plaintiff claimed that the plot was rightfully his because his grandfather had originally mortgaged, not sold, it. The judge cited the statute of limitations and also rejected his argument because the plaintiff offered only a contract for a different plot to support his claim: "If he says the land was inherited, he should have a land register or a will that can be consulted. If he says it actually was mortgaged by his ancestors, he must have a contract or a mortgage agreement that can be consulted. But he has nothing." Nor did the plaintiff know the selling price, the broker's name, or the original buyer's name (*Qingmingji* 9:313–314). The judge was adamant that the plaintiff should be able to provide documentary proof—after all, the contracts for each of the five sales had been submitted to the court.

As riled as the judges were by the widespread use of contracts, they could, as here, rebuke those without adequate documentation. In another land dispute, the judge chided someone else who failed to provide sufficient proof of ownership: "Today when people take their clothes to the pawnshop to borrow 10 or 100 coins, they use a ticket to redeem their clothes. According to the principle that one cannot redeem clothes if the ticket is lost, how can one redeem land or a house with no proof of ownership?" (*Qingmingji* 5:149). The judge describes a society in which contracts are so widespread that pawnshops use them for even small transactions. In such a document-oriented society, it was unthinkable that anyone could put up land as security for a loan and not use a contract to record the exchange.

Some people making claims in *Clarity and Lucidity* had no contracts proving ownership. Others drew up two different contracts for the same plot. One of the contracts was a straightforward buyback (*zhengdian*) contract. Geoffrey MacCormack (1990:238–242) calls this type of sale a conditional sale, which allowed the person borrowing money to buy his own land back within a certain time. The other type of contract simply recorded the loan of money and the amount of land put up as collateral without granting the moneylender any claim to the land (*didang*). Then, depending on the circumstance, the two parties could show one or the other of the contracts, explained a judge at the beginning of a decision.

In the case at hand, a Mr. Li had borrowed 450 strings of coins from Mr. Ye in 1218 and had given 33 sixth-acres of land as collateral. In 1220 he returned 300 strings and subsequently gave one pear-and-sparrow painting mounted on a screen, four large hanging scrolls of landscapes by Gao Dafu, four bamboo-and-magpie scrolls by Tang Quenei, and two pieces of calligraphy carved in two styles, to pay off the rest of the debt. For fifteen years neither man sued the other, but after their deaths, the moneylender's family took the opportunity to make a claim on the Li family's land, arguing that the original loan had been a conditional sale. The judge ruled that all the evidence pointed to a loan with the land as collateral, not a buyback loan, but he did allow that the paintings might not have been worth 150 strings, a price so low that it implies that these were paintings by local artists, not well-known masters. The judge ordered the Ye family to return the paintings to Mr. Li's son and have him pay back the money originally due them in cash or paper money (*Qingmingji* 6:170–171). In this case the two men who were parties to the original transaction thought the paintings could be exchanged for the money, but their descendants did not. The judge concluded that there would be fewer suits if a debt originally in money was repaid in money.

Disputed Engagements

Like sales of land, engagements and divorces both produced documents and thus prompted contract disputes. As described in a memoir about life in Kaifeng, written in 1147, marriage simply consisted of taking vows before the ancestral altar. The only documents signed were those during the engagement: a couple agreed to marry when the man's family sent a notice asking the woman's hand, and when her family sent back an affirmative letter (*Dongjing menghualu* 4:32–34; Ebrey 1993:83–88; Sheng 1990:129–133).

Song law set a punishment of sixty strokes for any bride's family who broke an engagement, whereas if the groom's family called off the engagement there was no penalty other than that the bride's family kept the gifts. Reflecting the original oral nature of marital agreements, the law stipulated that the exchange of gifts was just as legally binding as the exchange of letters. The commentary to the law specifically notes: "There is no limit on the value of betrothal gifts. If more than one Chinese foot of cloth is given, neither side can cancel" (*Song xingtong* 13:213). This is an extraordinary law, especially since it defines engagements as "private agreements," from which the state usually distanced itself. The wording of the law raises the issue of consideration in modern legal terminology. A contract is not binding unless one party pays something, even something of token value, to the other for some service. In the same way, engagements were binding only if a gift of some value, however slight, had been exchanged.

Liu Kezhuang wrote one decision in which he interpreted the law about engagements literally and tried to apply it strictly. Even though the groom's family denied sending a notice of engagement and refused to acknowledge receipt of the woman's reply, a professional scribe confirmed that the handwriting was indeed that of the man proposing. Liu remarked, too, that the notice of the engagement named the man and the woman and included several mirror boxes, a clear indication that the man was proposing. With the man refusing to marry and the woman demanding marriage, the two sides appealed the decision six(!) times. Liu remained adamant: given that the law called for someone who had married to annul a marriage and return to his original fiancée, surely the two still-unmarried parties in this case had to go through with the marriage. Liu later asked someone to mediate the dispute and urged the two heads of family to reach an agreement. He was sure that the two should marry, but could not force the man's family to proceed inasmuch as they had not broken the law. Finally, the two sides gave up the dispute, presumably after having agreed not to marry (*Qingmingji* 9:347–348).

Judge Liu's decision and the wording of the Song penal code view the breaking of an engagement very seriously, but a contemporary play suggests that families, even brides' families, could find ways to call off engagements provided no presents had been exchanged. *The Romance of the Western Chamber* (*Dong Jieyuan xixiang ji*) was written sometime around the turn of the thirteenth century by a Mr. Dong (Ch'en Li-li 1976:x–xi). It tells of a young scholar and a woman of good family who fall in love. At the beginning of the play, Yingying is already engaged to her cousin. Once the girl's mother discovers that her daughter and the scholar have been sleeping together for six months, the girl's mother cancels the engagement, saying, "Even though my husband promised Yingying to Zheng Heng, we never received any engagement presents" (*Dong Jieyuan xixiang ji* 6:124; Ch'en 1976:169). When the scholar asks the mother for Yingying's hand, he has to borrow money from a monk so that he can make an engagement gift of a piece of gold. Otherwise that engagement would not be binding either. When the original fiancé hears that his engagement has been canceled, he sues in court; but the judge, a friend of the scholar, rules that he could not have married Yingying anyway, as she was his first cousin.

Contested Divorces

Just as the groom's family could break off an engagement more easily than a bride's family, so too could a husband initiate divorce more easily than a wife. The Song inherited the Tang divorce law, which allowed a husband to end relations with his wife for seven reasons, the "seven outs." Like the Dunhuang bills of divorce, the judges in *Clarity and Lucidity* do not even mention the seven reasons. Instead, the judges must establish first that the husband did indeed write the bill of divorce, and they tailor their judgments depending on which of the parties, if either, has remarried.

Liu Kezhuang heard one case in which a man wrote a bill of divorce on the instructions of his father, whose own wife was having an affair with a clerk. Judge Liu criticizes the son for allowing his father to order him to divorce his wife when he has no grounds for doing so, but he upholds the divorces of both the son and the father. Judge Liu does not revoke the son's divorce, for his ex-wife has already remarried and the son himself has become engaged to another woman in the year since the divorce (*Qingmingji* 12:447; Qu Chaoli 1991:99). The speed with which the two parties have arranged their second marriages may seem surprising, given later support for widow chastity, but the people involved in these divorce disputes remarried quickly.

Judge Liu heard another dispute in which a man who suddenly did well in the civil service examinations ordered his brother-in-law to divorce his sister, who returned to her brother's household. Liu criticized the successful candidate but allowed the divorce to stand because the husband drafted the notice of divorce himself. He did recommend that the couple reconcile, or, barring that, that the successful family give the former husband money so that he might remarry (*Qingmingji* 9:345–346). This case ran directly counter to the spirit of the law that did not allow a suddenly wealthy man to divorce his wife, even though in this case it was the suddenly wealthy wife who abandoned her husband. Still, Liu upheld the divorce.

Judge Liu's decisions indicate that men enjoyed the support of the law in drawing up bills of divorce and that the courts did not examine their motives too closely. In his notes on poetry contained in his collected papers, Liu explained the divorce of Lu You (1125–1210), one of the most famous and most prolific writers of his time. Lu You's parents worried that their daughter-in-law was disturbing their son's studies, and they rebuked her several times. "Then Lu did not dare to contravene his parents' opinion and parted with his wife" (*Houcun xiansheng* 178:1591; Qu Chaoli 1991:107n9). Interfering with one's husband's studies hardly constituted grounds for divorce according to Song law, but Lu was able to divorce his wife easily. The story is a sad one, for the two apparently continued to love each other and write poems to each other, even though both remarried without suffering any stigma (*Qidong yeyu* 1:17–18).

The law allowed women to divorce their husbands only under very limited conditions: if the husband had been exiled or if he had failed to communicate with his wife for more than three years. One judge allowed a woman to divorce her husband, who had been exiled for six years without communicating with her. The woman had drawn up a contract with her husband, permitting him to take 45 strings' worth of paper money from her original dowry. Her husband had approved the contract, the agreement was witnessed and signed, and the woman had registered the agreement with the authorities. The presiding judge rejected her ex-husband's claim. "Since he has taken her paper money and permitted her to remarry, and since she has already married someone else, how can he claim her?" (*Qingmingji* 9:353). The court was struck by the agreement they drew up and by the payment she made to him. Most salient was her remarriage. The court was not going to overturn a divorce when one party had already remarried, which may account for the rapidity of remarriage in such cases.

Husbands may have enjoyed the right to divorce their wives at will, but the law did not grant them absolute rights over them. Married women were not the chattels of their husbands. Selling one's wife was tantamount to divorce, according to the law. One man, unable to support his wife, sold her to another man for 300 strings. Her first husband drew up the bill of divorce, collected 100 strings and stamped his thumb on the contract, but was still short 200 strings. Unable to pay the entire price, the new husband forcibly kept the woman prisoner. Judge Weng Fu rejected the entire arrangement and sentenced all the people involved to beatings or hard labor. The woman was given to a broker, who was to find her a new husband (*Qingmingji* 9:352). The court reached a similar decision in the case of a high official's descendant who left his wife in her uncle's house, where she earned her keep as a seamstress. One night her husband took her drinking with him at someone's house. He returned home but left her there overnight alone. The next day he drew up a contract selling her to his drinking companion. The court refrained from probing more deeply into the extent of "unrighteous activities"; it ordered the contract destroyed and the girl returned to her own mother, who could arrange for her remarriage (*Qingmingji* 10:382–383). This was, in effect, a court-ordered divorce. Although the judge felt great indignation at the husband, he did not order him punished, probably because he was descended from a high official.

Overturning Contracts Used in Wrongful Sales

As the judges felt free to override contracts and overturn engagements or divorces they found immoral, so too did they overturn land sales, even those with correct documentation. The besieged Song government's enthusiasm about contracts as a source of revenue could not erase traditional prejudices against contracts on the part of the magistrates, and the magistrates writing in *Clarity and Lucidity* were more prejudiced than most. Most of the decisions in that book reflect the judges' attempts to reconcile written law, including both the code and all subsequent amendments, with their own sense of what was right—to reconcile what Hu Ying called the intent of the law (*fayi*) with human feelings (*renqing*).

The judges did not restrict themselves to disputes involving written contracts. An oral agreement could also be binding. A man who rented a house without using a lease tore it down to build a new one. Five months later, the owner sued. The judge in the case, again Hu Ying, doubted the owner's motives, saying that when the tenant tore down the store five months earlier, he had done nothing to prevent him then. Hu therefore supposed that the two men must have made an oral agreement. Moreover, the owner had written the tenant a note suggesting ways to cover the cost of building a new house. Judge Hu concluded the dispute by ordering that the neighbors be questioned (*Qingmingji* 9:334–35). Because, in an unusual circumstance, neither party presented a written contract, the court was forced to assume the existence of an oral agreement.

Hu Ying did not hesitate to ignore contracts when it suited him. In one case he heard, the owner of a pawnshop sued a man for failing to repay his debt in full and maintained the debtor had signed a note saying he had borrowed 270 strings from the pawnshop eight years earlier. The debtor gave a different amount. Both agreed that the amount given in the contract was not accurate. Hu commented, "Even though officials are obliged to examine the contract, how could each detail match the contract?" Because determining the actual amount loaned would waste the time of the neighbors (and of the court), Hu noted that the original debtor had no money anyway and ordered the case closed (*Qingmingji* 9:335–336).

Hu Ying overturned another series of contracts because he was particularly outraged by an adopted son who schemed with his mother to cheat his stepfather's natural sons out of their inheritance. He quoted the neighbors who testified: "The son, Li Ziqin, came with his mother in 1208 when she married Tan Nianhua. They brought nothing with them, and his father had no land. After Li Ziqin grew up, he never did any work. Tan Nianhua gave him food and clothing and arranged his marriage."

Hu Ying shares their indignation that, even after he had grown up, the son had found no livelihood and depended on his adoptive father for food, clothes, and the money to get married. Even though the stepfather had acceded to his second wife's scheme to disinherit his own children, and had placed his personal mark on four of eleven contracts selling all his property to his stepson, and even though all eleven contracts had been stamped, Hu Ying rejected the contracts as violating both the intent of the law and human feelings. He ordered the head of the father's lineage to divide the property among his sons (*Qingmingji* 4:124–126).

Hu Ying may have been more volatile than the other judges in *Clarity and Lucidity*, but they too were willing to overturn contracts. A frequent justification stemmed from one Song law that land could not be sold in order to pay off debts or the interest accruing on debts (*Qingmingji* 5:142–143).[6] This law reflects the widely held belief that land was more valuable than money: the law was too biased in favor of the male family line to allow someone to discard his family's future in one instant. The ban on such sales to pay off debts does not mean they did not occur. Surely people heavily in debt had to resort to selling their land to repay the money they owed. But this provision of the law allowed a family to sue a buyer for the return of its land if the family could prove it had been sold under duress.

Song law afforded special protection to those who had just inherited land by forbidding them to sell the land too quickly. One judge called the sale by a son of his father's land only one year after his father's death a wrongful sale (*daomai*). *The Tang Code* used the term in its strict sense of selling land that did not belong to one (*Tanglü shuyi* 13:245 [article 166]). By the time of *Clarity and Lucidity*, wrongful sale did not mean merely that the correct procedures had not been followed—it could mean wrongful in some broader, moral sense, as in harmful to a family's interests. In this instance it ordered the land returned to the mother, whose signature had been forged, and the money paid for the land given to the government. The decision was a surprising one, given that the buyers, who were the family of a pacification commissioner (the equivalent of a regional commander), had refused to appear in court for the past fifteen years (*Qingmingji* 9:297–298)! This judge faced exactly the problem Huang Gan had in 1210: he could reach the correct judgment, but he could not enforce it.

In the same way that the judges wanted to protect a man's property from his profligate children, so too did they try to protect it from the schemes of his widow. Women were not considered part of a man's lineage. They could provide a man with sons who belonged to his lineage, but their loyalties were always assumed to be with their natal families or their children, not with their in-laws. In contrast, a widow could not necessarily depend on her husband's family for support. The law recognized her need to support herself and her children, but it limited her right to sell her

---

6. Land could, however, be confiscated to pay off debts to the state (Paul Smith, personal communication, March 1993).

husband's land. "If a widow has no children or grandchildren, and she mortgages or sells land or a house, she will be beaten one hundred strokes and the land returned to the owner" (*Qingmingji* 9:304). In short, the sale of land by a widow was a wrongful sale and could be reversed. The law made no provision for the widow's support in this case, assuming she could return to her own family. If she had small children to raise, she was allowed to sell the land, but the law was phrased in the negative: "If a widow has no children or grandchildren sixteen or under, she cannot sell or mortgage her land" (*Qingmingji* 5:141).

The decisions about widows and contract disputes were all by the same judge: Weng Fu (advanced degree 1222), who served as magistrate in Chuzhou and Juzhou, both prefectures in the interior of southern Zhejiang. In each decision Judge Weng tried to balance the needs of the widow to be supported against the right of her husband's family to keep their land. The thirteenth century was a time of disagreement about women's property rights, and Weng tended to see the property rights of the husband's lineage as outweighing those of women (Birge 1992:180n46, 251). These were sensitive cases too, involving family conflicts that would not have occurred had the people concerned adhered to traditional family values. Strikingly, the families in these cases differed sharply from stereotype of the nuclear family: they were the products of remarriages and adoptions and remind us of the difficulty of producing a male heir in an era when life expectancy was so low.

Judge Weng reproached one man for suing his stepmother and thereby violating his obligations to be filial. The man objected to the division of his family's property arranged by his stepmother, his father's second wife, and her younger brother: the man received land with an output of 170 piculs; the second husband's and stepmother's own daughter, 31 piculs for her dowry; and the stepmother, 57 piculs to support her in old age. Judge Weng ruled that the daughter was entitled to her share, usually one-half that of her brothers, and that the stepmother's share was hers as long as she did not mortgage or sell the land, remarry, or leave it to her daughter. He took the opportunity to explain his views about women's property: "The land a woman brings as her dowry when she marries is land that her parents give to her husband's family. Once her husband has heirs, how can she be permitted to keep it?" Here, her land would revert to her son on her death. Judge Weng concluded this decision by urging the second wife and the stepson to get along—and ordered the son to be given twenty strokes with the light cane, presumably to provide real incentive for him to do so (*Qingmingji* 5:141–142).

If a son suing his stepmother was distasteful to Magistrate Weng, a widow marrying her husband's brother was positively repugnant, and, according to Song law, illegal. Widows, the judge explained, were supposed to mourn their husbands, till their land, and raise the children of the dead man so they could make ancestral offerings to him. Even worse in this case was that, after marrying, the widow Ashao and the uncle Zizhi had cast off all the children from the first marriage, and wrongfully sold off all the land of the first husband. Magistrate Weng could barely contain himself: "Although a stranger could not bear to break up someone's family, destroy his children, or cut off his ancestral offerings, this is just what Zizhi and Ashao have done!" Of the six plots of land they sold, the court allowed one to remain in the possession of the second husband Zizhi's children. The remaining five plots were to be returned to the children of the deceased first husband. The brother was ordered to leave Chuzhou, and the widow was to terminate relations with him (*Qingmingji* 10:389–390).

Judge Weng's decisions nicely capture society's suspicion of widows and their motives. These cases both involve remarriages and show the hostility between the surviving children and the father's second wife. Modern Americans are accustomed to this animosity, but it was upsetting to a society that took seriously Confucius's teachings to revere one's parents and, by extension, the second wife of one's father.

Buying land was an uncertain act in thirteenth-century China. If a judge determined that a wrongful sale had taken place, the buyer had no recourse but to appeal the decision, even though he and the seller might have carried out all the procedures for buying the plot, including paying the contract tax. In the above cases, Judge Weng does not even consider the buyer's rights. A wrongful sale has taken place—not because the contract law has been broken, but because the moral code has—and the only way to rectify it is to return the land to its rightful owner, regardless of what contracts have been drawn up.

Because land was popularly viewed first as a family's property, second as belonging to a community, and only in the final resort as a transferable commodity, since at least the Tang the right of first refusal had been limited to kin and neighbors. By the time of *Clarity and Lucidity*, as Hu Ying explains, the right of refusal was limited to those who were both kin and immediate neighbors. If someone's house, or a river, or a ditch, or a road separated two plots of land, the two parties were not neighbors and did not have the right of refusal. A time limit was also applied: neighboring kin had to make their claim within three years of a sale or they forfeited their right to the land (*Qingmingji* 9:308–309; Li Jiaju 1988:27; Schurmann 1956a:514).

Since graves were the most conspicuous physical manifestation of a family's ties to the land, the law granted special rights to those whose family graves were near a given plot. The three-year limit on making claims was suspended, but claims had to be made within the lifetime of the parties involved in the dispute (*Qingmingji* 9:323). In 1142 the Department of State Affairs ruled that within 18 five-foot lengths of a tomb, other people could build houses or other structures, cultivate fields or orchards, and plant mulberry or fruit trees, but they could not dig any new tombs (*Qingmingji* 9:323). In 1173 another directive explained that within this restricted area, no one could dig into the soil or pile it up, because the displacement of the soil might disturb the tombs (*Qingmingji* 9:324). Of course, people faked the presence of tombs when it could be to their advantage (*Qingmingji* 4:133–134; 9:318–319)! Not everyone shared the law's respect for ancestral tombs. Liu Kezhuang expressed contempt for a son who opened his grandfather's tomb, not to give him a more auspicious reburial but in order to sell the bricks, stones, coffin, nails, and funeral plot (*Qingmingji*, fulu 3:619).

The judges writing in *Clarity and Lucidity* held that land was not just another commodity that could be bought and sold. Families had a right to keep their land from those who were not related to them, and communities had a right to keep land from outsiders. These were ideas that fit a time in which land was bought and sold infrequently, a time that did not exist in Turfan and Dunhuang—a time that may actually have existed only in the far recesses of mythical Chinese antiquity. But as the cases in *Clarity and Lucidity* show, land did change hands frequently, especially as people were drawn into producing for market and moved away from self-sufficient farming. In this and many other instances, the judges' views did not accord with those of the people who brought their disputes before them. The judges, particularly Hu Ying, were willing to put human feelings, as they understood them, ahead of contracts. Yet they lacked any means of enforcing their views in contract disputes. It is doubtful that they persuaded litigants to abandon their heavy use of contracts for the more moral, yet much less predictable, course they advocated.

Land Contracts from Huizhou

For all that *Clarity and Lucidity* shows about the willingness of judges to ignore contracts, it always omits the texts of the disputed contracts. In fact, very few Song contracts survive. Five of the extant Song contracts are from Huizhou, a commercially developed, mountainous district in Anhui famous for its lumber and the paper made from its trees.[7] The first one dates from 1215 and records the sale of a hill plot in Qimen county.

> The records are attached: taxpayer Wu Gong's ancestral land includes one hill with the family's ancestral graves on it. The plot is in Yicheng district, fourth division, under the Yang character, number 27 on Shang Mountain by the wall behind the houses on Slanting Seven Mountain. Behind the tombs is a high mountain with one fertile plot. From it they take three-quarters of a sixth-acre and today sell it to Zhu Yuanxing. The land is one-half of Wu Gong and his brother Wu Han's inheritance, and they sell it for paper money with a face value of 6 strings. The plot's borders are: to the east, the top of the peak and the border of the third division; to the west, behind the tombs; [northern and southern borders illegible]. The plot originally had the long wall by the Slanting Seven Mountain as its border. That has collapsed.
>
> Now, once the sale has taken place, Zhu Yuanxing will obey the officials and pay taxes. He will hoe the land and plant cypress saplings for a living. If any outsiders obstruct or occupy the land, Wu Gong is responsible for resolving the matter, and neither is the concern of the buyer. Of the two copies of the original stamped contract the owner and his brother used to buy the land from Zhang Mincheng, one is given to Zhu Yuanxing as proof. His copy of this contract also serves as proof. Wu Gong will write no other contract under Zhu Yuanxing's name. Today, for fear that people's hearts are not trustworthy, this contract for a sale is drawn up as proof.

7. The texts of fourteen Song and Yuan contracts from Huizhou have been reprinted in a collection of contracts from Huizhou (*MingQing Huizhou*), and eight unpublished contracts held in the rare book room of the Beijing Library have been microfilmed under the title *SongYuan diqi jicun.* The unpublished Beijing Library contracts are partially cited in Zhang Chuanxi (1982:28–29) and Jiang (1991:94). Three Song contracts are on the Beijing Library's microfilm, and two, dating to 1242 and 1248, are transcribed in *MingQing Huizhou.* Color photographs of these two contracts appear in *Huizhou qiannian* as plates 1 and 2.

1215. Fourth month. Day 20   (Wu Gong's mark)

Now at the end of the contract I verify that the price for the
mountain land on the high mountain by the wall behind the houses
on Slanting Seven Mountain is complete. Moreover, nothing is
lacking. Now, at the end of the contract, I certify that I approve this.

Same day, month, and year as above   (Wu Gong's mark)
Guarantor   (Huang Xihe's mark)

(*SongYuan diqi jicun* unpaginated)

Although long, this contract is quite simple. Most of it is taken up with
the location and borders of the plot. It uses an unusual phrase for the
guarantor or cosigner, literally "the person who helped to stamp the contract" (*zhuyaqi ren*). The marks of Wu Gong and Huang Xihe, the character
ya (stamp), are in the same controlled hand as the rest of the contract,
suggesting that the person who drafted it also drew their marks for the
seller and the guarantor. It allows for only one contingency: if another
party makes false claim to the land, the seller, not the buyer, must resolve
the problem. The Turfan and Dunhuang contracts contained a similar
clause, although the exact phrasing varies, because Anhui residents had
their own local models for contracts. This contract was stamped, as are the
four other Song contracts from Huizhou. The note at the end of the
contract, saying that the money was paid in full, occurs in all the Song
contracts from Huizhou. It was intended to forestall suits claiming
underpayment.

A 1242 contract for the sale of fields and hill land includes the four
borders of the plot and the price. It specifically authorizes the buyer to pay
all future taxes, and its use of the phrase, "evaluated and discussed by three
sides," suggests that brokers were present when the price was set by the
buyer and seller. An unusual clause then occurs: "If the fields or hills have
any grave plots, the buyer Hu Yingchen may move them at his convenience,
and the original owners will not provide any further obstacles" (*MingQing
Huizhou* 3–4). The presence of tombs could complicate land sales enormously. A shorter 1248 contract holds the seller responsible for any errors
in the dimensions and the buyer responsible for future taxes (*MingQing
Huizhou* 4). The latest Song contract from Huizhou, dated 1270, from the
final years of the Song dynasty, resembles the others but explains that the
sale is taking place because the owners lack money. It adds one more
provision: the seller is also responsible if the four borders are not clear.

Except for the clauses about tax obligations, these contracts retain many of the clauses of the contracts from Turfan and Dunhuang.

Conclusion

When the Song dynasty took power in 960, it adopted the hands-off policy of the Tang toward contracts, expressed so clearly in *The Tang Code*. The one extant contract from the late tenth century, from Ding county, Hebei, echoes the insistence of the Turfan contracts on the separation of private contracts from official matters. Unlike the Tang, though, the Song sought to mine contracts as a source of revenue.

The tenth through thirteenth centuries were a time of great commercial growth and correspondingly increased use of contracts. Country folk in Fujian used contracts to record small loans of just two strings of cash, while traveling merchants used them for consignments of goods worth tens of thousands of strings (*Yijianzhi* 4:5:575; 2:7:242–243; Elvin 1973:162–163). Farmers drew up contracts every year with the brokers who bought their crops at harvest time. The author of a famine relief manual bemoaned the reluctance of villagers to sell rice to their hungry neighbors or relief officials because they were contractually bound to sell to merchants from outside their districts at exploitative rates (*Jiuhuang huomin shu* 2:11a–b). Song sources tell of these contracts for salt, for tea, for rice, for lichees, even for some rare peonies that cost 5,000 cash each (*Song huiyao* shihuo 31:26a, 32:10a; *Yijianzhi* 15:7:1609; *Lizhi pu* 1:2b; *Mudan ji* 1:6b; Jiang 1991). People drew up contracts every time they pawned a possession, hired a maid, adopted a child, announced an engagement, purchased a cow or a horse, and, of course, rented or bought land.

Bureaucrats raised the tax on contracts higher and higher and extended the period between signing and registration longer and longer; but the populace still did not pay the tax. The history of the dynasty was in many ways that of a war between officials strenuously trying to register the land and the populace doing its best to evade registration. The battle over collecting the contract tax was part of that war. The decisions in *Clarity and Lucidity* record the last skirmishes between those using the contracts and those taxing them. The users forged contracts with impunity and inserted artificial prices to minimize their liability. On occasion they drew up two contracts—one a buyback loan and one putting up the same plot as collateral—and held onto both so they could use whichever better supported their case in court. And the judges employed their own artillery. They cross-examined everyone possible about agreements. They scrutinized contracts, and went so far as to call handwriting experts into court to verify calligraphy.

The disjuncture between government and private views persisted in the Song. Filled with reservations about contracts, officials sought to regulate their use even as they taxed them. The judges in *Clarity and Lucidity* found many types of wrongful sale, but the populace continued to use contracts in ever increasing numbers.

The government kept pressure on local officials to collect the tax because it needed the revenue to finance its armies in the war against the north. In 1126 it lost all of northern China to the Jin and stepped up the demand for revenue. In the thirteenth century an even more powerful enemy appeared on China's northern borders. The Mongols took northern China from the Jin in 1234 and fought forty years to take southern China, whose terrain was inhospitable to their cavalry. They were able to do so in 1276, once they had constructed their own navy. The Song dynasty came to an end in 1279, with the death of the last boy emperor. Having conquered China, the Mongols faced exactly the same challenge the Song had: collecting the tax on contracts.

5

Contracts

under Mongol

Rule and

Afterward

The Mongols finally succeeded in conquering southern China in 1276 and ruled all of China until 1368 (map 3), when the founder of the Ming dynasty ousted them. Although in power for less than one hundred years, they took a very different approach to the collection of the contract tax than the Song had. For instance, they lowered the tax to one-thirtieth the value of a given transaction. Although scholars doubt the efficiency of Mongol rule and see this century as a time of great chaos, the surviving evidence—some of it in contracts, some of it in new vernacular sources—suggests that the Mongols were better able to collect the contract tax than their predecessors had been.

The Mongols did not recruit officials in the traditional way. They suspended the civil service examinations until 1315 and thereby undermined the tutors and schools that taught classical Chinese, the language tested on the exams and used only for reading and writing. Even after the exams were reinstated, only a few bureaucrats were recruited from them. Many more were recommended by local officials—or promoted after long periods of clerking for those officials. One of the unanticipated side effects of suspending the exams was a boom in vernacular Chinese and the publication of almanacs (leishu) to guide clerks and office holders in their duties. The first almanacs dated to the Song, but many more were written in the Yuan and later periods. They were designed as aids for literate people—some highly educated, some less so. Their readers would have needed help with drafting an appropriate letter to an official, cooking a particular dish, using a certain medicine, or drawing up a contract. While the often anonymous authors of these almanacs railed against the litigiousness of the society they lived in, they went on to supply their readers with model plaints they could use to bring suits.

Map 3. China under Mongol Rule, 1260–1368, also showing modern provincial
boundaries. The Chinese at this time continued to use contracts written in Chinese.
Surviving documents suggest that the Mongols were successful in collecting the
contract tax. (Drawn by Donna Perry.)

The decline in classical studies coincided with the rise of a new literary
genre, drama. Theater had flourished in northern China under Jin rule and
continued to gain in popularity under the Mongols. Some of the plays
concerning extraordinary contracts suggest the legal sophistication of the
audience, while others shed light on how ordinary people—including
women and non-Chinese speakers—used contracts in daily life. Perhaps the
most revealing source is a Chinese-language textbook that follows a group
of horse traders from Korea to Beijing and devotes pages of text to the
process of finding a broker, finalizing a price, drawing up a contract, then
canceling the deal, and undoing all the paperwork. These sources allow us
to see how all types of contracts, not just those for the purchase of land, but

also of children, women, and horses, functioned in the century of Mongol rule and afterward.

When the Mongols took southern China, they had already governed northern China for forty years. There they followed many of the practices of the Jin, who had promulgated a modified version of *The Tang Code* in 1201 and who retained much of the Chinese law concerning contracts (Ratchnevsky 1937:9–11; Chen Gaohua 1988:45). Because the Mongols allowed the conquered peoples to continue their own way of life as much as possible, they permitted them to worship their traditional gods, they often hired local bureaucrats to administer their government, and they tended to follow the taxation policies of the conquered governments. The Mongol dynasty in China, the Yuan, appointed Mongols and other Central Asians to office, but they often had Chinese counterparts and their clerical staffs remained Chinese.

Little evidence about the use of contracts from the period of Mongol rule in northern China survives, but one lone contract for the purchase of a tomb for a Daoist teacher in Datong, Shanxi (map 3), shows that the Mongols instituted some reforms in the north, following the conquest of 1234, before carrying them out in the south. The contract reads:

> A contract for the purchase of a tomb for the Teacher in the west of the city.
>
> Wu Junfu, who serves under Liu Xuan of the western capital, today needs money to use and otherwise has no means of raising it, so he puts up one plot registered under his name in the southwest part of the Song Family-Estate Village. The plot has a footpath running north to south and totals 25 sixth-acres. The east reaches to Han Lao's land, the south to the official road, the west to Han Da's land, and the north to the small road.
>
> He draws up a contract to sell the above plot with its four borders to Great Teacher Feng of the Longxiang Daoist monastery in the same city, who will be the owner of the plot permanently. The two sides have discussed and agreed on a price of 25 ounces. On the day the contract is drawn up, each pays in full. If afterward there is any obstacle to the sale or anyone encroaches on the land, the seller of the land Wu Junfu must resolve the problem alone without going to court. Once this is agreed, no one can change his mind about the transaction. Whoever does so first must pay a fine of 10 ounces of silver. For fear that people will not believe this, we accordingly draw

up this document as proof on the twenty-eighth day of the ninth month of 1265.[1]

Seller of land, Wu Junfu	(mark)
Joint seller, his mother, A Gu	(mark)
Neighbor Han Lao	(mark)
Neighbor Han Da	(mark)
Witness Wang Zhen	(mark)
Representative of tax office in western district on [ ] year,	
[ ] month	(mark)

(*Wenwu* 1962.10:40)

Most of this contract closely follows the pattern we have come to expect, with the seller responsible for the accuracy of the borders and resolving any subsequent claims. One clause is noteworthy, that which explains how the price was determined: it was "discussed and agreed on." This clause refers to the Mongol practice of having the seller first post an asking price before the buyer responds. The signatories include two of the neighbors, who have chosen not to exercise their right of refusal, as well as a representative of the tax office. Their marks are not reproduced in the published transcription of this contract. The last signature on the contract hints at what was the most pathbreaking change under Mongol rule. The Mongols were able to link land sales with payment of taxes, ensuring that they could collect the contract tax at the time of sale and the newly assessed land tax thereafter.

The Mongol emperors did issue several edicts ordering changes in the process of buying and selling land. Mongol law, like Tang and Song law, consisted of imperial edicts, rulings by important branches of the government, and decisions on local cases. Because a decision in one part of the country was binding in all other regions, the Mongol government regularly promulgated its decisions throughout China (Chikusa 1973:30). Periodically, the central government gathered the precedents and edicts (Ch'en, Paul 1979:30–33). One such collection, *Yuan Institutions* (*Yuan dianzhang*), compiled sometime between 1320 and 1322, reproduces the edicts delineating the changes in contract law introduced by the Mongols.

In 1271 Qubilai Qan announced the founding of the Yuan dynasty, and in the years leading up to and following the announcement his officials

1. The text gives the incorrect cyclical date, but the epitaph on the back of the stone gives the date of death as 1265. Thomas Lee helped me with this translation.

issued a series of decisions defining Mongol policy toward contracts. Continuing many of the earlier policies of the Tang and Song, they limited the interest on money and grain debts to 100 percent and prohibited the compounding of interest, while allowing brokers to collect a 2 percent fee on sales of slaves, cattle, and land, all of which required a contract (*Yuan dianzhang* 22:86a; 27:4a, 7a; 57:52b; Cleaves 1955:48–49). They forbade the intermarriage of free people with slaves and the selling of wives (*Yuan dianzhang* 18:20b, 21a–b, 44a, 45a–b; 57:12a, 15b; *Nancun chuogeng lu* 17:208). They set penalties for breaking engagements (*Yuan dianzhang* 18:18a–19a). They allowed a man to divorce his wife for the same seven outs but forbade it for the same three protections the Tang and Song codes had, and even summarized the law in tabular form (*Yuan dianzhang* 18:29a).

Because the people they governed were descendants of the same wily folk who had outwitted Song officials, Mongol bureaucrats complained about many of the same tactics the judges in *Clarity and Lucidity* had. Moneylenders inserted false amounts in contracts, even ten times the actual price, with the goal of collecting after the debtor had come into his inheritance (*Yuan dianzhang* 27:4b–5a). They pasted contracts onto already stamped contracts so they could evade the contract tax (*Yuan dianzhang* 22:84a). Localities devised ways to retain more revenue from the contract tax than the central government thought they were entitled to (*Yuan dianzhang* 22:84a). Officials continued to blame the large number of suits on poorly drafted land and marriage contracts (Ch'en, Paul 1979:124). And, like the Song officials before them, they extended the grace period between the signing of a contract and the payment of the contract tax in hope of increasing compliance (*Yuan dianzhang* 19:24b–25a; Ratchnevsky 1972:101–102).

The similarity of these complaints to earlier complaints masks the very real changes the Mongols instituted in China. They divided the population into four groups: Mongols, others from central Asia, northern Chinese, and southern Chinese, and these terms appear in *Yuan Institutions*. One decision specifically forbade central Asians from using their children to pay off debts, and another forbade the sale of Mongols to pay off debts (*Yuan dianzhang* 57:14a, 15b). The government may have dictated how the Chinese were to marry, but the Mongols and the central Asians followed their own marriage customs, hints of which survive (*Yuan dianzhang* 18:1a). Many cases in *Yuan Institutions* deal with runaway fiancés, and officials consistently ruled that if men were gone for sixty or one hundred days, as nomad warriors could well be, their engagements could be terminated (*Yuan dianzhang* 18:11b–12a).

The Mongols also instituted important changes in contract law. Most notably, they reduced the contract tax to one-thirtieth the value of the land, animal, or slave sold (*Yuan dianzhang* 22:85b, 96a, 99b; Schurmann 1956a:218–219). They urged the annual renewal of contracts for those who had used their own labor to pay off a debt (*Yuan dianzhang* 57:13a). They required contracts to be drawn up at the time of engagement that specified the value of gifts to be exchanged (*Yuan dianzhang* 18:3a; *Tongzhi tiaoge* 3:39). They required a bill of divorce or notice of adoption to be registered with local officials (*Yuan dianzhang* 17:19b, 18:44a). And they gave right of first refusal on land sales to relatives and neighbors (Ratchnevsky 1972:103n2). The sellers were to draw up a full description of the plot for sale, which was addressed to interested parties. One had three days to say no, or five days to say yes and agree on a price (*Yuan dianzhang* 19:21a). Here the Mongols were following Jin practice and ignoring the Southern Song attempts, recorded in *Clarity and Lucidity*, to limit the right of refusal to those who were both kin and neighbors (Schurmann 1956b:514; Chen Gaohua 1988:36).

Most surprising, and the strongest evidence of the Mongols' desire to continue Song policies, was their decision to recognize contracts from the Song. In 1286 the Department of State Affairs responded to the query of the prefect in Ruizhou (now Gaoan, Jiangxi) to rule that Song contracts granting the right to buy back land should be upheld as long as they were not forged (*Yuan dianzhang* 19:24a).

In 1299 the Department of State Affairs followed the recommendation of the Ministry of Rites and revised its earlier decision to recognize Song contracts granting the right to buy land back. Given the many changes in currency since the Song, and the difficulty of detecting forgeries, the ministry ruled that it was too difficult to determine fair terms for redeeming land that had been mortgaged in the Song. It also felt that some had taken advantage of the 1286 decision to bring endless numbers of cases before the local courts. The ministry therefore ruled that such Song contracts should not be honored (*Yuan dianzhang* 19:30b–31a).

Significantly, these two rulings concern only the redemption of mortgages, not contracts for the sale of land. In 1302 a Chinese commoner in Tanzhou (now Changsha, Hunan) sued a high Mongol official for encroaching on his tangerine orchard. The case was referred to the Ministry of Rites, possibly because it involved relations between Mongols and the local

Chinese. The ministry ruled that the contested land belonged to the Chinese plaintiff because he showed a stamped contract from 1241 in addition to documents permitting him to buy the buildings on the land. Although the previous owner, an assistant grand councilor (*canzheng*), claimed to have been awarded the orchard in 1289, he offered no documentary proof. The current occupant of the land, a midlevel executive official in the Secretariat (*pingzhang*), had simply seized the land. "This is a case of the house of a bullying official who takes advantage of and pillages from the common people and who is not willing to purchase land," concluded the Ministry of Rites, which ordered the land returned to the original owner. The Department of State Affairs concurred (*Yuan dianzhang* 19:31a–32a). The Mongols may have found it too difficult to honor Song buyback contracts, but they fully accepted sale contracts from the Song as proof of ownership. The principle the ministry used to reach its ruling is evident: those who had contracts, even from the Song, had stronger claim to a plot of land than those who had no documentary proof of ownership.

People continued to avoid registering their contracts, not because the contract tax was too high but because the Mongols succeeded in linking the tax assessment with the price of the plot to be sold. In 1300 the Imperial Secretariat listed the procedures for buying and selling land that were to stand until the end of the dynasty in 1368. An official in each district was to draw up a register showing ownership and the tax assessment on each plot. When someone wished to sell a plot, that person was to go to the government office to request certification that the land to be sold was his or her own (*tiji*). At this point, although this particular regulation does not say so, relatives and neighbors would be given an opportunity to buy the land. The time limits for a decision, three days to say no and five days to say yes, were too brief and were extended in 1315 to ten and fifteen days, respectively (*Yuan dianzhang* 19:21b–22b). Presumably people buying land needed time to raise the capital. The government office would then issue a certificate verifying that the land had been investigated and could be sold. This certificate would be laid on the government register, which was a piece of paper. It was stamped so that half the stamp was on the certificate, the other on the register, and it could be subsequently checked. Then the buyer and seller would go to the tax office to determine the new rate at which the land would be taxed. As an inducement to comply, the officials were authorized to seize half the unregistered land if the buyer and seller failed to obtain the half-stamped certificate or if they did not go to the tax office (*Yuan dianzhang* 19:27a–28a).

Fifteen surviving contracts from Huizhou, Anhui, spanning the years 1289 to 1353, allow a glimpse of how Yuan policies affected the drawing up of contracts.[2] All follow the Song texts closely, suggesting strong continuity between the Song and the Yuan, which may help to explain the Mongol government's decision to recognize contracts from the Song (Liu Hehui 1984:32). Of the fifteen Huizhou contracts, only one is unstamped. It is not obvious why these contracts survive—whether government offices or private individuals stored them for seven centuries, but Joseph McDermott (personal communication, July 1994) thinks it likely that individual families held onto them because of their potential use in land disputes. Because stamped contracts would have had much greater evidentiary value, they had a better chance of survival than the unstamped white contracts. Accordingly, it is impossible to generalize about the empire-wide rate of compliance with the contract tax on the basis of how many of the Huizhou contracts are stamped.

After giving the dimensions of the plot, one of these contracts, dated 1315, reads as follows:

> Today, because I am short of money, I willingly have applied to the
> authorities for a receipt, to draw up a contract for the fields and hills
> within the above four boundaries and for the cedars, big and small,
> on the hills, to be sold in full to my fellow sector resident, Li [   ].
> As evaluated and discussed by the three sides, the price is paper
> money from the Zhongtong reign (1260–1264) with a face value of 13
> ingots. The money must be exchanged at the time the contract is
> drawn up. Once the contract is written up, no other documents will
> be written. The fields, hills, and trees, today from the time of the
> sale, will be the exclusive responsibility of the buyer to cultivate and
> to manage. Before the time of the sale, none of these goods had
> previously been traded or sold outside of the family. If the four
> boundaries are not clear, or someone outside of the family makes a
> claim, both are the responsibility of the seller to resolve, and neither
> shall involve the buyer. We put our hand to two stamped copies of

2. Five unpublished contracts held by the Beijing Library are available in the microfilm set *SongYuan diqi jicun*. Ten Yuan contracts are transcribed in *MingQing Huizhou*, with photographs in *Huizhou qiannian*. Four additional items (a tax receipt, a tomb contract, an agreement to divide family property, and a receipt for lumber) also appear in *Huizhou qiannian*.

the contract, one of which is attached. Today, for fear there will be no proof, we draw up this contract to serve as such.

On the fifteenth day of the seventh month of the second year of the Yanyou reign

Wang Zixian	(mark)
His son who drew up the contract, Wang Youde	(mark)

(*MingQing Huizhou* 8; *Huizhou qiannian* 10, plate 4)

The father's mark is an awkward squiggle, but his son's hand is well schooled and clear. The contract gives the location of the land to be sold in several ways: the name of the plot, its location on a grid (presumably that used by the authorities for tax purposes), and the four boundaries. The reason it gives for the sale, lack of money, occurs in almost all the Huizhou contracts, as does the phrase "as evaluated and discussed by the three sides." The three sides are the buyer, the seller, and the broker, who could set a price only after refusal of the option to buy by the relatives and neighbors. All succeeding contracts absolve the buyer from any responsibility should either the boundaries or the original claim to the land turn out to be fraudulent (*MingQing Huizhou* 7–13).

The Murder of First-Victory

Both *Yuan Institutions* and the Huizhou contracts suggest that disputes over land could be resolved if they arose. A rare report captures one result when conflicting claims to land were not resolved: murder. A few primary documents survive from the archives of local governments in the Song and the Yuan only because of an accident. Government officials printed books on the backs of discarded documents, largely because they could make extra income by selling the paper to their own presses (Chikusa 1973:12–13). When the binding of one book of this type, a Yuan edition printed on Song blocks of the *Ougong benmo* (*A short history of Ouyang Xiu*), was cut open by the Seikadō Library, the Japanese scholar Chikusa Masaaki (1973:15–24) was able to examine the back of each folded page. Chikusa transcribed the records about the murder of Zheng First-Victory (*Shengyi*), including the depositions of the main criminal, Zhu Ten-Thousand Seven (*Wanqi*); his wife; his son Fifth-Wisdom (*Xianwu*) and his wife; the two men who helped him carry the corpse and hang it from a tree; and the dead man's brother Second-Victory, who brought the charge against Zhu Ten-Thousand Seven.

The local officials do not charge Zhu Ten-Thousand Seven with murder, but with the crime of moving a murdered body from the scene of the crime, possibly because the body was too decomposed to be examined properly and sustain a murder change—possibly, too, because of Zhu Ten-Thousand Seven's high social standing within the community.

These depositions make it possible to reconstruct the events leading up to the murder. In the fourth month of 1318 the government of Lishui county, Zhejiang (shown on map 3), conducted a survey of the fields and their yields in the district as a preliminary step before raising land taxes. On the nineteenth day of that month, Zhu Ten-Thousand Seven submitted a claim to a plot of land. He presented a group of contracts showing that his father had bought a plot of land from Zheng First-Ever (*Cengyi*), the father of First-Victory. Two low-level officials verified the claim, and Zhu Ten-Thousand Seven sent them wine as thanks. Fifth-Wisdom reported that eight days later First-Victory came to their house, cursed Zhu Ten-Thousand Seven, who refused to see him, then said to Fifth-Wisdom:

> I have a field of 80 *ba* located in this county in the [   ] district, named [   ]. My father, Zheng First-Ever, sold it to your grandfather, Zhu Forty-Eight. Afterward the field filled up with sand and rocks during a flood. Your father, Zhu Ten-Thousand Seven, sold the field back to me. I repaired it and have tilled it for many years.
>
> Then your father goes and registers this land with the district officials. I came to ask why and saw that your father was ill with a cold and wouldn't see me.[3]

Fifth-Wisdom then testified that First-Victory decided to stay the night in the empty room on the second floor of the store belonging to his brother, Fifth-Longevity. Did he hope to see Zhu Ten-Thousand Seven in the morning? Or did Zhu Ten-Thousand Seven feign illness in order to trap First-Victory? The son does not say. His narrative resumes in the middle of the night when his brother woke him to tell him First-Victory had died. He got up and saw his father holding a pine torch and First-Victory's body hanging next to a grain bin.

The accessories to the crime reported that they wrapped the body in a bedspread on a plank, carried it to a nearby mountain, and strung it up on

3. Because the last two characters of each line are missing where the book publishers cut the page, my translation is based on Chikusa's brilliant transcription and reconstruction of the text.

a yew tree to make it look like suicide. One of these men was a tenant of Zhu Ten-Thousand Seven, the other a man staying at his house, quite likely a field hand. Their ties as Zhu's subordinate tenants were such that they could not refuse his request, although they surely knew that moving the corpse was illegal. As suited their different social positions, they carried the body, while Zhu Ten-Thousand Seven carried the torch. Four days later, after he had first gone to look for him at the Zhus' house, Second-Victory discovered his brother's rotting corpse. The investigation took a long time, four months, because the murderer and his victim lived on the border of two prefectures. The investigating official, a Mongol registrar, took the accused to the home of the victim to gather the testimony of his neighbors and family.

The depositions provide a fascinating glimpse of legal procedure on the local level in the Yuan. The names of the people involved are peasant names: Fifth-Wisdom and Fifth-Longevity are brothers, as are First-Victory and Second-Victory. Not for them were the elaborate naming practices of those who thought in terms of descent and who reserved only one component of a character, or a radical, for members of the same generation. These people simply chose one auspicious word, be it "wisdom," "victory," or "ever," then added a number as each son was born. Numbers occur frequently in Chinese names, but with different, poorly understood meanings. What did Zhu Ten-Thousand Seven mean? The other sons in his family could have been named Ten-Thousand, or the name could have been one assigned by the court to prevent mistaken identity. Sometimes the parents named a child with the sum of their ages at the time of birth, which may be why Zhu's grandfather was named Forty-eight (Hansen 1990:100*n*22).

The language of the depositions is a mixture of colloquialisms and the terseness that resulted from transcribing oral speech into classical Chinese. They use a measure of yield, literally a handful (*ba*), to give the area of the field, and because the one place where the area is transcribed in the standard sixth-acre units is blank, we do not know the size of the field.

The Zhengs felt ties to their land even after they had sold it to the Zhus. The Zhengs must have sold in hard times and were able to buy back the plot only after it had been flooded and filled with rocks. When they did so, they must not have drawn up a contract; for if they had, they certainly would have cited it to support their claim. Buying and selling land were relatively straightforward transactions; selling with the option to buy back was positively murky. No wonder the Yuan officials refused to consider Song buyback contracts. No wonder they set a hundred-day limit on buying land back (*Yuan dianzhang* 19:21a). But the law could not eradicate common practice. People may have mortgaged and even sold land to those who had more money than they did, but they continued to think of the land as theirs and to hope for the day they could again formalize their ownership. That is why Zheng First-Victory was so incensed when Zhu Ten-Thousand Seven laid claim to the plot. And it was this intensity of feeling that led to his death.

An obviously apochryphal story from a Yuan collection of tales, set around 1330, confirms the strength of ties between people and their land, even after they had relinquished ownership and moved away. Farmer Si was the tenant of the village rich man, Mr. Chen, in Taixing county, Yangzhou, Jiangsu. One year Farmer Si was so poor that he was unable to pay his rent, so he had to pawn his right to cultivate his land, which carried with it the right of occupancy. A neighbor, Mr. Li, who was also a tenant, bribed Mr. Chen's son to sell him the rights to Farmer Si's land. Farmer Si then lost his right of occupancy. Mr. Li drew up a contract and urged Farmer Si to eat some chicken and to drink a glass of wine with him, but Farmer Si refused. The custom of having a feast on the signing of a contract must have been deeply entrenched, if, even under these circumstances, the buyer and seller were to share a chicken and some wine. Farmer Si was so enraged that he took a torch that night to burn down Mr. Li's house, but he abandoned his plan when he heard a woman in labor. He thought to himself: "The person I want to get revenge on is the master of the house. What reason do I have to kill his wife and child?"

Forced off his land, Farmer Si began to peddle bean-curd milk and wine and eventually prospered. At the same time, Mr. Li lost money. After ten years Farmer Si used the same stratagem Mr. Li had used to buy back the rights to his land. They drew up a new contract. This time the enraged Mr. Li was about to torch Farmer Si's house when he heard Farmer Si's wife giving birth. He too threw away his torch, but Farmer Si found it the next day and saw Mr. Li's name on it. He decided this was a sign from heaven and went to Mr. Li to give him 5 strings of cash as a token of friendship. As the two men were drinking, they drew up an engagement contract for their children. From that day on, both families prospered (*Nancun chuogeng lu* 13:162–163).

This story with its fairy-tale ending indicates that Zheng First-Victory's experience was typical. It was typical for people to feel ties to their land even after they had mortgaged it, after they had left it, and after they had lost their legal rights to it. It was typical for people to feel deep anger at those who took their land from them, even if they did so legally. And it was typical for very poor tenant farmers, even those who peddled bean-curd milk and wine, to draw up contracts to record both the transfer of land rights and the engagement of their children.

Model Contracts in Almanacs

This frequent use of contracts, even among the rural poor, meant that there was a real need for model texts, a need that almanacs helped to fill. Some of the almanacs are clearly aimed at an audience of literati, with the most rarified of them listing different, more elegant ways to request that a contract be stamped (*Jie jiangwang*, jia 8), more than a hundred elaborate engagement letters according to the parents' professions (*Hanmo quanshu*, ding 7), classical citations for different terms to be used in drawing up a plaint (*Hebi shilei*, waiji 26:1a–14a), or terms to be used in writing up legal decisions (*Shushu zhinan* 18:36a–38b).

Other almanacs contained information of a more practical nature. *A New Collection of Topically Ordered Documents, Letters, and Essential Texts*, dated 1324, provides texts of model contracts for both final and conditional sales of land, to hire men and women servants, and to buy a boat, a horse, or a cow. It also gives the texts of a promissory note to pay crops or rent to a guarantor, a notice putting hill land up for sale, a public plea to stop others from encroaching on the family's tomb land, a receipt for the loan of money and of grain, and a bill of adoption (*Qizha qingqian*, waiji 11; *Yuandai falü ziliao* 1988:238–250). These models indicate the basic uses of contracts in daily life had not changed since the time of Turfan or Dunhuang. They were still used to acquire land, people, animals, or commodities—for various lengths of time and under various circumstances. The contracts in this almanac are quite different from contracts in earlier periods, as can be seen from this model for the final or conditional sale of land:

> A model contract for the mortgaging or purchase of land. *** Name of *** district in *** village.
>
> The above-mentioned *** has purchased or inherited so many plots of fertile land, totaling so many sixth-acres and so many five-foot lengths. The tax on crops is so many strings. The first plot is located in *** district. The name of the land is *** place. The eastern border reaches to [   ], the western to [   ], the southern to

[   ], the northern to [   ]. This is cultivated by ∗∗∗ name, who pays a rent of so many piculs each winter.

Today because of financial trouble and because of the burden of the corvée, he has willingly sought the services of [∗∗∗] name to serve as broker and write a contract to put up the entire plot of land within these four borders for sale (or mortgage) to ∗∗∗ name from ∗∗∗ village. The three parties have discussed and set the price at so many strings of paper money from the Zhongtong reign (1260–1264). It is all cash. It is not extorted or the product of debt. This money should be paid in full at the time the contract is signed. Nothing should be left over. The land to be sold (or mortgaged) is land that has been rightfully bought or inherited. It has not been obtained by deceiving the old or the young. The private transaction is within the provisions of the law and there should be no obstacles. If there are, then [∗∗∗], the seller, is responsible for resolving them and should prepare other land to make up the loss. It is not the purchaser's (or the mortgager's) concern.

Once the contract is signed, it is up to the owner to assume responsibility for the taxes and tenants of the field. (In the case of mortgage, one writes, it is agreed that there is a limit of three winters to prepare the same amount of cash to redeem the land. If the seller does not have the money to redeem the land, it will be according to the original agreement.) The land will be permanently his. Once it is sold, the children and grandchildren of the seller cannot use this contract to claim the right to redeem the land.

All the agreements and stamped contracts will be taken to the government office to be stamped. The above-mentioned lot and tax obligations will be entered under the name of the buyer to pay and to be answerable for. The tax and corvée obligations should be carried out as before. This is to be used as proof. Respectfully dated [   ] year, month, day.

Seller	∗∗∗ name, number
Guarantor	∗∗∗ name, number
Broker	∗∗∗ name, number
Witness	∗∗∗ name, number

(*Yuandai falü ziliao* 1988:238–239)

This contract assumes the payment of taxes. It records the price as set by the three parties of buyer, seller, and broker, who give both their names and the number they use to identify themselves to the state. The guarantor, called the person familiar with the contract (*zhiqi*), also signs his name. This contract aims to preclude suits because of ambiguous borders. It seeks to block suits claiming that the money was obtained by force or the land extracted from a debtor. It promises that, provided the land is rightfully the seller's to sell, the buyer can buy it and know that it will be his permanently and that he will be obliged to pay taxes on it permanently, too. This is a contract with an agenda, and that agenda is exactly that of the government. Designed to establish a national standard, the contract leaves no room for First-Victory's claim against Ten-Thousand Seven or for any other claim. It does not have the same feel as the Dunhuang writing exercises copied by students into small booklets. Those may have been riddled with scribal errors, but they were concise and they were usable. This is a land contract as the authorities wanted one, and it was much too long to be suitable for daily use. The later Huizhou contracts were duly stamped and registered at the government tax office, but they do not include all the provisions and provisos of this model.

Other almanacs share the normative thrust of *A New Collection*. One encyclopedia, *Wide-Ranging Notes from the Forest of Life* (*Shilin guangji*), was reissued and reprinted repeatedly (Morita 1992). Its 1330–1332 edition contains a section listing punishments for abuses of land contracts under the penal law section (*Shilin guangji* [Zhiyuan edition] bieji 3). This section reprints the law specifying the number of beatings to be given should relatives, neighbors, and those who have mortgaged the land fail to exercise their right of refusal within the set periods or should the buyer fail to obtain the proper certificate authorizing the sale (*Yuanshi* 103:2641-42; Ratchnevsky 1972:103–104).[4]

Surely only officials or clerks who were ghostwriting decisions would consult such an encyclopedia. A 1699 Japanese reprint of the 1325 edition reinforces this impression of the encyclopedia's readership. It warns about contracts in which the government stamp precedes the text, for that indicates that the sale never took place and that the change in ownership was never recorded in official registers (7:27a). It takes the same distrustful tone about commoners when advising readers how to draw up contracts, explain-

---

4. The 1331 law code, *The Great Compendium Spanning Generations* (*Jingshi dadian*), survives as the monograph on penal law in the official history of the Yuan (*Yuanshi* 102–105) and has been translated by Ratchnevsky (1937, 1972, 1977, 1985).

ing that "many of the people's suits start here [from inaccurate borders in wills and contracts]" (7:28a–29b). The author does not spell out who "the people" are, but his list of the ways in which they distort contracts certainly implies that they are different from the reader. Sometimes, because of uneven terrain, one hill could be rendered as two, or two hills could be rendered as one. The land beneath a house could be called a paddy field and a paddy field could be foundation land. Some contracts change the course of roads or rivers. Although officials may have maps and records of land surveys, many have been eaten away or are no longer extant. The catalogue of abuses goes on and on, and the readers are urged to accept only stamped wills and contracts. The section concludes: "These are the products of a lesser man's mind. When he encounters an enlightened official, it is up to him to correct his crime." For "lesser man," we should read "commoner," and for "enlightened official," "the reader." Judging from the frequency with which this encyclopedia was reprinted, *Wide-Ranging Notes* affirms that officials' struggle to tighten up contracts and minimize suits continued through the period of Mongol rule and even after it.

This same encyclopedia, in spite of its calls to stay out of court, in the 1330–1332 edition contains forms for drafting different types of plaints (*Yuandai falü ziliao* 1988:227–237). Most are requests to officials to lower or forgive tax or corvée obligations because some untoward event—be it an attack by locusts or the disappearance of a laborer—has occurred that makes it impossible to pay the usual taxes or perform the usual corvée duties. The forms for reports describing site visits and the extent of damage would be consulted only by officials or their clerks. Some of the forms, though, are for bringing suit against other people. One form sues to get back money from a debtor who has repeatedly failed to make interest payments. Another describes the circumstances leading up to a beating. The attacker was drinking, but not drunk, and struck the victim with a cudgel when he refused to buy the attacker more to drink. The inclusion of these forms for drafting plaints follows a frequent pattern of these books. The same almanac author who in one chapter rails against the proclivity of the masses to bring suits in another chapter includes the very forms needed to do so. For all of the Confucian rhetoric about the ideal conflict-free society, officials who lived under the Mongols realized how much a part of daily life lawsuits had become and how urgently their readers wanted to know how to bring them.

Contracts in Yuan Plays

No source testifies more eloquently to the importance of contracts in daily life than the plays written under the Mongols and performed for centuries after Mongol rule. In vernacular Chinese, and filled with slapstick, they depict the lives of ordinary people, officials, and often their sons who were unable to pursue, or uninterested in pursuing, official careers. The language of these plays is startlingly fresh; one can feel the playwrights enjoying the fun of breaking the conventions governing classical Chinese. Determining exactly when sections of the plays were first written down poses enormous difficulties. A 1330 source, Zhong Sicheng's *Roster of Dead Souls (Luguipu)*, gives the titles but not the texts of over a hundred plays. Partial texts, giving arias, of only thirty plays survive from the Yuan (*Yuankan zaju*), and actors probably improvised the dialogue. Over two hundred years later, between 1573 and 1619, the full texts, *Selections from Yuan Drama (Yuanqu xuan)*, were published—in a version revised for a sophisticated reading audience (Idema 1985:33). While the actual speeches date to the end of the Ming, the basic plots are probably close to those of the original Yuan-dynasty plays.

The plots of three of these plays hinge on atypical contracts, as unbelievable as Shylock's for a pound of flesh in *The Merchant of Venice*. Because the timing of the dramas depends entirely on the fulfillment of unconventional contracts, they reveal the audience's familiarity with contractual language and logic. These plays would not have engaged an audience who knew nothing of contracts. But those who did would have been intrigued to hear of a contract that was not read aloud at the time of signing, of a contract postponing the division of family property to an unnamed later date, and of a contract for the sale of a child that did not give the price. The pleasure of these plays consists in watching, or reading, how these unusual contracts were implemented.

One play, *The Elder of the Eastern Studio (Dongtanglao)*, stars a contract that, contrary to usual practice, is not read aloud until the end of the play. In the opening scene a dying merchant gives a contract to his friend and neighbor, Mr. Li, who is so upright and wise that everyone calls him the Elder. The merchant makes his mark on the already completed contract and asks his son, whose nickname is Yangzhou Boy, to put his mark on the back (Niida 1937:352). He does not read it aloud. The merchant then gives the contract to Mr. Li, the Elder, leaving the boy—and the audience—ignorant of its contents.

Once the father dies, the wastrel son proceeds to sell off everything he has inherited. The playwright is sufficiently skillful that he does not bore the audience by showing all these transactions, but presents the first one, the sale of the house, in some detail. Yangzhou Boy decides to sell his house when he runs out of money at an inn. One drinking companion offers to register the transaction with the government,[5] while another draws up the contract (*Yuan quxuan* 210). Yangzhou Boy sells the house to Mr. Li, the Elder, who makes one payment of 250 ingots and promises another, in the vain hope of curbing Yangzhou Boy's spending. Instead, Yangzhou Boy finances a banquet with the proceeds and thereby begins his descent down the social ladder. His former associates, failed examination candidates, abandon him when his money runs out. Yangzhou Boy ends up living in a broken tile kiln peddling vegetables for a living.

Mr. Li, the Elder, then invites everyone to a birthday banquet and asks Yangzhou Boy to read his father's contract aloud. This event is something the audience expected at the time of signing and has been waiting for since the beginning of the play:

> Today, I, Zhao Guoqi, resident of Commemorative Arch Alley, inside the wall of Yangzhou, because I am ill and unable to get up, and because my son, Yangzhou Boy, is not prudent, secretly place 500 ingots of silver in the care of my old friend to give to my son, Yangzhou Boy, to use when he has difficulties and is in need of money. (*Yuan quxuan* 226)

This remarkable contract is not a loan to his friend, which would be usual, but a request to safeguard money until his son needs it. Nor was it the norm to entrust the care of a thirty-year-old orphan to another adult. The contract follows the standard form, though, in giving the reason for the request and has been validated by the marks of the father and the son. Mr. Li, the Elder, reveals what he has done with the money. Each time Yangzhou Boy sold off part of his inheritance, Mr. Li, the Elder, secretly bought the item back. So he has purchased the house and the land, the oil press, the mill, the pawnshop, the animals and slaves, the furniture, musical instruments, books, and paintings for Yangzhou Boy. The play ends happily, with the contract having been fulfilled, and the virtues of saving money extolled. Contracts have so penetrated society that no one even suggests that the merchant should have been able to give his trusted

---

5. The first *gongju* seems to be a printer's error for the correct *gongju*, meaning official receipt.

friend the money to safeguard without drawing up a contract. That scenario would have been even more unbelievable than the contract they did draw up.

A play entitled *The Contract* (*Hetong wenzi*) is named for the unusual contract it features: one drawn up by peasants to divide their family's household property at some unspecified time in the future. Its interest hinges also on the audience's expectation that the terms of the contract, no matter how unconventional, will be carried out.[6] *The Contract* tells of a Kaifeng peasant who takes his wife and son with him on the road during a famine year. Before he goes, Liu and his elder brother draw up two copies of a contract stating that they have not yet divided the family property. At the time of the signing, the elder brother prophetically remarks that the contract will serve as proof when the two brothers meet again. Here is the text of the contract he drew up the night before:

> I, Liu Tianxiang, resident of the Yiding quarter of the West Gate of Kaifeng, my younger brother, Liu Tianrui, and his son, Anzhu, because the harvest has failed, obey the instructions of officials to split up the household and lower the number of mouths by going to different places to seek the harvest. Younger brother Liu Tianrui willingly takes his wife and child to another place to seek the harvest. All the family property and land has not been divided.
>
> Today we draw up two copies of the text of this contract, and each takes one copy as proof.

Person who drew up the contract	Liu Tianxiang
Younger brother of the same household	Liu Tianrui
Witness	Community Head Li

(*Yuan quxuan* 421)

The elder brother reads the contract aloud so that all present (and the audience) understand its contents. Then the community head, a functionary who governs about fifty families and who ranks below the village head, puts his mark on the contract. On the face of it, this contract does not make

---

6. Because the title of the play is mentioned in another dated Judge Bao play, *The Ghost of the Pot*, the rough outlines of the plot must predate 1398 (Hayden 1978:118, 179–181, 209n33; Iwaki [1959] 1972:458–460). The early plot was also rewritten to become a short story, extant in a 1498 edition (Hanan 1973:4). Two brothers, with the same names as those in the play, come to an identical arrangement, but the story does not give the text of the contract.

sense. Surely the two brothers would divide the family property at the time one brother leaves home. But the audience accepts the premise of the play: because the family property could not be sold for a good price during a famine, it is more logical to wait. This is a surprisingly complex contract for a typical peasant to draft, and we learn later that both of the brothers have attended school.

The younger brother and his family say goodbye. They get as far as an inn in Shanxi, where the brother and his wife fall ill and die. Once the boy comes of age, the innkeeper sends him home with the contract to find his aunt and uncle. His aunt tricks him into giving her his copy of the contract and beats him, saying he is not her nephew. She wants her daughter and her husband to inherit the land, but because the inheritance law privileges her nephew's claim over her daughter's, she cannot afford to recognize him. The nephew complains to the community head who witnessed the original contract. The official takes him to Judge Bao, a figure based on the historical magistrate whom we encountered early in chapter 4. Judge Bao summons the aunt and uncle, who again deny the boy is their relative. Then the judge and his clerk spread the word that the boy has died in prison. If a relative has killed him, the penalty will only be a fine; but if a stranger has killed him, the punishment will be death. The aunt admits that the boy is her nephew, and when Judge Bao expresses doubt, she shows him the two copies of the contract. Then Judge Bao announces that the boy, still alive, is entitled to his full inheritance. This is, of course, the denouement the audience has been waiting for since the contract was first signed. The fun of the play has been watching Judge Bao enforce the contract.

Another play, *The Moneywatcher* (*Kanqiannu*), features a contract that omits the price. It works because the audience knows more about contracts than the protagonists. The action opens with a mud-and-daub workman praying for money to the god of Mount Tai, who promises him the use of some money for twenty years and tells him where it is. The workman steals the buried inheritance of an examination candidate. The impoverished candidate is forced to sell his son to the workman, and a broker suggests they draw up a contract:

> The person who draws up the contract, Examination Candidate
> Zhou, because he has no money to spend, cannot buy food, and has
> difficulty eking out a living, willingly sells his son, ••• name, so
> many years old, to rich man Mr. Jia the Elder to be his son.

At this point, the broker interrupts to object to the label "rich man." Mr. Jia then dictates the rest of the contract:

> Today the three sides [broker, buyer, and seller] agree on a price of so much. Once the contract is drawn up, the buyer and seller are not permitted to change their minds. If anyone does, he will be penalized 1,000 strings' worth of paper money to be given for the use of the person who has not changed his mind. For fear that there will be no evidence later on, we draw up this contract to serve as proof forever. (*Yuan quxuan* 1593)

This contract contains the usual clauses explaining why the sale is taking place, who is being sold to whom, and the penalties for reneging on the agreement (Niida 1937:375). A version of this play in which the stage directions instruct the characters draw up a contract, and in which the boy's parents go unpaid, was published in the Yuan (*Yuankan zaju* 103). Because the text of the contract is not given, the actors must have been sufficiently familiar with contractual language to improvise a suitable text.

Everyone hearing the contract would immediately note a major omission: the contract does not give the price to be paid for the child. The innkeeper reassures the boy's parents that Mr. Jia is very wealthy and will pay them handsomely, and they agree to sign. When the boy's parents meet again with Mr. Jia, they have filled in the boy's name and age. Mr. Jia asks why the parents have not yet left, and the innkeeper explains that they are awaiting payment. Mr. Jia feigns surprise and says that if they want to cancel the transaction they must pay him 1,000 strings' worth of paper money, money they patently do not have or they would not be selling their child to him.

This development stretches the audience's credulity. Who in such a contract-conscious, litigious society would sign a contract that leaves out the price? The lesson of the play is clear. The parents were fools to sign the contract and to trust Mr. Jia. When they ask the innkeeper to intervene on their behalf, he obtains a mere 2 strings of cash for them, far less than they expected, because the middleman is nearly powerless to intervene once the contract has been signed. The disappointed and, of course, saddened parents take their leave, and meet their son again only in the last act after he has inherited Mr. Jia's wealth. The meaning of the god's prophesy, that the money will have to be returned after twenty years, is suddenly clear.

None of the contracts in these three plays typify the contracts in use in

Yuan society. The editors of the Ming editions have exercised literary license to draft unrealistic contracts that drive the plays to their resolutions. Although these dramas succeed only because audiences knew how contracts worked, other plays reveal much more about actual practices when they mention contracts only incidentally, as when a character buys a house or divorces a wife. Equally informative are the situations in which contracts are not used.

In a later play (*Huolangdan*), named for a singing technique used by peddlers from Shandong province, two adoptions occur—one with a contract and one without. After his wife's death, a man takes a concubine who then plots, with her lover, to kill him and his family. They are all on the Luo River on a boat that overturns. Just as the man's child and his milknurse are pulled out of the water, a battalion commander sends an intermediary to offer to buy the boy (Idema and West 1982:283–298). The commander's unusual name, Niange, suggests non-Chinese origins, and his last name, Wanyan, is that of the Jurchen ruling house. The milknurse is hardly in a position to turn down the offer, and, acting as de facto guardian, she accepts a price of one piece of silver. The intermediary then asks an elderly singing peddler if he can draw up the contract, since the nurse, the general, and the intermediary are all illiterate. He asks the nurse to dictate the contract, which she does aloud:

> This boy, a native of Changan, resides in the district west of the government office. His father is Li Yanhe. His milknurse, Zhang Sangu, willingly sells the boy Chunlang, who is seven years old with a red mark on his chest, to Commander Niange to be his son. For fear there will be no evidence later on, we draw up this document as proof.
>
> | | |
> |---|---|
> | Person making the document | Zhang Sangu |
> | Person writing the document | Zhang Biegu |
>
> (*Yuan quxuan* 1645, 1650)

This contract is simpler than the one between the former workman and the examination candidate. It does not give a reason for the sale, or a price, or a penalty for canceling the sale. Even so, it is a sound contract, one that is impressive—too impressive?—for an illiterate milknurse to dictate. The singing peddler writes down what she has dictated. The commander and the nurse draw their marks. Then the singing peddler agrees to adopt the nurse, but they do not draw up another agreement. At the end of the play the boy grows up, inherits his adoptive father's rank, and punishes his father's concubine and her lover for their crimes.

Why does the singing peddler not use a contract to adopt the milknurse? The line between engagement and adoption of a girl child is a blurred one, and playwrights frequently omit a contract in the case of engagements, even if the marriage is far in the future. In Guan Hanqing's *Dou E's Revenge* (*Dou E yuan*), a widow returns the contract for an exam candidate's debts, gives him 10 more ounces for travel expenses, and says they have become relatives. She then takes custody of the seven-year-old Dou E, who will eventually grow up to marry her son (*Yuan quxuan* 1499; Liu Jung-en 1972:120–121). The exchange of gifts makes this a legitimate transaction, and the characters do not register the engagement at the government office. This marriage follows the pattern of Tang and Song law, which recognized the exchange of wedding gifts as binding, but does not accord with Yuan law, which required the registration of engagements. The implication is that the Mongols may not have succeeded in enforcing this requirement.

Like the Yuan plays that mention divorce bills (*Yuanqu xuan* 203, 866–868, 937), a novel written at the end of the Yuan or the beginning of the Ming confirms the awareness of divorce among the lower social strata. Set in the last years of the Northern Song, *The Water Margin* recounts the adventures of a band of 120 brigand heroes, several of whom divorce their wives before leaving to join the group (Niida 1937:110–114). Even those who do remain married talk about divorce as if it were an everyday event. The infamous wife of a bun seller, Golden Lotus, falsely accuses her brother-in-law of making a pass at her and tells her husband his brother has moved out. When her husband questions her account of his brother's conduct, she responds: "Just give me a bill of divorce and you can keep him here. That will be better" (*Shuihu quanzhuan* 24:287; Shapiro 1980:371). In another incident a butcher, Shi Xiu, urges his companion Yang Xiong, a prison guard who works in the local government office, to confront his wife with murder charges and divorce her (*Shuihu quanzhuan* 46:581; Shapiro 1980:743). In neither of these instances do the characters actually divorce— they kill their spouses instead.

The most detailed account of a divorce occurs when Lin Chong, who has been framed by the son of a powerful official, is exiled to Cangzhou (now Cangxian, Hebei). Lin writes the bill of divorce in the presence of his father-in-law but without his wife's knowledge. While drinking, he calls for someone who can write and for a piece of paper, and the alacrity with which both are supplied suggests that drawing up a contract must have been an everyday event in inns. He dictates the following:

> I, Lin Chong, teacher of eight hundred thousand palace guards in
> Kaifeng, because of having committed a great crime, am sentenced to
> be exiled in Cangzhou. Once I leave I cannot guarantee if I will live
> or die. I have a wife, surnamed Zhang, who is young. I willingly draw
> up this bill of divorce. Should she remarry, I will never contest it.
> This is done of my own free will and not coerced. For fear that there
> will be no evidence later on, I draw up this contract as proof. Year.
> Month. Day. (*Shuihu quanzhuan* 8:98; Shapiro 1980:133)

Once the writer has finished the contract, Lin Chong grabs the brush, writes his mark, and traces his hand on it. His wife is not present when he draws up the bill of divorce, nor is she consulted. When he informs her of what he has done, she responds that she has never been unfaithful to him and asks why he is divorcing her. Both her father and Lin reassure her that they have set aside enough money so that she will not have to remarry. Nevertheless, she bursts into tears when she sees the bill of divorce. This poignant scene captures the helplessness of a wife whose husband has decided to divorce her against her wishes.

The Use of Contracts among Non-Chinese Speakers

Intended for a largely Chinese-speaking audience, these literary sources were all in Chinese and depict the use of contracts in all strata in Chinese society. China under Mongol rule was home to other peoples also, and several sources suggest that non-Chinese speakers were quick to adopt Chinese contracts. We have already seen how one non-Chinese battalion commander depended on an intermediary to draft an adoption agreement. In a milieu filled with professional letter writers and literate people for hire, ignorance of the Chinese language, like illiteracy, posed no obstacle to drawing up contracts. The scribes either wrote down what was dictated to them, as in the adoption of the shipwrecked boy and Lin Chong's divorce bill, or they drafted a contract from scratch. In both cases, as we have seen, they read aloud what they had written.

One group of eight Yuan contracts is especially interesting because they are signed by resident Arabs in the major southeastern port of Quanzhou, in Fujian, shown on map 3. These Arabs formed a separate community with its own laws, but in this instance followed Chinese contract law to the letter. Attached to the Ding family genealogy as proof of the family's landholdings and published after 1949, the eight copies of original documents spanning 1336 to 1367 record step by step the many procedures for buying and selling land in the Yuan dynasty (Shi 1957:79–82; Chen Gaohua 1988:36–47). [7]

The first document is a half-stamped certificate, as described in the 1300 legislation. The county office issued this license only after it had received the report of a local leader and elders who stated that Mahemo (quite possibly the Chinese transcription of Muhammed) and his father were the rightful owners of the property and nothing prevented them from selling it. The second document, dated the seventh month of 1336, is the official announcement of the sale of one orchard, one pavilion, one house, and the trees located on the grounds as well as the foundation of another house. The asking price is 150 strings of cash. Those who want the land are asked to approve the price (*pijia*) and those who do not want it, to refuse it (*pitui*) (Ratchnevsky 1972:104). The notice is signed by Muhammed, his mother, and the official broker. At the bottom of the document are the names of three aunts and one uncle who do not want to buy the property, showing that the right of first refusal extended to non-Chinese as well. The third document is the contract itself. After giving the dimensions, it explains that a man named Alaoding—Aladdin—has agreed to buy the property for 60 strings of cash, only 40 percent of the asking price. The contract states that the property is Muhammed's to sell, that he is not wrongfully selling any of his relatives' land, that there are no obstacles to the sale, and that the property has not been previously mortgaged to anyone. The contract includes the standard clause that should any of these conditions not be met, then it is the obligation of the seller, not the buyer, to resolve them. The buyer agrees to pay the tax on the land: 2.8 pecks of grain as of that year. The contract is signed by the seller, Muhammed, his mother, the go-between who found the buyer, a witness, and a scribe. As was common, the buyer does not sign the contract. The final document in the series is simply Muhammed's acknowledgment that he received 60 strings of paper money from Aladdin. This note is meant to prevent any subsequent suits on grounds of nonpayment.

7. Chen Gaohua (1988:36) argues convincingly that these documents are published in the wrong order, and that the permission to sell must have preceded the posting of the official announcement. The first and second documents, and the fifth and sixth, should therefore be reversed.

Thirty years later, in 1366, Aladdin's grandson Puayou puts part of the hill up for sale. He follows the same procedures as his grandfather and draws up a contract setting the price at 90 ounces of stamped silver with a tax obligation of 1 peck. This contract is dated the eighth month of 1366 and signed by Puayou, but it must not have taken effect because a nearly identical contract is dated the second month of the following year. This document describes the property for sale as a lichee orchard, and it gives new southern and northern borders. The plot must be smaller than the one originally put up for sale, because the price has been lowered by a third and the tax obligation halved.

This revised contract reveals Yuan officials were able to monitor the sale of the plot and set the tax assessment when it changed hands. Too few contracts from the Yuan survive to draw any firm conclusions about the extent of compliance with the regulations about the sale of land, and the contracts from Huizhou and Quanzhou were hardly typical. For fear of being expelled, three generations of Arabs—foreigners in Quanzhou—may well have adhered to Chinese law much more faithfully than locals. Surely some people continued to buy and sell land illicitly without registering contracts, much as First-Victory did when he mortgaged his family's land back from Ten-Thousand Seven. Still, barring the introduction of new evidence, the Huizhou and Quanzhou contracts indicate that in some instances Yuan officials succeeded in linking tax assessment with the sale of land.

Two rare contracts surviving from Juyan (Edsen-gol) show that non-Chinese peoples, in this case a Tangut, used Mongolian translations of Chinese contracts to record transactions among themselves. Found together were seventeen Mongolian documents, which included a booklet describing lucky and unlucky days and how to make medicine for horses, letters to accompany gifts, a complaint about the theft of a horse, and two contracts for the loan of grain (Cleaves 1957:7). These documents were taken to Leningrad in 1908 by General Piotr Kozlov. Only one of the contracts has been published, and Francis Cleaves translates it as follows:[8]

> Saying, "On the ninth day of the fourth moon, the year of the
> dragon, we, Sing Quli and Sing Ishinambu, Sochqul-a being in need
> of wheat, have borrowed without interest from Suu Degür, according
> to the iron-bound pint measure, 3 piculs and 7 pints of wheat. It has

8. I have altered his philologically much more accurate translation to improve the readability.

been agreed that, with no excuses, on the fifteenth day of the seventh moon, the same year, we shall give them back completely and integrally. If instead of giving back this wheat, Sochqul-a, who received it, should abscond with his tent-cart and his animals, it has been agreed that the guarantor Nambu, with no excuses, will integrally give back exactly double the quantity borrowed as compensation."

This is the mark: I, Sing Quli	(mark)
This is the mark: I, Sing Isinambu	(mark)
This is the guarantor: I, Nambu	(mark)
This is the mark: Sambu Ox-Iron	(mark)
Witness: Suu Sarambabaq	(mark)
Witness: Chang Süng	(mark)
Witness: Master Sod Shi	(mark)

(Cleaves 1957:24–25)

This contract for the loan of grain is actually a Mongolian translation of Uighur translations of Chinese prototypes, which is not surprising because the Mongolian contracts were found on the Chinese-Mongolian border on a lake about 1,000 kilometers west of Turfan. A few years after Turfan fell to the Uighurs, their language replaced Chinese as the language of commerce, and the same shift occurred once again when the Mongols conquered the region. The contract follows the Chinese practice of beginning with the date, but it gives only the year of the animal, not a reign-date. (Cleaves dates it to before 1368, so this contract could be from 1304, 1316, 1328, 1340, or 1352.) It then names the borrowers, who are brothers or relatives, and the reason for the loan. Like the loans of grain to individuals from monasteries at Dunhuang in the ninth and tenth centuries, and like a 1325 contract for the loan of money from Dunhuang (Maspero 1953:217), the loan is interest free provided it is paid back on time, suggesting that the borrower is already in some kind of dependent relationship with the lender.

The usual proviso, if the debtor absconds, is given as "if he goes inside or out," instead of the more usual, "if he cannot be found in the east or west," but this phrasing is still certainly a translation of a Chinese phrase. The term for guarantor, *baosin*, is the Mongolian transliteration of the Chinese word *baoren*. The contract omits the obligatory final remark about the contracts standing as proof should anyone doubt the transaction, but the signatures come at the end, followed by the mark of each person. The marks are indistinct, but Cleaves believes they may be Tibetan letters. The names indicate that this is a loan from one Tangut to two others, on behalf of a fourth person and guaranteed by a fifth. The fourth signature is that of a Mongol named Ox-Iron, and the second witness is Chinese. We see here the appeal of Chinese contracts to the non-Chinese. Contracts were so convenient that these nomadic peoples translated and used them to record even such small transactions as this loan of grain.

Non-Chinese were so aware of the importance of contracts to the Chinese that two Chinese-language textbooks, dating to the Yuan dynasty or to just after its fall in 1368, contain long sections on the use of contracts. The textbooks, *Old China Hand* (*Lao qida*) and *Interpreter Pak* (*Pu tongshi*), survive today in bilingual Korean-Chinese versions, but they were probably first written in Mongolian and Chinese (Dudbridge 1970:60; Dyer 1983:3–8; Fang Chao-ying 1969:258; Kang 1985:21–22; references courtesy of Ellen Widmer). The books were carved into woodblocks in Korea, on the basis of manuscript texts, in 1423, and again in 1480, when readers already complained that they could not understand the dated colloquial Chinese. The books seem to have fallen out of use before being reprinted in the seventeenth century, when they were translated again into Mongolian, Manchu, and Japanese. The earliest extant editions of these books are from the seventeenth century, and certain changes have obviously been introduced since they were first written. Some place names are changed to reflect Ming Chinese geography, whereas others retain Yuan usage (Dudbridge 1970:62). Eighteenth-century versions of the two books change individual phrases and some pronouns, but retain the overall sense of the dialogues, indicating that whatever linguistic changes took place after the fourteenth century, the contents remained largely the same. The textbooks were so helpful that they continued to be used in the Ming and Qing dynasties.

Interpreter Pak consists of a series of unrelated dialogues meant to teach students the phrases they would need to know. Recognized as the source of one of the earliest versions of *Journey to the West* (*Xiyouji*), the book also contains forms for bringing suits or reporting thefts and tells of someone dictating a letter to a professional scribe. It gives the full texts of three types of contract: those to rent a house, to borrow money, and to purchase a child (*Pu tongshi* 1:34a–35a, 2:9a–11a, 38b-40a). The contracts to rent a house and for the loan of money give the landlord or the moneylender the right to seize the household possessions of those who are in arrears. Otherwise they are straightforward. The contract for the sale of a child is more detailed than those in the Yuan plays. In the lesson, the purchaser explains that the child's parents have drawn up the contract and that he would like to have it checked, presumably by a professional scribe.

> Qian Xiaoma, resident of ∗∗∗ village in Beijing, today, puts up for sale his own son, whose nickname is Shennu, and who is five years old with no illness. Because I have no money, am in debt, lack food, and cannot raise my son, it is a great inconvenience. Subsequently I have inquired of a ∗∗∗ official, who lives in ∗∗∗ district within the city walls, to sell him the child. The two sides agree. The payment for generously raising the boy is 5 ounces of silver. The new owner will be the permanent master of the boy, whom he will raise as his servant.
>
> If, after the sale, the background of Shennu is not clear, or distant or close kin or relatives or other people come to contest the sale, the seller is fully responsible for resolving any claims without going to court. Such claims are not the concern of the buyer.
>
> For fear that afterward there will be no proof, we draw up this document to be used.

∗∗∗ year, month, day	
Seller	Qian Xiaoma
Coseller	His wife, Woman He
Witness	∗∗∗
Middleman	∗∗∗

(*Pu tongshi* 2:9a–11a)

Notable is a frequent euphemism for the price paid to the parents of a child to be sold, "payment for generously raising the boy," which does not obscure the parents' failure to raise the child to maturity. It also contains the familiar clause holding the seller, not the buyer, responsible for resolving any future claims on the boy. The scribe says that everything is in order and then asks if the foreigner has any further concerns. He does. He explains that because the guarantor's word is good for only one hundred days, he is planning to take the boy home immediately. Other sources do not mention a time limit on the validity of the guarantor's support, but such a limit may in fact have been common practice.

The other manual, *Old China Hand*, follows a group of Korean horse traders on a selling trip to China. They are accompanied by one all-knowing native speaker, a familiar figure in Chinese-language textbooks, even those

in use today. The language is old-style vernacular, but some of the phrasing
and sentence patterns are surprisingly modern. Everyone the traders meet
wants to know where and with whom they studied Chinese. On the way to
Beijing, they struggle with innkeepers who constantly try to cheat them,
and they continually ask if they are being charged the "actual price." They
meet friendly peasants, who give them and their horses a free meal, and
they meet starving peasants, whom they persuade to part with some gruel.
They order a lavish banquet once their trading is done. When they get sick
afterward, they call a doctor, who prescribes betel nut pills, which help
them to recover. In short, *Old China Hand* is a travel survival kit for
businessmen going to China in 1400.

The primary goal of their trip is to sell fifteen horses. One innkeeper
they meet offers to sell the horses illegally, by not using a broker, but they
politely decline his offer (Dyer 1983:397).[9] Later that day an innkeeper
introduces the Koreans to two men who want to buy horses and one broker
(*yazi*). The buyer describes the horses in a speech that could only come from
a language textbook intent on introducing all possible ways to describe a
horse in the same lesson:

> Let's negotiate a price for the good and bad horses together. Among
> the horses here are geldings, red horses, brown horses, sparrow-
> colored horses, chestnut horses, horses with black manes, white
> horses, black horses, metal-colored horses, loess-colored horses,
> horses with embroidery markings on the front legs, horses with
> battered faces, smart horses, horses with peach-blossom markings,
> speckled horses, horses with sunken noses, mares, pregnant horses,
> horses with ring markings around their eyes, and defective horses.
> These horses walk in small circles with oxlike steps, and there are
> horses who hide, and dull-witted horses, and horses with an untamed
> look, horses that buck, horses who were formerly lost, and horses
> with hard or soft mouths.
>
> Among these horses are ten inferior ones. One is blind, one is
> lame, one has a crooked hoof, one paws the ground like an inkstone,
> one has a broken back, one is always kicking, one has scabies, and
> three are emaciated.
>
> However, there are five good horses. (Dyer 1983:408–411)

9. Dyer (1983) provides a full translation into English of the original Chinese
text and on facing pages reproduces the most reliable edition, that in the
Keishōkaku sōsho. After checking the original, I have adopted her admirable
translation, with minor alterations.

The author has succeeded in including ten colors, nine physical attributes, six personality traits, and eight flaws in one speech! The Koreans ask 140 ounces—60 for the five good horses and 80 for the ten bad ones—but they settle for a total of 105 ounces, negotiated by the broker after a counteroffer of 100 ounces. The Koreans are forced to accept the price, especially when a group of bystanders concurs (Dyer 1983:415).

Once they have agreed on a price, the broker asks if he can write up one contract for all the horses, but the buyer requests individual contracts, saying "If you write up a group contract, how are we going to resell the horses to others?" He needs proof that each horse is rightfully his before he can dispose of the horses in Shandong. Those who bought an animal planning to resell it had good reason to pay the contract tax, for it would have been difficult for them to sell an animal without proof of the original sale. The broker then asks who the owner of each horse is and whether the horses were bought or born into the seller's household. This distinction goes back to the rules of *The Tang Code* about selling slaves and livestock: a seller had to provide the contract if the person or animal was bought, but, as Monk Huiyuan reminded his kidnapper in the Dunhuang tale, the seller could simply vouch for a slave or an animal born into his own household.

The broker now draws up one contract, which he reads aloud, for the benefit of those who are parties to the transaction:

> Wang ***, resident of Liaodong city, today, because he needs money, sells the five-year-old red gelding with a brand on its left leg, which he originally bought. He relies on Zhang Three, a broker who lives on the north side of the Jiaotou street near the sheep market in the capital, to act as intermediary. He sells the horse to Li Five, a merchant from Jinan, Shandong, who will be the new owner permanently. The two sides agree on a current price of 12 ounces of silver. The money is to be paid in full on the day the contract is drawn up, with nothing owing. It is up to the buyer to determine if the horse is good or bad. If the horse's antecedents are not clear, the seller alone takes responsibility.
>
> After the exchange, neither side may change his mind. The party that first changes his mind must pay a penalty of 5 ounces of official silver to the party that has not changed its mind, so there will be no suits. For fear that afterward there will be no evidence, accordingly we draw up this contract to be used.

* * * Year, month, day

Person who made the contract, Wang * * *   (mark)

Broker Zhang * * *   (mark)

(Dyer 1983:418–421)

This contract is the direct descendant of all the contracts discussed so far. Its distant ancestor is the brief Turfan contract for the exchange of camels dated A.D. 367, which included a penalty of ten carpets for the first party to change its mind. A much closer relative is the contract of 822 from Dunhuang for the sale of a bull, which gives the reason for the sale, names the price to be paid in full on the day of the exchange, and holds the seller responsible for resolving any subsequent claims of ownership. The *Old China Hand* contract also forbids either party to change its mind, penalizes the party that does, and gives the reason for drawing up the contract. The price is set, as is a penalty for reneging. This fourteenth-century contract does not include the three-day waiting period originally stipulated by *The Tang Code*, probably because it was unworkable. As we saw in the previous chapter, the anonymous author of *Self-Admonitions* recognized the dangers of the three-day trial period. He cautioned officials that country folk exchanged animals simply on the basis of an oral agreement. If an animal fell ill, there was no contract to consult in the ensuing dispute. It made much more sense to draw up the contract at the moment the animal changed hands and to dispense with the trial period, as the traders do in *Old China Hand*.

The foreigners' poor Chinese poses no obstacle to drawing up a contract because the broker does it for them—for his usual fee. Once the contract is signed, the problem of fees must be addressed. The all-knowing Chinese companion of the Koreans explains that the buyer must pay the contract tax, while the seller covers the broker's fee. The Korean calculates that he owes the broker 3.15 ounces on a purchase of 105 ounces, or a fee of 3 percent, as opposed to the 2 percent Yuan law stipulated in the *Yuan Institutions* edict of 1271. The Koreans ask when the contract tax will be paid, and the broker offers to go immediately and return with the receipt, but he does not reveal the amount. Without the receipt, the sale will not be valid. Here too the government seems to have succeeded in inserting the procedures for paying the contract tax into the normal order of selling horses as *Old China Hand* depicts it. Of course, one innkeeper did offer to evade the tax, but the buyer's insistence on individual contracts for each horse indicates that Chinese, as well as foreigners, were concerned about following the law.

The contract given in the textbook omits one familiar clause from Tang contracts. Rather than giving a three-day grace period for the buyer to discover any defects in the horse, it states that the buyer is responsible should the horse turn out to be ill. Remember that the author of one Song manual for magistrates complained that many suits occurred because local people drew up contracts only after the grace period was over, so they had no evidence if an animal did fall ill within the three days. The new form of contract is simpler and minimizes the possibility of suits.

Old China Hand is too thorough a textbook, though, not to address the problem of what to do if the buyer discovers the horse is ill. Just after the broker has returned from the tax office with the stamped contract, the buyer notices that one of the horses he has bought has a runny nose. The broker responds by reading aloud the clause holding him responsible for detecting any flaws and then says, "Officials take a stamped contract as evidence, and individuals take the agreement as evidence" (Dyer 1983:422–423). He instructs the seller to tear up the contract and ask 5 ounces as compensation. The buyer pays the 5 ounces and asks for 8 ounces back from the Korean seller and 0.12 ounce back from the broker (the commission on a horse costing 4 ounces). The numbers do not tally. Did the horse originally cost 8 ounces? Is it the custom to take back only half of the original commission? *Old China Hand* does not explain. The book ends with the Koreans saying goodbye to their Chinese companion and returning to Korea laden with goods and books to sell.

Of all the topics covered, *Old China Hand* devotes the most space to drawing up a contract for the sale of horses. That was, after all, the quintessential Chinese experience of foreign merchants, and that was the Chinese vocabulary they had to know to do business successfully in China.

The sources of the Yuan underline the frequency of use of all types of contracts among both the Chinese and the non-Chinese. Had contracts become more common since the Tang? The sources do not permit us to assign an absolute number showing what percentage of the population used contracts, but the growth of the market economy under the Song and the Yuan must have prompted even greater use of contracts than at Turfan or Dunhuang. Under Mongol rule, government officials were able to insert themselves into the process of buying and selling more successfully than their Tang or Song predecessors: surviving evidence from the Huizhou and

Quanzhou contracts, and literary sources as well, suggest that the Mongols actually succeeded in collecting the contract tax. In short, contractual language and ideas deeply permeated Chinese life under the Mongols, and, as the second part of this book will demonstrate, figured just as importantly in the world of the dead.

Part Two

*Contracting
with
the Gods*

6

Tomb

Contracts

One type of contract differs from those described in the first part of this book. Buried in tombs, these contracts for the purchase of grave plots were with gods, not with people. They were usually called *maidiquan*, literally, contracts to buy land. Although they retained many features of real-world land contracts, some telltale signs marked them off as contracts for use in the netherworld. They were meant to resolve an age-old danger in China: the risk of encroaching on land that belonged to the gods when digging deep in the ground to build a grave. They were also meant to prevent lengthy suits in the courts of the underworld, the subject of the next chapter. Tomb contracts were in use from the first to the twentieth centuries, with the largest number dating from the tenth to the fourteenth centuries.[1]

A look at appendix A, a master list of tomb contracts, shows many more from the Song, Jin, and Yuan than from dynasties either earlier or later.[2] The compilation provides a rough guide to the geographic and temporal distribution of tomb contracts. For one thing, the list is biased in favor of tombs made of durable materials. Second, this

---

1. Ina Asim, a member of the Sinology Department at the University of Würzburg, in 1993 published a dissertation on Song tomb contracts in which she translates and explains many of the terms that occur. In 1994 she summarized her findings in an English-language volume by the research group studying Chinese tomb culture and directed by Dieter Kuhn, also at Würzburg. This project was first described in Kuhn (1990).

2. Appendix A gives the date, location, and original source of the known tomb contracts. My sample includes a disproportionate number from Jiangxi, because Chen Baiquan in 1991 published forty from that location, many of them translated in Asim (1993, 1994). Similar compilations from other provinces do not yet exist.

list shows only tomb contracts reported in the archeological literature, not all those that have been excavated. As Asim (1994:317–318) points out: "While in Sichuan I asked archaeologists about the frequency of land deeds occurring in tombs from Song dynasty. The answer was quite astonishing: almost every grave excavated from the Song, Yuan, or Ming dynasties contained a deed. But only those are registered and archived which are fairly undamaged and have legible inscriptions. The others are thrown away." Tomb contracts may have been popular in the tenth to fourteenth centuries, but not everyone used them. Of forty-nine Song tombs excavated in Taiyuan, Shanxi, in 1963, only one is reported to contain a tomb contract (Xie 1963:250–258). Cremation was a popular means of disposing of the dead in the Song (Ebrey 1990), and only rarely were tomb contracts buried with the ashes.[3]

Still, contemporary observers confirm the popularity of tomb contracts at the time. One of the first literati to comment on them was Tao Gu (903–970). In the section of his notes concerning mortuary customs, he wrote the following entry, entitled "Earth Banquets":

> Those in mourning hear religious practitioners say, "It is customary to use red writing on iron contracts, as in the contracts of ordinary people, in which one writes the markers for the four borders and the owner's name." They say this is intended as proof of ownership for the dead person for his or her tomb. I do not know who would contest ownership of the land. In front of the tomb, they build a wall of stone or bricks with a square face and not taller than 3 Chinese feet, and call it the contract platform.
>
> The poor do not have the means, so they use grass mats and worship a small painted wooden stand. This is called "earth banquets." (*Qingyi lu* 2:64a)

Tao Gu assumes the usual detached, slightly ironic stance of the literati in discussing popular customs, but his comment reveals that tomb contracts, like this-world contracts, included the plot's four boundaries and the owner's name. He raises an important question without giving the answer: who could contest ownership of a given funeral plot and in what forum?

Tao's account is most informative for what it tells us about the cost of tomb contracts. He explains that the well-off wrote their contracts in red

---

3. In 1186 the concubine of a member of the imperial clan was cremated, and her ashes were buried with a tomb contract.

ink on iron, while the poor used grass mats and wooden stands because they could not afford iron. Since neither grass nor wood is durable, few tombs of the poor survive. People used other materials as well. Paper was the cheapest material one could use to make a contract. Carving the text into soft brick or writing it with brush on wood cost more, and incising the characters on iron or stone was still more expensive.

The use of tomb contracts continued, and catalpa wood became a popular material, if a thirteenth-century account is to be trusted. Writing after the fall of the Song, Zhou Mi (1232–1298) said: "Today when people make tombs they always use a contract to buy land, made out of catalpa wood, on which they write in red, saying: 'Using 99,999 strings of cash, we buy a certain plot, and so forth.' The customs of sorcerers in villages are like this and are especially laughable" (*Guixin zashi*, bieji 2:7a–b).

Zhou uses the twentieth-century term for such a contract: a contract to buy land (*maidiquan*). Although this term retains the older usage for contract, *quan*, rather than *qi*, which came into use in the late Tang, it does not distinguish grave contracts from real-world contracts. Tomb contracts followed the format of real-world land contracts quite closely, giving the name of the purchaser, rarely that of the seller, the location and area of the plot to be sold, the price, and the conditions of sale. Zhou Mi is right to focus on the number 99,999, which does occur in many of the contracts. Three was a yang number, which could counteract the yin forces of the underworld, so nine was even more powerful, and 99,999 more powerful still. "Nine" (*jiu*) was also a pun on "long-lasting" (*jiu*).

After the usual expression of skepticism, here even derision, Zhou Mi concludes his entry on tomb contracts with: "This dates to Emperor Ai of the Tang. Therefore the origins of this practice go way way back" (*Guixin zashi*, bieji 2:7a–b). The Song was the first period in Chinese history during which the literati took an interest in archeology. They knew tomb contracts had a long history, but it is only recently that scholars have established the first century A.D. as the date of the earliest authentic tomb contracts.

The First Tomb Contracts

In the earliest examples, from the first and second centuries A.D., sometimes the only difference between tomb contracts and real-world contracts is what Terry Kleeman (1984:3) calls corpse clauses, clauses specifying that bodies previously buried in the plot were to serve as the servants or concubines of the newly buried dead. Yet because many early contracts do not include this clause, identification can be difficult. In later centuries, tomb contracts become easier to tell from real-world contracts as some of the witnesses to the contract are divine, or the neighbors are gods, or the amount paid for the land (often 99,999 strings of cash) cannot be taken literally.

The Chinese belief that the land under the surface of the earth belonged to the gods is documented as early as the first century A.D. when Wang Chong (27–97) described a ceremony to placate the gods who might be disturbed by the construction of a house. Although he does not mention tomb contracts, his description provides solid evidence of the belief that the gods controlled the region underground:

> When people build or repair a home or hall, they pierce the earth and dig up land. When the work is completed, they propitiate and ask for pardon from the earth god in a ceremony called appeasing the earth. They make an earthen figure in the shape of a spirit and ask a wizard to invite the figure in order to appease the earth god. Once the worship is over, they feel happy and glad and say they have propitiated and asked forgiveness from the ghosts and gods and driven away the bad spirits and dangers.
>
> If one examines this more closely, one realizes that it is empty trickery. How can one test it? Now, the earth is like a human body, with everything in the empire forming one body with head and feet at different ends some 10,000 third-miles apart. People live on the surface of the earth, much as lice live on a person's body. Much as lice eat and steal human skin, people pierce the earth and steal the earth's body. If some of the lice understood and wanted to propitiate the person, and they gathered together to propitiate and ask for pardon from what they were going to eat, would the person know? Much as the person could not know the sound of the lice, so too can the earth not understand the speech of people (*Lunheng* 25:6b–7a; Forke 1908:144–45; Stein 1979:74).

This passage, with its equating of lice and people, captures Wang Chong's iconoclasm perfectly. His account is important not for what it reveals about his skepticism, which few shared, but for what it tells us about the beliefs of his contemporaries. Digging into the earth, they felt, posed certain dangers that could be averted only by first performing a ceremony.

Digging tombs must have posed the same types of dangers as building houses because tomb contracts began to be buried in the first century A.D. Experts debate which are the earliest contracts and which are forgeries, and which are real-world contracts and which are underworld, but the earliest authentic other-world contract seems to be dated 82 from Xinzhou, Shanxi (Fang Shiming 1973; Kleeman 1984; Li Shougang 1978; Seidel 1987).[4]

> On the sixteenth day of the eleventh month of the sixth year of the Jianchu reign [82], Miying, the son of Wu Mengzi, buys land for a tomb from Ma [name unclear] and the two brothers Zhu Shao and Zhu Qing. The southern border is 94 five-foot units long, the western 68, the northern 65, the eastern 79, totaling 23 sixth-acres, 164 five-foot units of land. The price is 102,000 strings, with the eastern border extending to the Chen fields, and the northern, western, and southern borders to Zhu Shao's land.
>
> Witnesses to this contractual agreement: Zhao Man and He Fei, who provide 2 pecks of wine each.

Here we see the essential clauses of all land contracts: the date, the name of the buyer, the type of land, the borders and the area, the price, the names of the neighbors, and the names of the witnesses. The unusual price, the sum of 99,000 and 3,000, is a particularly auspicious number. The price is also the main evidence that this is an underworld contract, because it is a price to be paid not in real money, but in facsimile money that could be bought for a fraction of its face value and buried as an offering to the gods. No such facsimile money has yet been found in any Han tomb.

Before the year 150, most of the tomb texts were phrased as celestial ordinances, to use Anna Seidel's term, in which the highest deity, usually the Yellow Emperor (Huangdi) or the Celestial Emperor (Tiandi), notified the underworld deities of someone's death. The Celestial Emperor was thought to be in charge of keeping the registers of both the living and the dead (Seidel 1987:30–32). He thus knew the exact moment when someone was to leave the world of the living and go to the world of the dead. These ordinances took the form of an imperial edict (*chi*), usually delivered by an emissary of the Celestial Emperor to lower officials, who included the deputy of the grave mound (*qiucheng*), the earl of the tomb (*mubo*), and the netherworld 2,000-bushel officials (*dixia erqian dan*). A 2,000-bushel offi-

---

4. Sources for all tomb contracts mentioned in this chapter are in appendix A under the year of the contract.

cial, one whose annual salary was 2,000 bushels of grain, served as the real-world governor of a commandery. Deputies assisted local magistrates. Although modeled on real-world titles, the underworld bureaucracy did not completely mirror the Han bureaucracy, for "earl" was not a bureaucratic title but a title of nobility, dating to the period before China was unified in 221 B.C. and not in use in the Han dynasty (Hucker 1985:205, 13, 387).

The nature of the documents buried in tombs changed at the end of the second century A.D., as Seidel (1987) and Kleeman (1984) have demonstrated. Celestial ordinances fell into disuse and were replaced by tomb contracts, in which someone actually bought land from the earth gods. The first texts that can definitely be identified as tomb contracts date to A.D. 161 and 168. The contract from 161 uses the verb "to buy" (*mai*) to obtain a plot with a price of 99,000, and the one from 168 names the divine seller as the Lord of the Hill (Shan Gong).

The Rise of Organized Daoism

Did this change from celestial ordinance to tomb contract occur for religious reasons? Yes, if we accept Seidel's argument that the tomb ordinances provide the last evidence of indigenous Chinese beliefs before the rise of organized Daoism at the end of the second century A.D. Before that time, scholars are not sure what constituted Daoism, or if there was any kind of organized Daoist church. The famous Daoist texts *Daodejing* and *Zhuangzi* testify to the belief in longevity and the existence of breathing exercises which could extend one's life, but they do not shed light on the organization of Daoists. We do not know if there was more to Daoism than a few individuals teaching their disciples.

An organized Daoist church arose at the end of the second century because of two religious movements: the Celestial Masters, who were active in Sichuan, led by Zhang Daoling; and the Taiping rebels, who rose up along coastal China in A.D. 184. Like these rebels, the organized church also viewed Laozi as a god and the text usually attributed to him, the *Daodejing*, as scripture (Seidel 1989-90:237–238). The organized Daoist church began in 142, when the divine Laozi appeared to Zhang Daoling. The two made a pact, according to which Zhang assumed Laozi's role as the instructor of emperors (Seidel 1983:315, 347). As was the custom at the time, Laozi and Zhang sacrificed a white horse and wrote the agreement on an iron tally. This pact, perhaps the most dramatic instance of an agreement between people and gods, is reported for the first and only time in a fifth-century text. The agreement also included a promise on the part of the people to worship only the gods of Daoism, not other gods, and on the part of Daoist practitioners neither to perform blood sacrifices nor to accept fees for performing religious services. In return, the gods were to grant their followers good health and long life (Seidel 1983:311–315; *Santian neijie jing* 1:5b–6a). From this time on, the Daoists struggled to differentiate themselves from indigenous Chinese religion, a struggle in which they were only partially successful (Stein 1979). Different schools of Daoism offered solutions to the problem of digging into the earth to make graves, including the use of certain forms for tomb texts. As we shall see, however, not everyone used the suggested texts.

The Danger of Digging in the Ground

The Daoists were not the only people to recognize the danger of digging into the earth. A minister named Jiang Tong (d. 310), who served as attendant and mentor to the heir apparent (*taizi xima*), wrote a remonstrating memorial that urged the heir apparent to behave more virtuously, to spend less on gardens and buildings, and to stop the sale of vegetables, chicken, baskets, and noodles on the palace grounds (*Jinshu* 56:1535–37). His last point concerned an order forbidding all digging into the earth:

> I have heard that people use earth primarily to sow and to plant, to build houses, to construct cities, and to establish districts. There are clear regulations about this written in the classics, with no mention of breaking any taboos or causing any harm. It is only a recent decadent custom espoused by lesser sorcerers, who have the view that their sorcery books forbid entering the earth more than 3 Chinese feet. Because they dig according to the calendar at different times, not all digging is forbidden.
>
> I think the order forbidding the use of the earth that says "it is forbidden to repair earthen walls or to move tiled houses" violates the intent of our laws and cannot be a lasting law. (*Taiping yulan* 735:5b)[5]

5. A variant of this text occurs in the official history of the Jin (*Jin shu* 56:1537). The text is difficult and possibly corrupt, and I have found Peter Nickerson's reading very helpful (personal communication, February 1992). Nickerson is currently writing a dissertation at the University of California at Berkeley on these texts and their relationship to the real-world bureaucracy.

Minister Jiang Tong does not name the sorcery book with its ban on digging more than 3 Chinese feet into the earth, but dismisses it as a "decadent custom espoused by lesser sorcerers." Yet even these lesser sorcerers did not go as far as the government had in banning all digging; they allowed digging on some days, unlike the law Jiang opposed, which forbade it at any time.

One Daoist school active in the fourth century near Nanjing offered its own solution to the hazard of cutting into the earth to make tombs. In 499 Tao Hongjing transcribed a series of revelations originally dating to 364–370 in his *Declarations of the Perfected* (Seidel 1989–90:239; Strickmann 1981). The original teacher, Yang Xi, suggested that one could transform all the malevolent consequences of digging a tomb into good fortune by following his advice:

> The tombs of marquises and kings excite too much notice, so they should be hidden 9 Chinese feet in the ground. One should take a stone cube, 3 Chinese feet on each side, write this text on it, and bury it 3 Chinese feet in the ground:
>
> > "The Celestial Emperor announces to
> > the gods in the tomb, Wang Qi, and of the
> > Five Directions under the earth, Zhao
> > Gongming and others:
> > "A noble of ∗∗∗ state, who
> > was so many years old in a certain year,
> > while living encountered the ether of Pure
> > Perfection. He has returned in death to the
> > Palace of the Gods and concealed his body in
> > the land of darkness, plunging into quietude
> > and penetrating the void. He has avoided and
> > driven back the prohibited and the tabooed.
> > He will not be assaulted by harmful spirits.
> > His children and grandchildren will flourish,
> > in literary arts praised for their nine
> > accomplishments, in military matters
> > complete in the seven virtues. They will be
> > high ranking and kings generation after
> > generation, and live as long as heaven and

earth. All in accordance with the laws and
edicts of the subterranean nine heavens."[6]

The phrasing here is high-flown, but the general import is clear: the
Celestial Emperor is informing the gods of the earth and the tomb of
someone's death and warning them not to interfere with him or cause his
descendants harm. He identifies the dead man by name, by place, and by
age—all to avoid confusion with someone else. This text takes the form of
a celestial ordinance, not a contract. The tomb goes deep into the ground,
but this ordinance is to be buried only 3 Chinese feet underground—do the
Maoshan Daoists agree with Minister Jiang Tong that the gods' jurisdiction
starts 3 feet under the ground? They do not say so explicitly, but they shared
the view of the nameless sorcerers quoted by Minister Jiang Tong: the top
3 Chinese feet of soil belonged to humanity, and people could use that land
freely. If they dug any deeper, and to make tombs they did, then they had to
secure the permission of the gods. The tomb according to the Maoshan
Daoists was deep in the ground, but the order to the gods was to be buried
just where the human jurisdiction ended and the god's jurisdiction began, 3
feet below the surface.

One copy of this Maoshan Daoist text, dating to the eighth century, has
actually been excavated in Fugou, Henan (Stein 1979:72n67). Daoists continued to use the format of a celestial ordinance in later model documents
and in actual tomb texts (dated 506, 520, and 520, from Zixing, Hunan). It
is striking, though, how few texts along Daoist lines have been excavated
from tombs. Perhaps not many people followed the Daoist models in drawing up tomb texts. It must be also admitted as a possibility, though less
likely in early periods when paper was scarce, that Daoists ignored the
instructions given in the *Declarations of the Perfected* to bury a stone in the
ground and instead burned the funeral texts. Burning documents is the
accepted mode of communication in twentieth-century Daoism, and in
contemporary Taiwan dual copies of contracts to purchase a plot are indeed
burned, with the god's copy burned on one day and the dead person's copy
on the final day of the funeral (Schipper 1974; 1989:32).

In the centuries following the fall of the Han dynasty, few people, then,
used tomb ordinances to notify the gods of the death of a family member.
Many more used a contract to buy land from the gods of the earth. Given
that the god selling the plot was in a superior position, analogous to that of

6. With a few modifications, I have adopted Kleeman's (1984:24–25) excellent
translation of the original passage (*Zhengao* 10:16b–17b).

the person who had money in a real-world contract, in many cases the god was not named. The contracts that give the god's name show considerable regional variation. It turns out that people in different regions bought the land from different gods, most frequently the lord or god of the earth, sometimes the immortals who were thought to rule over the other world, the Queen Mother of the West and the King Father of the East (see appendix B).

One anecdote from a Tang collection of miscellaneous notes confirms the multiplicity of views about divine ownership of land below the surface. In 727 an Academician of the Scholarly Worthies requested permission to bury his wife. He asked the advice of a local man, who quoted the theory of a monk from Huangzhou (now Huanggang, Hubei):

> Under the surface of the earth, 1 Chinese decafoot and 2 Chinese feet
> is the realm of earth. Another decafoot and 2 feet underneath that is
> the realm of the water. Each is guarded by dragons. The dragon of the
> earth explodes once every six years, and that of the water explodes
> once every twelve years. Underground passages disturb them, and the
> paths to tombs will not be peaceful, thus one can build the vault of a
> tomb to a depth of 2 decafeet and 4 feet under the ground. . . . One
> can use iron to make images of cattle and pigs to protect oneself
> from the two dragons (*Da Tang xinyu* 13:195; Xu Pingfang 1963:93).

Given that 1 decafoot was about 3 meters, and twice that 6 meters, it seems unlikely that many people followed that particular monk's advice about the ideal depth for burial. In 1022, when the emperor's advisers discussed the potential depth of imperial tombs, they considered several possibilities: 90, 81, or 200 Chinese feet. They were not sure where the underworld actually began, but they agreed not to exceed a depth of 140 feet (*Song huiyao*, li 29:24a–b; Xu 1963:98).

The residents of different regions in China may have agreed that they had to buy funeral plots from the gods of the earth, but they did not agree on the exact identities of the gods who could sell them the land. Nor did they agree on which text to use for their tomb contracts. To be sure, almost all the contracts included the same elements: price, area, identity of the new occupant, and perhaps name of the seller. On occasion, almost identical contracts have been excavated from the same region (the 487 and 519 contracts, both from Guangxi; or the 506, 520, and 520 examples from Zixing, Hunan). The language in other contracts varies considerably. To cite one example, a contract from 814 excavated in Zhuoxian, Henan, uses the second person to address the spirits of the dead directly: "If trespassing occurs, you (*ni*) will be beaten nine-thousand strokes and you will be made a slave." This is a surprising departure from the third person address so usual in the formal language of Chinese contracts (Gernet 1957:326n3).

The Most Common Tomb Contract

Most tomb contracts show a surprising convergence of language and intent. One illustration of this uniformity is a tomb contract text that first survives on paper from a 769 tomb in Astana, Xinjiang, and of which forty-three other examples have been found (map 4). Another document in the grave identifies the dead man as General of Mobile Cavalry Zhang Wujia. The full contents of the grave have not yet been published, but a preliminary report highlights an unusual funerary object: a paper coffin 2.3 meters long, with a wooden frame, made from discarded receipts for horse feed at two postal stations and covered with painted red paper.[7] All of these paper objects were able to survive only because of Turfan's unusually dry climate. The dead man was laid on a mat underneath this coffin (Xinjiang Museum 1975b:12–13). The use of a grass mat bespeaks poverty, as Tao Gu noted, and indeed General Zhang's daughter was forced to apply to the central government to cover his funeral costs, which it did (*Tulufan chutu wenshu* 10:8–9).

The Tang practice of giving officials tomb contracts is documented in a twelfth-century collection of miscellaneous notes. An entry dated 1255 reports that grave robbers opened a tomb in Quyang county (Hebei) and found more than one hundred pieces of silver, one ink-stone and one mirror, and an iron contract bestowed by the last emperor of the Tang (r. 904–907). The contract said, "The emperor orders the late honorable minister Wang Chucun to be given 99,999 strings, 999 coins of money" (*Xu Yijianzhi* 3:61). Minister Wang fought the rebel Huang Chao, and when Wang died at the age of sixty-five, he was given the rank of Grand Preceptor of the Heir Apparent (*Xin Tangshu* 186:5418–19; *Jiu Tangshu* 182:4699–700). This account testifies to the interest of Song and Yuan literati in archeology (Zhou Mi included it in his notes) but, alas, does not cite the full text of Minister Wang's tomb contract.

The Tang instituted the practice of paying for the funeral, and tomb contract, of dead officials. Some of the regional rulers during the Five

---

7. These documents have since been reconstructed and published as volume 10 of *Tulufan chutu wenshu*.

Map 4. Distribution of Tomb Contracts Written as in *Earth Patterns*. Forty-four almost identical contracts, all based on the same model, have been excavated at sites thousands of miles apart and spanning a millennium. (Drawn by Donna Perry.)

Contracts Written as in *Earth Patterns*

Date	Place (Province, County)	Material	Accompanying Goods	Social Status of Deceased
769	Xinjiang, Astana	paper	paper coffin 2.3 meters long (disturbed)	General of Mobile Cavalry
946	Anhui, Hefei	wood	19 pottery and porcelain vessels, 6 silver vessels, 1 bronze mirror, 19 wooden figurines, 6 gold and silver dangling hair ornaments	woman of high-ranking family
953	Anhui, Hefei	wood	lacquer and pottery fragments, 1 bronze mirror, 4 porcelain bowls	
955	Sichuan, Pengshan	stone	1 stone coffin, 5 pottery jars, 10 clay figures, 1 pottery dog, 1 bronze mirror (disturbed)	woman
1055	Jiangsu, Jiangyin	cedar	11 Buddhist and Daoist sutras, 33 wooden figurines, lacquerware, lead mirror	woman with posthumous title, relative of vice-minister of works (rank 3b)
1056	Henan, Zhengzhou	brick	1 porcelain jar	
1069	Sichuan, Huayang	sandstone	5 pottery vessels	
1072	Sichuan, Pujiang	sandstone (2 copies)	11 stone figurines, 4 pottery drums, 86 pottery figures	married couple
1086	Jiangxi, Xinyu	stone	10 porcelain pieces, 1 bronze mirror, 1 stone epitaph, 1 iron pot	
1099	Henan, Baisha Shuiku	brick	rectangular iron block	
1104	Hubei, Xiangyang	brick	1 pottery jar, 4 porcelain vessels, 2 lacquer vessels, 1 bronze mirror, 2 hairpins	
1119–1123	Jiangsu, Jiangdu	stone		woman
1121	Jiangxi, Dexing	stone		secretariat drafter (4a)
1126	Hubei, Xiaogan	iron	2 iron dogs, 2 iron cows, 2 porcelain plates	
1128	Gansu, Longxi	stone	brick carvings, pottery grain vessels, 1 porcelain bowl, 3 lacquer plates	
1133	Jiangxi, Ruichang	stone	2 porcelain pieces, 1 pottery vessel, 2 bronze implements	
1138	Henan, Jiaozuo	copper	brick tomb with murals (disturbed)	

Map 4 (*Cont.*)

Date	Place (Province, County)	Material	Accompanying Goods	Social Status of Deceased
1162	Shaanxi, Hanzhong	stone	2 porcelain pieces, 10 pottery figurines, 7 pottery animals, 8 pottery vessels	office manager to prefect
1175	Jiangxi, Fuzhou			
1183	Neimeng, Dongsheng			
1183	Shanxi, Yuanqu	brick	pottery bowl, 3 brick figures, elaborate brick carvings	
1186	Fujian, Nan'an	iron	1 porcelain jar for ashes, 4 pottery jars, 4 incense burners, 1 epitaph	imperial concubine
1188	Jiangxi, Xingan	stone		
1191	Henan, Luoyang	brick		
1198	Jiangxi, Fuzhou	stone	2 bronze mirrors, 5 gold items, 7 crystal items, 5 jade items, 1 pottery vessel, 1 stone pillow, 1 bronze brush stand, 1 epitaph, 70 figures	prefect
1210	Shanxi, Houma	brick (2 copies)	model of stage, 5 porcelain vessels, 4 wooden implements (disturbed)	two brothers
1226	Zhejiang, Wenzhou	stone		woman
1237	Jiangxi, Yugan	brick		wet nurse of Ministry of Personnel supervisor
1243	Fujian, Fuzhou	brick	334 silk garments, 7 lacquer pieces, 7 silver pieces (disturbed)	wife of imperial clan member, daughter of prefect
1272	Jiangxi, Ruichang	stone	2 porcelain pieces, 1 hairpin, 1 bronze mirror, copper coins	wife of doctoral candidate awaiting departmental examination of Board of Rites
1288	Henan, Jixian	brick		
1298	Hebei, Weixian	polished green brick	13 porcelain funerary dishes	
1301	Jiangxi, Nanchang	brick		vice-commissioner, weaving and dyeing service
1303	Shanxi, Fencheng	brick		

Map 4 (*Cont.*)

Date	Place (Province, County)	Material	Accompanying Goods	Social Status of Deceased
1457	Shandong, Penglai	brick		
1457	Jiangsu, Nanjing	stone	1 stone table with 53 lead vessels (disturbed)	director of ceremonial directorate
1515	Beijing	stone	12 jade pieces, 83 silk garments (disturbed)	father of empress
1553	Jiangsu, Jiangdu	brick		
1568	Jiangsu, Yangzhou	stone		
1631	Jiangsu, Taicang	wood	2 bronze mirrors, 1 bronze ear ornament, 1 jade cup, 4 books	
1714	Jiangsu, Suzhou	brick		
1759	Jiangsu, Shuyang	brick		

Dynasties continued this practice, as suggested by three contracts identical to General Zhang's which have been excavated from tombs: two from Anhui (dated 946 and 953) and one from Sichuan (dated 955). And the Song adopted the practice, once it reunified the country in 960. The official history of the Song includes a summary of the detailed regulations specifying which funeral expenses the government would cover for high officials before 1068:

> Many meritorious members of the imperial family and high officials will receive an official burial when they die. An imperial emissary will be sent to supervise, and the government will pay the costs, so as to demonstrate imperial benevolence at the time.
>
> All funerals will have a path to the tomb, spear-carrying guardians to frighten away ghosts in four directions, a cart to pull the soul, incense, an umbrella, paper money, goose feathers, a sedan-chair for the tablet of the deceased, a brocaded model chariot, a big sedan-chair, a flag with the name of the dead on it; a ceremonial structure over the coffin and a moving curtain, one each; mourners, sixteen. Mortuary objects, including bed netting, clothing and carts for clothing, and festooned beds have no fixed number. At the tomb, stone sheep, stone tigers, and viewing columns, two each. For those having a rank of three and higher, add two stone people. To be placed in the tomb are five types of guardians, twelve animals of the year, a biography carved on stone, *a contract in stone, and an iron contract,* one each.
>
> The officials supervising the ceremony will conduct rituals on the day before the funeral facing the coffin until the time the coffin is lowered into the ground. (*Songshi* 124:2909–10; emphasis added)[8]

Determining the meaning of all the objects listed in this text, as well as the reasons for their use, is difficult because one has to work backward from excavated tombs and surviving burial manuals. Still, this text provides a rare sketch of the elaborate paraphernalia required for a lavish funeral in the eleventh century. During the funeral ceremony a cart covered with an umbrella would pull the coffin to the tomb, along the spirit path where stone animals, and possibly stone men, would be in attendance. A cloth flag

8. Although the *Songshi* cites the *Song huiyao* as the source of this regulation, the passage is not extant in the modern edition of that work.

with the name of the dead official on it would be flying. Incense and paper money would be burned. A funeral structure would be built, and sixteen professional mourners would be in attendance. Into the tomb would go clothing for use in the afterlife, furniture, guardians, a set of the twelve animals for the years (chicken, dog, dragon, and so on), a biography based largely on the deceased's record of officeholding, and two tomb contracts. The regulations do not explain why two copies of the tomb contract were needed or what the tomb contract should say. After 1068, this detailed list concludes, the regulations were changed to allow more mourners and to restrict the type of coffins, but surviving texts do not refer to the new regulations concerning tomb contracts.

The practice of burying stone contracts in the tombs of officials must have continued after 1068, for the tomb of a very important and famous grand councilor (the Song-dynasty equivalent of a prime minister), Zhou Bida, who died in 1204, included a stone contract. When he died at the age of seventy-nine, he was given the posthumous title Lord of Literature and Loyalty, and Emperor Ningzong himself drew the characters on the heading of his tombstone (*Songshi* 391:11971–72). Appended to Zhou's collected works are five chapters of documents from his funeral, including the prayers said on his behalf, his official and unofficial biographies, and the text awarding him his posthumous title (*Zhou Bida wenji*, fulu 1–5). Nowhere is his tomb contract mentioned. Since Zhou Bida is one of the best-documented officials of the Song, this silence cries out. If his own collected papers do not mention the tomb contract, no one else's will. Excavation is the only way to determine if a tomb contains a contract, and to date very few officials' tombs have been excavated. All the evidence suggests that Song officials, like Grand Councilor Zhou Bida, did bury contracts in their tombs, as the official regulations prescribed—even though the practice generated no documentation in the historic record.

In the course of the Song, and continuing into succeeding dynasties, one funeral text appears over and over again. It is similar to the one in General Zhang's 769 tomb in Astana. The text was used eight times in the eleventh century, in places as far apart as Jiangxi, Jiangsu, Henan, Hebei, and Sichuan. The most recent example dates to the nineteenth century. In all I have found forty-four examples of the text, including some that shorten it and some that embellish it (see map 4). The text of the contract says:

> ••• year, month, and day. An official of this title, this name, died on
> ••• year, month, and day. We have prognosticated and found this

auspicious site, which is suitable for the grave, in this plain, in this district, in this county, and in this prefecture. We use 99,999 strings of cash as well as five-colored silk as offerings of good faith to buy this plot of land. To the east and west, it measures so many steps; to the south and north, it measures so many steps. To the east is the green dragon's land; to the west, the white tiger's; to the south, the vermillion sparrow's; and to the north, the dark warrior's.

The four borders are patrolled by the imperial guard. The deputy of the grave mound and the earl of the tomb sealed it off by pacing the borders and the thoroughfares; the generals made orderly the paths through the fields so that for one thousand autumns and ten thousand years no spirit will return from the dead. If any dare to contravene, then the generals and neighborhood heads are ordered to tie them up and hand them to the earl of the rivers.

We have prepared meat, wine, preserved fruits, and a hundred types of sacrificial food. All these things constitute a contract of our sincerity.

When the money and land have been exchanged, the order will be given to the workmen to construct the tomb. After the deceased is peacefully buried, this will forever guarantee eternal good fortune.

The witness represents the years and months. The guarantor is the direct emissary of this day.

Bad ethers and heterodox spirits are not allowed to trespass. Those formerly living in the residence of the deceased must forever stay 10,000 third-miles away. If any violate this contract, the main clerks of the subterranean government will be personally responsible for punishing them. The master of the tomb, and all his own kin and in-laws, whether living or dead, will enjoy peace and good fortune. Hastily, hastily, in accordance with the statutes and edicts of the emissary of the Five Directional Emperors, Nüqing. (*Dili xinshu* 14:13a)

This contract follows contemporary land contracts closely and has a distinct Daoist ring. It begins with the name of the buyer (the dead person), and the date of the transaction (actually the date of the funeral), and the location of the plot. The model does not name the seller, an omission that often occurs in real-world contracts when the seller is in a position superior to the buyer. One version found in 953 in Hefei, Anhui, alters the text to identify the recipient of the offerings as the generals of the underworld bureaucracy (*tufu jiangjun*).

Let us take a look at this contract, phrase by phrase.

"99,999 strings of cash" The price for the plot is twofold: 99,999 strings of paper money and bolts of five-colored silk. This familiar figure from other grave contracts is auspicious because of the yang power of three and nine, but this contract, like the others discussed, does not explain the relationship between real-world money and spirit money.[9] Another tomb contract from 1033 in Taiyuan, shown in figure 6, spells out the mechanism for converting real-world money into spirit money.

> The tomb was completed on the eighth day of the tenth month of the second year of the Mingdao reign [1033], when Tao Mei moved the graves of his grandparents. He lives in the first left district in Bingzhou and works in the big iron furnace for a living. He buys 2 sixth-acres of land in Yangqu county, Wutai district, Meng village, from commoner Liu Mi, and pays a price of 12 strings, 500 coins. The land has no tax or corvée obligations in this world. In the other world, where the King Father of the East and the Queen Mother of the West are, this converts to 99,999 strings, 9 coins. Within the plots are two walled graves, with a guard area in front. The aforementioned buys the plot, and the four borders are clear.
>
> We request that a ritual be conducted to select this sacred land and to establish that it is auspicious below. We build a spot to invite good fortune and leave nothing undone. We recognize the grave paths to protect the descendants so that each generation will attain honor and flourish and so that the wealth will increase each year. We clearly draw up this contract to show our respect for the value of ritual and to attain the reputation of having virtue in all quarters. No one shall encroach, this will be recorded forever, the descendants will also know of this, and the rich land will belong to the family. So that future generations will understand this intent, we have made this inscription.

9. The relationship continues to be a close one. In the summer of 1991 in Xian, I bought two types of spirit money that mirror real-world currencies: thousand-*renminbi* notes and ration coupons for grain that could be redeemed in the underworld.

墓至

維貳千歲次癸酉十月癸巳朔八日庚子閻美邊本三世者

□□□□左弟一廂大鐵爐為造墳到陽曲縣武曇鄉□符百建劉家

地貳畝就進作僧袋壹拾貳貫伍佰文市陌地陽間並無□□□司

東丑公西至毋陽折分九萬九千九百九十九貫九文内對土圓三廖廂旬

有簡地產□□到地四至□眼請當禮乃卜其聖地下封吉□蓬也

堤□並延福之鄉非为丁寧集承苹道孫子孫則世世榮昌金帛

立牢有盛明立募契禮居成員蓬四为有德之招無憂感

止万百以記子孫長知福地之家對明析田

後此款作銘記

陽世苹三人　趙三兒　　　　　男□吉

　　　　　陽世地主人劉□客　　男劉海

司隸地主人代保孫□　　　　　　　孫子洋男

This-worldly burial master Tao Mei
His son Yongji
His grandson Banjiu
This-worldly landlord Liu Mi
His son Liu Hai
Representative of landlord who is neighbor to
the west, Sun [   ]

This unusual tomb contract gives the occupation, not just the name, of the person paying for the funeral: a worker in an iron furnace. The text distinguishes between the real world, or the yang world of light, and the underworld, the yin world of shadows. It explains that the land has no tax obligations in this world. The names at the end of the contract are all identified as being of this world. (A very similar contract, also from Taiyuan and dated one year earlier, identifies the person paying for his parents' funeral as the owner of a restaurant. Here the handwriting is even, suggesting that this son was able to pay more to have the contract drafted.) The iron worker pays 12 strings, 500 coins, to a human landlord for the plot of 2 sixth-acres, which converts to 99,999 strings. The contract uses the verb *zhe*, the standard word for conversions from goods to money, and here, for conversions from one currency, that of the world of light, to another, that of the world of the shadows. The restaurant worker pays 9 strings for a plot of

Fig. 6. This-World Money and Underworld Money. This tomb contract, dated 1033 from Taiyuan, Shanxi, was designed for use in two court systems, one in this world and one in the afterlife. The document records payment by Tao Mei, a worker in an iron foundry, of $12\frac{1}{2}$ strings of copper cash for a grave plot, in which he will bury the remains of his deceased grandparents. He places this contract in their tomb to provide them with legal title, should another dead soul challenge their right to the space. Because land is more costly in the underworld, Tao Mei includes a second price, claiming that his $12\frac{1}{2}$ strings of cash convert to 99,999 strings and 9 coins of underworld money, the going rate for a plot in the underworld. Nine was a particularly auspicious number for the netherworld because it was the product of three multiplied by three. Three was a yang number, filled with the male cosmological principle and so with light. Nine was an even more powerful number, whose light was thought to counteract the dark of the underworld.

The handwriting on this rubbing taken from the original stone contract (measuring 42 by 27 centimeters) confirms the worker's low social status. The lines tilt to the left as would be typical of an inexperienced, and thus cheaper, scribe. The lack of decoration would also have kept the cost of the stone low. (Reprinted from *Kaogu* 1963.5:260.)

slightly more than one sixth-acre, and that too converts to 99,999 strings. In short, the rate of conversions is not a fixed one. Whatever the real-world price, the underworld price will always be 99,999 strings.

"Five-colored silk"   This so-called silk is actually made of paper. The five colors are those of the directions: east is blue-green, west is white, south is vermillion, north is black, and the center is yellow. Five-colored cloth was thought to have the power to combat evil forces and to protect its wearer. A Six-Dynasties calendar says, "On the fifth day of the fifth month, five-colored silk is tied to the shoulder; these pieces of cloth are called averters of illness, and make it possible for people not to fall ill or get the plague" (*JingChu suishi ji* 1:8b; de Groot 1892–1907:1059).

"To the east and west . . . to the south and north"   The dimensions of the plot are given in two ways: on a grid with the length of the north-south and east-west axes, and by naming the neighbors. The neighbors are the animals associated with the four directions—green dragon, white tiger, vermillion sparrow, and dark warrior—and cannot be taken as the literal occupants of the neighboring plots. The contract is saying that the neighbor to the north is the guardian of the north, and so on. The 955 contract from Pengshan, Sichuan, was buried in a tomb in which the guardians of the four directions were depicted on the four sides of the coffin.

"The four borders are patrolled by the imperial guard"   Following the dimensions of the plot is a classic encroachment clause. The deputy of the grave mound and the earl of the tomb, deities who have been associated with tombs since the Han-dynasty ordinances, police the borders of the

Fig. 7. The Most Common Tomb Contract. One version of a tomb contract, from the ritual manual *Earth Patterns*, has been excavated at over forty sites throughout China. This example, dated 955 and from Pengshan, Sichuan, divides the contract into sections, making it easier to follow. The rubbing was taken from a red sandstone tablet measuring 64 by 43 centimeters, with a depth of 5 centimeters.

The top of the stone shows clouds on both sides of a fiery sun; a pattern runs down the left and right edges. The first block of text, *E*, gives the date of death of the deceased and the location of the plot. The four neighbors to the east, west, south, and north, are indented, *D*. The next line begins with two additional dimensions: above reaches to the Blue-Green Heaven; below, to the Yellow Springs, or Chinese Hades. The next block of text, *C*, is the clause that warns all spirits of the dead not to encroach. At bottom left, *B*, are the names of the witness and the guarantor, in the same location as on a real-world contract. The final section, *A*, is an addendum exhorting spirits to leave the deceased undisturbed. (Reprinted from *Kaogu tongxun* 1958.5:25, fig. 5.)

grave, as do members of the imperial guard. Should any spirits encroach on
the plot, the contract spells out the enforcement mechanism. The generals
and neighborhood heads (borrowed from the Han bureaucracy) will arrest
them and transfer them to the earl of the rivers. In real-world contracts, the
buyer is never responsible for resolving challenges to his ownership of a
given plot. Here, too, it is the still unnamed divine sellers who must resolve
any subsequent claims to the plot.

"We have prepared meat..."   The meat, wine, fruits, and other foods are
offerings to be given to the gods in addition to the spirit money and the
paper cloth.

"Once the money and land have been exchanged..."   The timing of this
contract is the same as a real-world contract in which the land changes
hands when the money in exchanged. Here, the money must be burned and
the dead buried in the ground, in order for the exchange to take place. And,
as many land contracts assert that the sale the record is a permanent one, so
too does this contract affirm that the transaction is an eternal one.

"The witness... The guarantor..."   At the end of the contract come the
names of the witness, who serves as an intermediary should any disputes
occur, and the guarantor, who is liable should the buyer fail to pay the full
price. Their identities are clearly divine.

"If any violate this contract..."   Because this final paragraph follows the
names of the witness and the guarantor, it is not part of the contract but a
further exhortation to the souls of the dead. The 955 contract from
Pengshan, Sichuan, shows the break between the names of the witness and
the guarantor and this final section (fig. 7). It embellishes on the encroachment clause in the contract: should any spirit previously resident in the
tomb come within 10,000 third-miles of the plot, the clerks of the subterranean bureaucracy (*difu*), or underworld administration, will punish them. It
uses an unusual term for trespass, *ganlin*, which occurs in contracts from
Dunhuang from the tenth century (Yamamoto and Ikeda 1987:#277). This is
a slightly different enforcement mechanism than that discussed in the
contract: instead of the generals and neighborhood heads, the clerks punish
the offenders. Still, the clerks and the generals and neighborhood heads
are all part of the same underworld bureaucracy. This additional clause
expresses the hope that the dead person in the tomb, and the living, will not
be disturbed.

"In accordance with the statutes and edicts..."   The final clause suggests that this last section is really in the form of an order from the Five Directional Emperors to the spirits who reside under the earth. "In accordance with the statutes and edicts" occurs in many Han-dynasty laws and implies the existence of a body of written statutes and edicts for spirits (Seidel 1987:40–41). In the Han laws, bureaucrats are enjoined to follow a given order from the emperor without violating any other laws. Here, the spirits of the dead are similarly enjoined to follow this order not to disturb the dead. Nüqing, identified as the emissary of the Five Directional Emperors, is also the name of a precinct of the underworld.[10] The Daoist canon contains a text, possibly from around A.D. 400, called *The Spirit Code of Nüqing* (*Nüqing guilü*), which is organized as a list of gods over whom believers can assert power by naming them (Seidel 1987:41).

The New Book of Earth Patterns

The contract analyzed above raises more questions than even this detailed examination can resolve. Who exactly is selling the land? The two encroachment clauses indicate that the subterranean government, or underworld bureaucracy, is responsible for resolving any subsequent claims to the plot. In real-world contracts this obligation is always the seller's; so do these clauses mean that the underworld bureaucracy is the seller? And why was the contract used so many more times than any other contract? Copies of this text have been found all over China: to the northwest in Xinjiang, Sichuan, and Gansu; to the north in Inner Mongolia, Shanxi, and Shandong; in the interior in Hunan, Hubei, Henan, Hebei, Anhui, and Jiangxi; and on the southern coast of Jiangsu, Zhejiang, and Fujian (see map 4).

This contract turns out to be precisely the one recommended for use by an imperially sponsored grave-siting manual, *The New Book of Earth Patterns.*[11] According to its preface, *Earth Patterns* was completed only in 1071,

---

10. The origin of the term "Nüqing" is unknown. It is the name of a vegetable drug thought to have the power to return the near-dead to life (Barend ter Haar, personal communication, July 1994).

11. I first learned of *Earth Patterns* from a note in Su Bai (1957:3*n*8). The book is available, in an 1192 reprinting, in only three libraries in the world: the Beijing Library, the Beijing University Library, and the National Central Library in Taibei. I have examined the two copies in Beijing, and the Taibei edition is available in a 1985 reprint.

twenty years after a first draft was submitted by a team of four scholars and had been checked by others, and more than thirty years after Emperor Renzong had called for a revision. The original Song edition of thirty-two chapters, which included an extra chapter of maps, is not extant. During the Jin dynasty, the book was revised and reissued in fifteen chapters, with a preface dated 1192, in the edition available today. The survival of *Earth Patterns* greatly facilitates the task of interpreting this tomb contract, because it provides a ritual context. It gives extremely detailed directions for placing two copies of the tomb contract in the ground.

Earth Patterns is a grave-siting manual of the five-names (*wuxing*) school, which categorized all last names into five categories named for musical notes, which in turn are linked with the five elements (fire, earth, water, metal, wood) (Morgan 1990–91:52). It explains how to pick a suitable grave site for each group (*juan* 1). Like all practitioners of the ancient technique of grave siting, the authors insist that the correct site of a grave can determine a family's fate. A bad site will result in the daughters' turning to prostitution, while a good site will produce daughters who marry husbands who become high officials (*juan* 2). The manual goes on to illustrate patterns of water flow by graves, to explain the interpretation of divination sticks, to give historical examples of fortunate and unfortunate burials, and to instruct readers on how to select auspicious days for burial. All of this is standard for a text on divination, although the specifics differ from one school to the next.

This volume was not the first imperial ritual manual to be sponsored during the Song: Wang Zhu (d. 1057), the chief editor, mentions that when Emperor Taizu (r. 960–976) commissioned an earlier manual, he was following the example of the second Tang emperor, who had done so in the early seventh century (Song preface). The survival of one 769 tomb contract following the *Earth Patterns* model suggests that a previous version of the manual circulated at least as early as the eighth century, and a fragment of a tenth-century five-names siting manual, *Record of Burial (Zanglu)*, has been found at Dunhuang (S2263).

Compiler Wang reports that the book was intended as a demonstration of the emperor's benevolence to those resident in the underworld (literally, Yellow Springs). The Jin preface echoes his point, saying that the role of the government was to help the people to live long lives and to help the dead remain at peace under the earth. At the time of publication, Wang Zhu was an Academician Reader-in-Waiting at the Hanlin Academy, who served concurrently as the Secretarial Court Gentleman in charge of the Minister of Personnel. He was famed among his contemporaries for his knowledge of ritual (*Ouyang Wenzhong Gongji* 31:7a–9b). His was not a high rank, a 5 or 6 out of 9, and his appointment probably allowed him to work full-time on *Earth Patterns*.

The instructions in *Earth Patterns* vary according to the rank of the deceased. Officials of higher rank are to do a given task one way; those of a lower rank, a simpler way; and commoners, in an even more simple way (*Dili xinshu* 14:11a). This imperially sponsored manual could be used to conduct official funerals, but it was also written with commoners in mind. The chapter prescribing the funeral ritual ends with the statement: "The preceding is written on the basis of earlier official writings. Everything is done according to the customs prevailing in the world" (*Dili xinshu* 14:15a). The illustrated funeral instructions, shown in figure 8, add: "Officials will be sent to perform the rites for those who have received high posthumous rank. The children of the dead will perform the rites for those without official position or noble title" (*Dili xinshu* 14:12b).

Only the very highest officials, such as Grand Councilor Zhou Bida, who received posthumous titles of duke (*gong*) and marquis (*hou*), were entitled to state-financed funerals. The sons of those without such titles had to finance their fathers' funerals, but they probably did not perform the ceremony themselves. The manual is so detailed that it would have been almost impossible to follow its instructions exactly, especially when the well-being of the dead was at stake. Those paying for the funeral themselves must have hired a siting expert or a Daoist practitioner to perform the service. People chose a religious practitioner on the basis of reputation, availability, and cost—rarely because of the practitioner's religious affiliation. The dramatic economic growth of the twelfth and thirteenth centuries financed an explosion of self-educated practitioners who went from one marketplace to the next vending their services, one of which was conducting funerals (Hansen 1990:40–47).

Burial Objects

The wide range of grave goods buried with *Earth Patterns* contracts confirms the book's claim to serve different social strata. Occasionally the objects in the tomb, or the contract, state the rank of the deceased, which makes it possible to locate him exactly among the official class, already less than 1 percent of the total population. The material of the tomb contract

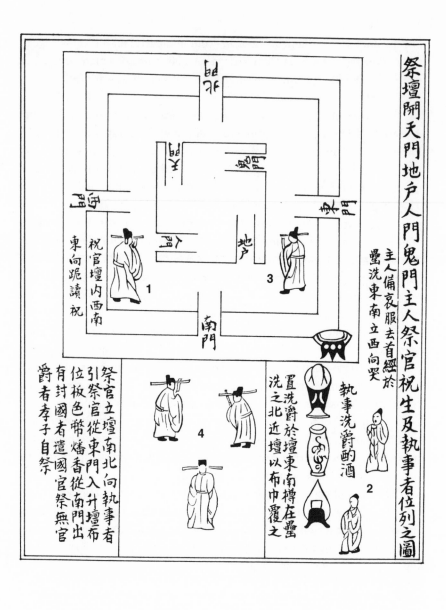

祭壇開天門地戶人門鬼門主人祭官祝生及執事者位列之圖

主人備哀服去首絰於盥洗東南立西向哭

祝官壇内西南 東向跪讀祝

執事洗爵酌酒

置洗爵於壇東南樽在盥洗之北近壇以布巾覆之

祭官立壇南北向執事者引祭官從東門入升壇布位板色幣燔香從南門出有封國者遣國官祭無官爵者孝子自祭

itself can be deceptive. Recall that the first excavated *Earth Patterns* contract, from the 769 tomb of a general, was made of paper, the cheapest available material.

Other rich people used contracts of cheap materials—for instance, the woman buried in 946 in Hefei, Anhui. Her tomb contract is made of wood, but the grave goods, especially the dangling butterfly hair ornaments, suggest great wealth, possibly that of an imperial concubine. Five hundred years later, the Director of the Censorial Directorate, the eunuch chief of the imperial household staff and secret police, was also buried with an *Earth Patterns* contract (Hucker 1985:451). This burial has since been disturbed, but the fine workmanship of fifty-three lead vessels to be used for underworld feasts leads us to believe that the funeral must have been lavish. At the opposite extreme, a highly abbreviated *Earth Patterns* contract written in brush on brick was found in Zhengzhou, Henan, dating to 1056. Only one porcelain jar was found with it.

People of different social strata were buried with *Earth Patterns*

Fig. 8. The Right Way to Bury Tomb Contracts. The ritual manual *Earth Patterns*, first published in 1071, gave detailed instructions for conducting a funeral. The procedures were meant for the services honoring high officials, but lower officials, and even those without official rank, could follow the step-by-step directions for the preparation of the grave, the types of offerings to be made, the prayers to be recited, and the use of tomb contracts. *Earth Patterns* instructs the mourners to draw up two tomb contracts, one for the deceased and one for the gods of the earth.

This illustration depicts the chief mourner, the reader of the prayer, the ritual officials, and the carriers, all positioned around a central altar, the luminous hall. The luminous hall has four gates, reading clockwise from the right: the gate for ghosts, the earthly door, the gate for humans, and the gate of heaven. At the end of the funeral, the gods' copy of the tomb contract is buried in the luminous hall. The surrounding interior wall has four additional gates, reading clockwise from the top, north gate, east gate, south gate, and west gate. The text, translated below, summarizes the tasks of those participating in the funeral ritual.

1. The reader of the prayer kneels to the southwest of the altar and faces east as he reads the prayer.

2. The carriers wash the wine pitchers and pour the wine. They place the washed pitchers in the southeast corner of the altar. The wine pitcher is to the north of the earthenware washing jars, close to the altar, which is covered with a cloth.

3. The chief mourner prepares mourning clothes, crosses southeast to the earthenware washing jars, and stands facing west, sobbing.

4. The ritual officials stand to the north and south of the altar. The carriers lead them from the east gate to ascend the altar, where they set out the ancestral tablet, lay out the varieties of paper money, and burn incense. They leave through the south gate. (Illustration from *Dili xinshu* 14:11a; redrawn by Liang Wei.)

contracts, and they showed decided individuality in what they hoped would accompany them to the next world. Sometimes they placed reading material in their tombs.[12] The surviving books reveal what personal libraries were like in the age of woodblock printing, when the cost of books was so low that individuals could afford to bury several of their favorites. The 1055 tomb in Jiangyin, Jiangsu, of a kinswoman of a Vice Minister of Works (rank 3a) contained eleven often-read canonical texts, some very brief (*The Diamond Sutra* and *The Heart Sutra*), some longer (*The Golden Splendor Sutra*). This woman also had a fortune-telling manual from the Buddhist canon that linked the year of birth with the seven stars of the Big Dipper and was supposed to keep the bearer from falling ill (*Foshuo beidou qixing yanming jing*). In addition, she had one text from the Daoist canon, *Lord Lao the Most High Explains How to Obtain the Dao Eternally* (*Taishang Laojun shuo changqing jingjing*). This library suggests a devout Buddhist who did not limit herself to Buddhist texts. She did not have a Buddhist funeral: she was not cremated, and she used an *Earth Patterns* contract to buy land from the earth gods.

Another tomb, also with an *Earth Patterns* contract (from 1631) and also in Jiangsu, contains books of a very different type: encyclopedias and letter-writing manuals. The grave goods are simple, and the deceased has no official title. He may have been a clerk in a military office. The books include two encyclopedias first written in the Song or the Yuan, a selection of model letters taken from the official histories, and a dictionary that gives various scripts, pronunciations, and meanings of characters. This library suggests an alternative view of the underworld. Rather than pass the days reciting Buddhist sutras, the deceased needed these reference books to write documents, perhaps even to draft legal plaints for the underworld courts.

The burial goods accompanying the *Earth Patterns* contract buried in 1210 in Houma, Shanxi, have attracted the attention of those studying Chinese literature because they include a finely carved brick model of a stage and five figurines who are the role-types of Jin drama (Idema and West 1982:xi). The stage and the contract are built into the top of the tomb wall, just where the roof begins (Liu Nianzi 1986:54). Chinese stages often faced temples, so that the gods could see the performance that

12. The most famous example is the books uncovered in the Han-dynasty tomb at Mawangdui, Changsha, Hunan. These have allowed scholars to reconstruct several previously unknown ancient texts and the *Daodejing*.

was conducted on their behalf. Here the tomb designer has the same idea. He has placed both the stage and the contract where the gods can see them easily.

Of interest to textile historians are two tombs containing many silk garments along with *Earth Patterns* contracts. Paper models were not enough to clothe the wife of a member of the imperial clan, herself the daughter of a prefect, who was buried in 1228 in Fujian with 334 silk garments. And the father of an empress who was buried in 1515 in Beijing took 83 silk garments with him.

The tomb contract these people used may have been standardized, much as real-world contracts were, but because their vision of their life in the underworld was not standardized (nor was that of their living relatives) they took very different items with them. The presence of a tomb contract along *Earth Patterns* lines does not necessarily mean that the deceased was buried according to the instructions there. The tomb contract text may have circulated as a model text separate from the ritual manual. Shortened or partial versions indicate that people felt free to stray from the model (in 946, 1055, 1056, 1072, 1121, 1128). We cannot know how many who used *Earth Patterns* contracts actually had a funeral along the lines prescribed. Still, the manual helps to resolve some outstanding questions about the contracts, namely the reason why two copies were buried, and the identity of the gods selling the land.

Wrongful Burial

Once the site of the grave and the day of the funeral have been selected, *Earth Patterns* instructs, the mourners must erect a structure over the future grave, called a luminous hall. This structure is a temporary home for the gods of the tomb (*zhongshen*) and also a place for the relatives of the dead to make offerings to the earth gods and to the deceased, who is represented by an ancestral tablet. The luminous hall is to house images of the Five Directional Emperors and the animal gods of the Chinese zodiac. The authors of the manual warn that failure to build such a structure is to commit a crime called wrongful burial (*daozang*) that will prompt great misfortune. The idea of wrongful burial directly parallels the legal concept of wrongful sale, so often cited by the judges of *Clarity and Lucidity*. Wrongful burial poses dangers for the unwary buyer, here the dead person and his family. Because they have, perhaps inadvertently, violated some fundamental law of dealing with the earth gods, such a burial will offer them no protection.

Earth Patterns cites the Blue-Green Crow (Qing Wuzi), the pen name of the author of the first book on grave-siting dating to the Qin and Han, The Classic of Burials (Zangjing). This book survives only in a Jin-dynasty edition, which mentions another type of wrongful burial: "To bury without beheading the grass, that is called wrongful burial" (Zangjing 1:6a). The tenth-century manual from Dunhuang, The Record of Burials, also mentions beheading the grass (S2263 unpaginated). It is the name of a ceremony in which three bundles of three stalks of either couch grass or rice straw are tied in five-colored thread and placed on the altar of the Yellow Emperor in the luminous hall. The Great Han's Secret Burial Manual for Plains and Hills, which circulated in the north during the Jin and Yuan dynasties, explains the link between the grass and the Yellow Emperor, the legendary first emperor who discovered so many things, including agriculture. He was disturbed by the cries of the dead who lay about on the surface of the earth, so he ordered them to be buried under the grass so that they could not be heard (Mizang jing 12a).

The Secret Manual also explains the concept behind the ceremony of beheading the grass. According to the legendary Duke of Zhou: "All grass is the hair and clothing of the land, and the children and grandchildren of the earth, so it is necessary to behead it. This is in order to bring peace to the dead souls and happiness to the living" (Mizang jing 12a). Earth Patterns gives a slightly different explanation: "Beheading the grass cuts off evil ghosts and brings peace to the dead" (Dili xinshu 14:11b). Whatever the details, the intent of the ceremony is clear. By cutting the grass first, the ceremony protects the dead from the dangers posed by the souls who reside in the grass and who might attack them. Beheading the grass meant beheading the souls resident in the grass.

Earth Patterns cites another text, which it calls a spirit code (guilü),[13] that equates failure to behead the grass with failure to use a contract: "To bury without beheading the grass, to buy land without drawing up a contract, these are called wrongful burial and will bring great misfortune" (Dili xinshu 14:11b). Seven tomb contracts from Jiangxi, including that of Grand Councilor Zhou Bida, open with a similar citation: "According to the spirit

13. This spirit code is not the same as the text in the Daoist canon called The Spirit Code of Nüqing (Nüqing guilü), but the repetition of the term guilü suggests the existence of other undocumented spirit codes as well.

code, to bury without beheading the grass or to buy the plot without drawing up a contract is called wrongful burial" (1204, 1232, 1254, 1260, 1293, 1319, 1446). Because these seven tomb contracts do not follow the model given in *Earth Patterns*, yet cite the same provisions of the spirit code, the spirit code may have circulated independently of the manual.

The Secret Manual spells out even more directly the consequences of not burying a tomb contract: "When all burials are complete, if one does not draw up a tomb contract, the soul of the dead will not be peaceful, the officials of the heavenly section (*tiancao*) will not be responsible, the subterranean bureaucracy (*difu*) will not accept the dead, the soul will wander without a fixed dwelling, and the living will not be fortunate. This will be an enormous disaster" (*Mizang jing* 27b).

The Funeral as Prescribed

On the same day that the grass is cut, *Earth Patterns* instructs all those with posthumous titles of duke or marquis, and those ranking above them, to bury in the earth two iron contracts with red writing, one Chinese foot high and seven Chinese inches across. The Song governmental regulations also specified two contracts, one of stone, the other of iron. According to *Earth Patterns*, one contract was to be buried in the luminous hall in front of the Yellow Emperor's image; the other was to be buried in the grave vault in front of the coffin (*Dili xinshu* 14:12a).

Incense was to be burned everywhere the grass was beheaded, and the ritual officials were to prepare paper money and paper models of thick, loosely woven raw silk fabric to offer to the gods. The dead received offerings of good faith including silk, cotton shoes, copper coins, paper and brush, and a stone for grinding ink (*Dili xinshu* 14:12b). These paper models, to be burned at the end of the ceremony, were very popular throughout China. A 1270 petition to the Mongol emperor called for a ban on the excessive expenditures of the Chinese on these paper funerary goods, which included money, houses, people, horses, cloth, and tents (*Yuan dianzhang* 30:10a). (Their use continues today, with the ethnic Chinese all over the world burning paper models of Mercedes cars and houses equipped with the latest appliances for the use of their deceased relatives.) *Earth Patterns* also lists food to be used in the ceremony: rice, horse feed, wine, dried deer meat, dried fish, millet, rice cakes, Chinese leeks, and three types of meat, all to ensure the comfort of the dead in the underworld.

Earth Patterns recommends that, on the day before the beheading of the grass, the luminous hall be erected and the images of different gods be put in the appropriate place. The manual provides a diagram showing the layout of the altar as well as the movements of the chief mourner (*zhuren*), the reader of the prayer (*zhuguan*), the ritual officials, and the carriers (*zhishizhe*) (fig. 8). After the ritual officials have marched past the altar and burned incense, and the wine has been poured, the reader prays:

> ✱✱✱ year, month, day. Chief Mourner ✱✱✱ reports to the Five
> Emperors of the Five Directions, the hundred spirits of the hills and
> rivers, the Empress of the Earth and officials of the underworld,
> deputy of the grave mound and earl of the tomb, gods of the paths
> through the fields: the relative of ✱✱✱ died on ✱✱✱ year, month, day.
> We kneel and are grief-stricken. The ritual system has auspicious and
> inauspicious times. We have prognosticated and found this
> auspicious site, which is suitable for his grave, in this plain, in this
> district, in this county, and in this prefecture. We move the tomb to
> here on ✱✱✱ day, month, year. We take today's auspicious time to
> behead the grass and make offerings of good faith. . . . [text garbled]
> We respectfully offer this to the Empress of the Earth and so bury the
> dead. In the future, forever, will be no disasters. Respectfully partake.
> (*Dili xinshu* 14:12b–13a)

This prayer is similar to the celestial ordinances of the Han: it simply informs the different gods, both those above ground such as the Five Directional Emperors and those below such as the Empress of the Earth, of the death, the burial, the identity of the dead, and the location of the tomb. It then asks them to forestall any disasters. The unstated hope is that these gods will protect both the dead and the living from the dangers resulting from digging into the earth to make a grave.[14] Then the ritual officials kneel before the Yellow Emperor and read aloud the text of the two contracts, which they have temporarily removed from their respective places on the altar and in the tomb.

The ritual officials place the two contracts together and write the characters for "contract" on the back of the two documents, so that when they are joined, the characters are complete (*Dili xinshu* 14:13a; *Wenwu* 1989.5:70). This ceremony replicates a contract signing between two people, but this ritual is between a dead person and the god(s) from whom

---

14. *The Secret Manual* contains a similar prayer (*Mizang jing* 30a–b).

he buys his funeral plot. Here the officials act as the proxies of the deceased and the divine. The moment they write the characters for "contract," *hetong*, must be taken as the moment the deities accept the offer of the dead to buy the plot. Could the gods reject the contract? Perhaps by causing some kind of disturbance, but no instances of this sort are recorded. The two contracts are returned to their original places in the tomb and on the altar.

The ceremony ends with offerings made to the several deities, whose images are located in different places. First the prayer reader goes to the altar of the generals of the paths through the fields, says the dead will be buried in their midst, offers wine, and expresses the hope that no calamities will occur. He then takes the beheaded grass from the altar of the Yellow Emperor and places it in front of the tomb chamber, addresses the neighborhood heads, the gods of the tomb and the grave mound, and asks them to accept the offerings, to protect the dead, "to keep the tomb chamber clean and quiet and to expel old spirits, and to ensure the peace of the newcomer." This ritual divides the gods into three groups: those above the surface (the Five Directional Emperors), those on the surface (the generals of the paths through the fields), and those below the surface (the neighborhood heads, the earl of the tomb, and the deputy of the grave mound). The sons of the dead take a knife and perform the three beheadings of earthly, heavenly, and human spirits. These three types of spirits correspond to the three gates at the altar; the sons then close off the fourth gate, that of the spirits. The ritual officials pray to the Yellow Emperor to protect the descendants of the dead. They place the remaining paper money, offerings of good faith, meat, wine, fruit, and one copy of the contract into the earth under the luminous hall. All are intended for the gods.

The practice of burying the gods' copy of a contract goes back at least to the blood covenant ceremony of the seventh and sixth centuries B.C. (Lewis 1990:43–50). Because the gods were credited with inventing Chinese characters, their copy of the contract could be written in Chinese. The gods could read Chinese, but they read characters in a different order, because "in the world of the dead (the 'underworld') everything is the other way round" (Werblowsky 1988:154). Both the gods who presided over the courts and the dead souls who stood poised to attack the living were thought to read left to right (the opposite of standard Chinese) or bottom to top. Two Five-Dynasties contracts are written left to right. Others alternate lines from top to bottom with those from bottom to top (1099 from Baisha, 1139, and 1272). The most ingenious even alternates these lines while reading left to right (1104). All of these variations were for the reading convenience of the gods.

At the end of the funeral, after the rest of the paper money and offerings were burned, after earth was tossed on the grave, and after everyone had dispersed, the other copy of the contract was buried in front of the coffin in the tomb (*Dili xinshu* 14:11b–13b). For whom was this copy intended? *Earth Patterns* does not explain, but two surviving contracts give hints.

An 1199 contract from Fenyi, Jiangxi, specifies that one copy is to go to Lord Lao the Most High, while a second will be given to "the dead woman herself in the netherworld to keep as proof." It then explains what will happen in the case of a dispute: "If anything of this type [violations of the contract] occurs, the great deity who erects the tomb (*likuang taishen*) should take the dead souls into custody and bring them to the court of Haoli [a precinct near Mount Tai], where Lord Lao the Most High will behead them." A 1233 text from Jiangdu, Jiangsu, echoes this warning, instructing that the dead woman receive a copy of the contract "to serve as proof forever."

Further information about the rationale for making two copies is given in *A General Record of Graves* (*Yingyuan zonglu*), a shorter and cheaper version of *Earth Patterns*. It survives in a badly damaged Yuan-dynasty edition housed in the Beijing Library. *Earth Patterns* must have spawned many imitators, for *A General Record* warns the reader against consulting spurious texts, of which it names some fifty. *A General Record* sites graves according to the five-names school, but it is much shorter than *Earth Patterns* (only five chapters) and more crudely produced, with lines of the text listing to the right or left.

It describes a burial much like the one in *Earth Patterns*, with the same beheading of the grass at the beginning of the funeral and the same three beheadings at the end. The text of the burial contract given is very similar to that in *Earth Patterns*, except that it has been updated to use the Yuan-dynasty term for land that is the owner's to sell, *tiji*. "Two copies of the contract are to be drawn up, one copy to be offered to the Empress of the Earth, and one to be placed in the tomb for the deceased, father of [★★★], to hold and to be prepared to keep on his person as proof forever." The second copy, then, is for the use of the deceased, who will need it to prove ownership of his own grave plot. *A General Record* proceeds to explain under what circumstances the deceased would need proof: "Then one separates the two contracts after writing the two characters for 'contract' on their backs. This is to ensure that bad ethers and corpses will never encroach on the grave or contest the deceased's claim to the land" (*Yingyuan zonglu* 3 unpaginated). The tomb contract will protect the grave plot both by threatening any bad ethers or corpses and by offering documentary proof of the deceased's claim to the grave plot. By implication the spirits of the dead realize that inasmuch as the deceased has a copy of the contract, the netherworld courts are bound to side with him.

A 1454 contract confirms that tomb contracts were placed in tombs for presentation in the courts of the underworld should a dispute arise. This document is from the tomb of Zhou Kuan (1361–1441), a member of the ceremonial guard attached to the princely establishment of the seventh son of Emperor Ren of the Ming (r. 1425), who was buried together with his wife, in Poyang, Jiangxi:

> If anything like this should happen, it is up to both Zhou Kuan and Lady Tian, the Mysterious Pure Lady of Suitability,[15] to take this land contract carved on a tablet immediately to the Gate of Three Heavens to ask for a judgment, to be carried out according to the heavenly code of Nüqing.

The heavenly code of Nüqing is a name for the spirit code. This contract looks to the Daoist practitioner who drew it up to serve as a witness in the underworld courts and ends with an unusual statement: "Today at this time we willingly hand over the price of the land. The dragon deity guards the tomb, and the earth receives the money and serves as a witness that 6 strings of 1,000 cash have been paid, with nothing owing." This statement provides extra protection from lawsuits. Tomb contracts were meant to prevent suits contesting ownership, and this statement, like the one that occurs at the end of this-worldly land contracts from Huizhou, offers additional protection from a suit claiming insufficient payment.

A 1568 version of the *Earth Patterns* contract from Yangzhou, Jiangsu, is unique in that both copies of the contract survive: that of the dead couple and that of the gods (both in *Taozhai cangshiji* 44:15b–17a).[16] The copies are mirror images of each other, but oddly the couple's copy reads backward

15. This honorific title was granted to wives of rank 5 officials (Hucker 1985:267).

16. Figure 9 is a drawing of the text from *Taozhai cangshiji*, with my emendations. The renowned Qing epigrapher Duan Fang reads the last line of the gods' copy as [ ] *shi zhi shen*, but I think *difu zhi shen* much more likely. Because the two texts are identical (except that the couple's copy adds the adjective "filial" in front of their son's name), the empty boxes, which contain indecipherable characters on the now lost original, can be easily filled in with the characters from the mirror image.

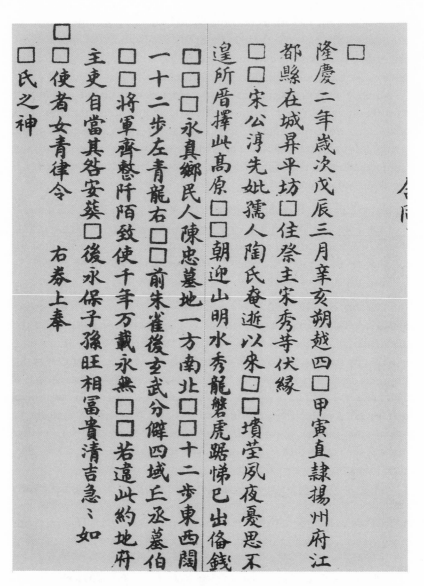

□
隆慶二年歲次戊辰三月辛亥朔越四□甲寅直隸揚州府江
都縣在城昇平坊□住祭主宋秀等伏緣
□宋公淳先妣孺人陶氏奄逝以來□□墳塋夙夜憂思不
遑所暨擇此高原□□朝迎山明水秀龍磐虎踞悕已出備錢
□□永真鄉民人陳忠墓地一方南北□□十二步東西闊
一十二步左青龍右□□前朱雀後玄武分僻四域正丞墓伯
□□將軍齊憝阡陌致使千年萬載永無□□若違此約地府
主吏自當其咎安葬□後永保子孫旺相富貴清吉急〻如
□□使者女青律令　　右券上奉
□氏之神

Fig. 9. A Contract in Duplicate—One Copy for the Gods, One Copy for the Deceased. This 1568 contract is unique in illustrating how mourners might follow the instructions given in the ritual manual *Earth Patterns* to bury two tomb contracts, one for the deceased and one for the gods of the earth. The two contracts are mirror images connected by the characters for "contract," *hetong*, which would be bisected when the two copies were cut apart during the ceremony. The halves could be fitted together later, should either party—human or divine—doubt the authenticity of the document.

先考宋公淳妣陶氏收執

五帝使者女青律令　　右券給付

主吏自當其咎安葬之後永保子孫旺相富貴清吉急急如

道路將軍齊整阡陌致使千年万載永無殃咎若違此約地府

一十二步左青龍右白虎前朱雀後玄武分擗四域正丞墓伯

財買到永真鄉民人陳忠墓地一方南北長一十二步東西濶

遑所晉擇此高原來去朝迎山明水秀龍磐虎踞悌巳出倚錢

先考宋公淳先妣孺人陶氏奄逝以來未卜墳塋夙夜憂思不

都縣在城昇平坊居住祭主孝男宋秀芽伏緣

隆慶二年歲次戊辰三月辛亥朔越四日甲寅直隸揚州府江

維

The deceased couple's copy gives their names on the last line, at right, while the gods' name on the last line, at left, reads "gods of the subterranean government." The person who drew up this contract grasped the idea that the gods read Chinese backward but confused its execution. He wrote the copy for the gods so that it follows the correct reading order for humans (from right to left), whereas the deceased couple's copy is inverted so that it reads from left to right—correct for the gods but wrong for people. (Reprinted from *Taozhai cangshiji* 44:16a–17a.)

(left to right), while the gods' copy reads forward (right to left; fig. 9). The couple's copy should read right to left, and the gods' copy left to right. The drafter of this text understood the convention that the gods did not read in the same order as humans, but he switched the gods' copy for the couple's, a readily understandable error! And he failed to modify the body of the reversed text to fit the new reading order. The last line of the couple's copy reads, "The contract to the right is to be given to the late father, Duke Song Chun, and my late mother, Lady Tao, to hold," while the gods' copy says, "The contract to the right is offered to the gods of the subterranean government." Note that both copies say "the contract to the right" (*youquan*), but the couple's copy lies to the left. Clearly, mastering the conventions of backward writing was not simple.

Only a people with a highly developed court system would have buried a contract for the purchase of their grave plot in duplicate, one copy for the gods and one for the deceased. We have seen that the Chinese placed many other items in their tombs as well. Some took books. Some took clothes. Some even took a miniature stage and actors. Almost everyone took food and money. No one knew exactly what dangers the next life posed, and certain precautions seemed worth taking. The state even financed them for its high officials, including Grand Councilor Zhou Bida, while other lower-ranking and ordinary families bore the costs themselves.

If the purchase of land was fraught with uncertainty in this world, it probably was in the next world too. Only by taking two copies of the contract for the purchase of the plot, which recorded all the details of the transaction, could one discourage the spirits of the dead from bringing suit. People hoped to spare the dead the agony of going to court. But if they should have to go, then the living wanted to arm them with the most detailed documentation available. What could afford better protection than giving the buyer (the deceased) and the seller (the gods of the earth) each their own copy of the sale contract?

1

The Courts

of the

Underworld

The Chinese envisioned the world of the dead to be much like the world of the living—governed by bureaucrats, filled with courts, and punctuated by lawsuits. Accordingly, they buried contracts as a precaution in case they were sued. Because the contracts do not reveal much, one has to consult other sources to explain how people viewed these subterranean courts.

Belief in the underworld court system was already widespread in the fourth and fifth centuries, when Daoist ritual manuals explained how to resolve an underworld suit. The Maoshan Daoists claimed they knew how to intervene in the courts on behalf of the living. Buddhists of different sects did not claim the same expertise, but because they firmly believed the courts would punish violations of Buddhist precepts, they included descriptions of the subterranean courts in their didactic tales. They saw the workings of karma in this system and described terrible hells for those who ate meat or failed to support monasteries. Other less partisan sources describe visits to the underworld, and a few Yuan plays are set there. During the Mongol era, Daoists continued to assert their authority over the spirits of the dead by drafting detailed law codes for them.

Many are the tales of people losing consciousness, visiting their kin or acquaintances in the world of the dead, and awakening to recount their experiences. (The Chinese word for "death", *si*, also means "to faint" or "to pass out.") Few of these accounts agree on the structure of the courts under the earth. Seemingly there were as many netherworlds as there were visitors, although all accounts concur that a judge—usually the Indian god of the dead, Yama, or his Chinese counterpart, Yanluo—sat in judgment on the humans brought before them. They agree, too, that a suit brought in these subterranean courts could affect the well-being of the living, either as party to a suit or as kin to those being sued. Structured much like this-worldly courts, and populated by many of the same corrupt figures, the courts of the dead differed in one important way: they usually implemented justice.

Early Daoist Views

One Daoist who claimed knowledge of the workings of the underworld courts was Yang Xi (fl. 364–370), the visionary who transmitted his teachings to Xu Mi (303–373), a leader of the Maoshan Daoist sect. Tao Hongjing restructured and rewrote Yang's and Xu's teachings in his 499 volume. *Declarations of the Perfected (Zhengao)* contains various examples of families whose sufferings stemmed from underworld suits (*zhongsong*) lodged against their dead relatives. The moment such a suit was lodged, regardless of its validity, the living began to suffer (Strickmann 1981:144–169). The only possible course of action, *Declarations* urged, was to hire a Daoist to intervene in the courts of the underworld on behalf of the living. "When someone falls ill or dies, is weak or in danger, awakes from bright or strange dreams or loses money," he or she should try to undo the underworld suit in which that person is involved (*Zhengao* 7:16b; Maruyama 1986:51; Strickmann 1981:144–169).

Master Xu Mi himself suffered because his uncle had unjustly killed a subordinate while serving as prefect, and the murder victim had sued the entire Xu family—living and dead—in the underworld courts. This is a textbook example of an underworld suit: unpunished murder in the world of the living could only be sentenced in the courts of the dead. Xu's wife had just died, and she was ordered to bring calamity to her husband's family. The Xu family was able to extricate itself from the suit only because of the timely intervention of the visionary Yang Xi (*Zhengao* 7:6a–9a; Maruyama 1986:50).

Declarations tells of underworld suits caused by failure to bury the dead (*Zhengao* 8:2b–3b; Strickmann 1981:161, 166) but does not list their causes. An undated text, *The Petition Almanac of the Red Pine Master (Chi Songzi zhangli)* lists eighty-one possible types of suits.[1] *The Petition*

---

1. Some scholars of Daoism who date this text to the Six Dynasties or Tang agree that it contains earlier material, while others date it to the second or third century A.D. It continued to be used throughout the Tang, and the same eighty-one suits are given in slightly different order in a Song text of the twelfth century (*Daomen dingzhi* 1:27b–38b; Boltz 1987:50–51; Schipper 1989:128; Maruyama 1986:47; Seidel 1987:41, Stein 1979:63).

Almanac gives two exceptionally lengthy model texts of petitions to resolve underworld suits. A suit of this sort could cause such problems as the inability to produce an heir, illness in the family, failure to prosper, or disturbances in the household. The first petition explains that some of the suits are caused by the same offenses that the drafters of tomb contracts feared: burial on top of someone previously buried in the same plot or burial underneath someone newly buried (*Chi Songzi zhangli* 5:19b). And when the presiding Daoist calls on a whole host of divine armies to disperse the spirits causing the trouble, he, like the tomb contracts, orders the ghosts to be arrested by the subterranean 2,000-bushel official, according to the edicts of Nüqing. This is a Daoist ritual document, transmitted only among Daoist practitioners, but the problems it addresses were not limited to Daoist believers. The fear of underworld suits was a real one, and lay people buried tomb contracts in the tombs of their kin for the same reasons that they hired Daoists to perform the rituals so copiously described in *The Petition Almanac.*

Immediately following the first petition for resolving underworld suits is a repeat petition, developed on an even larger scale should the first petition fail to end the original problem (*Chi Songzi zhangli* 5:23b–33b). The length of the text suggests desperation on the part of the living, while the list of materials needed indicates how costly a ceremony the repeat ritual was: 120 Chinese feet of plain cloth, 80 Chinese feet each of five-colored textured and pure white silk, 5 brooms, 5 manure baskets, 2 Chinese ounces of cinnabar, a mat, 200 sheets of paper for drafting memorials, 2 sets of brush and ink, a small knife for carving characters in bamboo, 5,000 strings of money (probably paper models), 1 Chinese catty of oil, 3 Chinese ounces of incense, 2 piculs and 4 pecks of rice, and all the equipment needed for ritual bathing the night before the ceremony (*Chi Songzi zhangli* 5:31a).

This repeat petition again contains a list of the eighty-one possible types of suits in which the living could be embroiled, providing a compressed view of widespread ideas about justice (*Chi Songzi zhangli* 5:26a–29a; Maruyama 1986:55–56). The dead could sue, it was thought, if they had died in an uncomfortable way, such as starving to death or in a plague. The dead could sue if they had been improperly buried without a coffin or if their skeleton was not intact. (Without an intact coffin they lacked shelter, and without an intact skeleton they would not have a whole body in the underworld.) They could sue for failure to raise a child to whom one had given birth, a traditional family obligation. They could sue for failure also to give birth to sons, the only children who could carry out ancestor worship and ensure that the dead were well taken care of. They could sue over the breaking of promises or disputes in love or hate. None of these were crimes according to the earthly law of the time, *The Tang Code*, but all were offenses against the natural order, against the way things should be.

The list of eighty-one suits ends with the stipulation that they could be combined into a hundred, a thousand, or ten thousand suits the dead could bring against the living, and the entire petition closes with the fervent request that no more underworld suits be brought against the family of the dead.

The petition has this to say about the underworld courts: "To make a plaint to the spirit officials prompts them to summon the living and make them suffer intensely. The courts of the dark, although enlightened, can also be twisted and swayed by rhetoric" (*Chi Songzi zhangli* 5:30b). These comments about the slow trials and warped outcomes of underworld suits could just as well have been applied to the courts of the living, but they reflected a distinctly Daoist view of underworld justice. Because the Daoists wanted fees to perform rituals, it was in their interest to paint the courts as just as corrupt as those on earth and to imply that plaintiffs would have just as much need for bribes as in this world. The workings of the spirit courts might be twisted and swayed by rhetoric, went the argument, but Daoist practitioners knew how to manipulate them. And for a fee—often a high one—they would bring their expertise to bear on whatever problem the individual presented. The Daoists were the underworld counterparts of those with brushes in their hats who encouraged suits in this world.

Buddhist Views

Other sources suggest that the spirit courts were basically just, if occasionally corrupt. In the mid-seventh century, a high official and Buddhist believer, Tang Lin, collected fifty-seven Buddhist tales on this topic in his *Records of Miraculous Retribution* (*Mingbaoji* 787–803; Gjertson 1989). Some tales about the underworld encouraged people to obey Buddhist precepts such as the prohibition on eating meat, while others described miracles performed by Buddhist deities. Unlike the Maoshan Daoists, the Buddhists made no effort to intervene in the underworld courts, but believed instead that the spirit judges evaluated the dead according to Buddhist precepts: those who hosted vegetarian feasts and sponsored the copying of Buddhist sutras were rewarded, whereas those who ate meat were punished. People visited the underworld, were warned about their sins, and reemerged in the real world to do good works in order to lessen their underworld sentences. The author of the collection named the people who told him the stories he recorded. This may have been a literary device to enhance the credibility of his tales, but some of his named sources were real historical figures. Although the tales are in classical Chinese, the written language of the time, they lack the complicated parallel sentences or frequent literary allusions typical of more sophisticated writing (Gjertson 1989:39). They may indeed have been transcriptions of accounts told to Tang Lin.

As is true of other descriptions from the Six Dynasties of trips to the netherworld, Tang's sources did not agree on all details, but they describe an underworld bureaucracy organized along lines very similar to those in the real world. King Yanluo presides and is aided by judges, recorders, clerks, messengers, and jailers (Gjertson 1989:136). One magistrate finds the documents in the underworld to be so like those in the real world that he is able to get to work on them immediately (*Mingbaoji* 801b; Gjertson 1989:260). The underworld courts have the power to summon real-world witnesses, who are able to return to life after testifying (*Mingbaoji* 796c–797a; Gjertson 1989:232).

The underworld clerks must be bribed just as their earthly counterparts must be, but with different currencies. One greedy clerk explains, "I have no use for your copper cash; I desire only cash made of white paper" (*Mingbaoji* 800b; Gjertson 1989:254). In another tale, a man well acquainted with the ways of the underworld explains: "The things that ghosts use are different from those of humans. Only gold and silk can be used by both, but even so, artificial materials are preferred. 'Gold' that is made by daubing tin with yellow paint and 'silk' that is made from paper are valued most" (*Mingbaoji* 792c; Gjertson 1989:198). This may be the earliest reference to spirit money, paper facsimilies of money that the living burned for the benefit of the dead (Seidel 1978:425; Hou 1975:5–6).

Almost all of these tales concern judgments on the newly dead issued by King Yanluo, but one tale mentions a suit against the living brought by the dead. A woman reports she has sued her husband in the Heavenly Section (*tiancao*) for murder without cause, but that a powerful supporter of his prevented the summons from being issued and delayed her case for three years. Only on the day the visitor came to the underworld was she able to have her case heard (*Mingbaoji* 799a; Gjertson 1989:245). These tales are in a collection that aims to show the power of Buddhist deities and the benefits of following Buddhist tenets, but the underworld court system it describes is Chinese—neither exclusively Buddhist nor exclusively Daoist.

Other Accounts

In these early accounts of the underworld courts, a murder victim accusing his or her unpunished killer is the most frequent type of suit. Tang literature reports that such an accusation was leveled against even the emperor Taizong (r. 626–649). A very short version of the story tells of the emperor's being summoned to hell and asked about the incident on the fourth day of the sixth month, the day the emperor took power. On that day he killed one brother and watched one of his officers kill another at the Xuanwu gate of Changan. He then forced his father to step down. The emperor was allowed to return to the living (*Chaoye qianzai* 6:148–149). The Dunhuang popular narrative *A Record of Emperor Tang Taizong's Entry into the Underworld* (*Dunhuang bianwenji* 2:209–214; Waley 1960:165–174) is much longer and much embellished, but gaps in the original text make it difficult to decipher every character.[2] When the emperor goes to the underworld courts, he appears first before King Yama, who assigns a lower official, the famous Prefect Cui (Cui fujun), to conduct his case.

While the Dunhuang version retains the subterranean questioning of the emperor from the earlier Tang tale, it introduces a new satirical theme. The interrogator, Prefect Cui, treats the emperor gently in order to secure a bureaucratic posting for himself. Prefect Cui explains that the emperor has been charged by his two younger brothers, one whom he himself killed and one whom he had killed when he took power. He tells the emperor that he can return to the living if he can answer one question: "The emperor of the Tang, Emperor Taizong, is asked why, in 626, he killed his brothers in front of the palace and imprisoned his kind father in the back of the palace? Please answer" (*Dunhuang bianwenji* 2:213; Waley 1960:172). The emperor is appropriately terrified. Because he cannot answer the question, he is not allowed to return to the living.

The story ends with Prefect Cui composing a concise answer for the

2. The manuscript bears the date 970, but the story probably goes back to the seventh or eighth century (Victor Mair, personal communication, May 1993). A later, altered version of the emperor's visit occurs in the Ming-dynasty novel, *The Journey to the West* (Yu 1977:237–253).

emperor: "The great sage will destroy his family to save the kingdom." Prefect Cui receives a promotion and the emperor returns to this world after being urged to publish copies of Buddhist sutras and to do good deeds. In this satirical tale, justice is not done; but it is noteworthy that the jurisdiction of the courts of the dead extends even to the emperor.

When the emperor arrives in hell, he first goes before King Yama. In this respect the emperor's experience is typical, for most people describe seeing only one judge in the underworld. Also from Dunhuang are visual depictions of the underworld courts, but they show ten kings altogether, only one of whom is Yama. In the first hand-scrolls from Dunhuang, the bodhisattva Dizang (Ksitigarbha) is surrounded by the ten kings. By the end of the twelfth century, artists in Ningbo painted each of the ten kings separately (Teiser 1988; 1993:129). Yama, the fifth king, is shown with a karma mirror, an implement he uses to view the past and future lives of those appearing before him (ter Haar 1992:169nn 155–157). In the painting the mirror shows the deceased killing a man in a boat (Fong 1992:335–342). The discrepancy between artistic depictions of the ten kings and written descriptions of just one king is puzzling. Is it possible that each person appears before only one king?[3] And that is why sightings of all ten together are so rare?

Later sources describe other types of suits in addition to those of murder victims. In one Tang-dynasty tale, a peasant in Anhui gives a ride on his boat to a spirit who goes from place to place presenting underworld summonses to the living. As he delivers one such summons in a village, the peasant glances at the list and see that his own name is next. He is horrified. The ghost scolds him for reading the list and asks: "Have you previously been in debt to anyone or not?" He thinks carefully and then replies: "In my lifetime I have stolen only 10 sixth-acres of land from Zhang Mingtong of my county. He subsequently lost his livelihood. He is already dead." The ghost replies, "This man is suing you" (*Taiping guangji* 339:2688–89, citing *Guangyiji*). The peasant's response at this point suggests he thinks any potential danger has passed with Mr. Zhang's death. In fact, as the ghost explains, Mr. Zhang's death has granted him access to a new court system. The protagonist then adopts a line of defense frequently used in this-world courts: as he is the only son of his parents, he pleads for leniency. The ghost

3. This suggestion is from Richard Barnhart, History of Art, Yale University, personal communication, March 1993.

grants him another ten years of life, provided that he remains inside his house for three years.

When the thief returns home, his father beats him for refusing to work in the fields, so he leaves the house to join his father. As soon as he steps outside, he encounters the spirit, who expresses regret that he has been unable to keep to their agreement. The man dies within the month, one can assume in order to serve his underworld sentence for encroaching on his neighbor's fields.

The Cypress People

The Anhui peasant knew immediately who was suing him in the under-world. The question of guilt and innocence was not always so straightfor-ward, though. Because the living could be punished by the underworld courts for crimes their dead relatives had perpetrated, they might have no idea who was using them in the underworld or why. The principle of mutual liability was borrowed from real-world laws that called for the punishment of anyone living in the same household with those who had plotted a rebellion or sedition (Johnson 1979:18).

The living were not defenseless against this type of suit. Three tombs in Jiangxi contain evidence showing what measures people took to protect themselves against punishments resulting from the crimes of their rela-tives. The first text, dated 890, was found in a tomb located in the suburbs north of Nanchang; the city is shown on map 5 (*Kaogu* 1977.6:401–402). The presence of a bronze mirror, a porcelain plate and bowl, three powder boxes, and a wooden comb point to an adequate but in no way extravagant burial for this middle-aged woman. Her tomb also contains a tomb contract. Written on wood, it records the payment of 99,999 strings of copper money and some cloth to buy her plot from the Elder of Haoli and King Wuyi. As was standard, the rest of the contract warns spirits not to encroach on her grave. Much more unusual, the other text in her grave is written on the back of a cypress figure (*bairen*), whose hands are folded in front of his chest and who wears an official's black hat and long gown with a row of circles on the inner robe. After giving the date, the difficult-to-decipher text says:

> The deceased, the seventeenth woman of the Xiong family of Jingde quarter, Nanchang, Hongzhou prefecture, was fifty-four years old. Today we use 99,999 strings of copper coins to buy this plot. If in the middle of the earth are spirits who call the deceased, her eldest son,

Map 5. Jiangxi Province. Famed in the Song (960–1276) for their love of lawsuits, the people of Jiangxi took extraordinary measures when preparing for the courts of the underworld. They went to their graves carrying contracts, sometimes on wooden figurines, to protect themselves and their living relatives from the dangers of the netherworld. (Drawn by Donna Perry.)

eldest daughter, middle son, middle daughter, youngest son, or youngest daughter, we depend on the cypress people to be informed of all of this. . . . If in the middle of the earth are spirits who call the deceased, and those born in the year of the rat, cow, tiger, rabbit, dragon, snake, horse, ram, monkey, chicken, dog, and pig, we depend on the cypress people to be informed of all of this. Slaves, cattle, houses, and livestock, we depend on the cypress people to be informed of all of this. If in the middle of the earth are spirits who call the eldest grandchild, the middle grandchild, the youngest grandchild, the great grandchildren, or the great, great grandchildren, we depend on the cypress people to be informed of all of this.

The last line of the text is not complete, but it too seems to call on the spirits to observe the "wood covenant" (*mumeng*), or tomb contract, also buried in the tomb.

Tomb contracts were designed to prevent any suits contesting wrongful purchase of a grave plot, but other types of suits could be brought in the

subterranean courts. This repetitive text takes on the quality of an incanta-
tion urging the cypress people to prevent those types of suits, yet it does not
explain who the cypress people are or why they should know of any spirits
calling the deceased or her kin. What powers do the cypress people possess
that make the seventeenth woman of the Xiong family want them to be
informed should any of her offspring be summoned?

One century later, a similar text was carved onto a tablet and buried on
a stone (40 centimeters by 30 centimeters) somewhere in Jiangxi; a rubbing
of both sides survives in the Beijing Library (Beitu, Muzhi 3712), but
because the provenance is unknown and no inventory of grave goods survives, it is impossible to locate the deceased either spatially or socially. The
handwriting on the tablet is rough, with the scribe often omitting the
wood radical in the character for cypress (writing *bai* ["white"] for *bai*
["cypress"]). The text contains additions in the margins, repetitions, and
omissions—all signs of an unschooled writer. One side of the tablet is a
tomb contract dated 995, which warns evil gods and malevolent ghosts
not to intrude on the grave and states that tens of thousands of strings of
cash have been paid to the King Father of the East and the Queen Mother of
the West to purchase the plot. The other side has more to say about the
powers of the cypress people:

> If evil gods and malevolent ghosts are present, then quickly inform
> Lord Lao the Most High (Taishang laojun). The sons and grandsons
> should produce (*chu*) ten thousands and ten thousands of strings of
> cash from the earth, which we depend on the cypress people to
> accept. More than ten thousands and ten thousands of live animals
> including horses, and the six types of livestock—horses, cattle, sheep,
> chickens, dogs, and hogs—which we depend on the cypress people to
> receive and give to the world of the living. The sons and grandsons
> should produce ten thousand fields and silkworms from the earth,
> which we depend on the cypress people to accept. The sons and
> grandsons should produce ten thousands and ten thousands of ingots
> of gold and silver from the earth, which we depend on the cypress
> people to accept. We should produce high ministers and rosters of
> officials, all of them knowledgeable and enlightened, which the sons
> and grandsons depend on the cypress people to receive and send to
> the world of the living.

This part of the text testifies that the cypress people can bring prosper-
ity and success to the living. Usually the living burn replicas of money,

cloth, houses, and servants for the use of the dead in the netherworld. This text speaks of a different type of transaction. The sons and grandsons of the deceased give facsimiles of money, livestock, fields and silkworms, gold and silver ingots, ministers and officials, all in the hopes that the cypress people will be able to turn them into the items they depict and then send them back to the world of the living.

> Should the names of the middle granddaughter and littlest granddaughter be produced (*chu*), we depend on the cypress people to block them. If after the deceased is buried and sent off, the earth should produce the names of the littlest grandson, we depend on the cypress people to cut them into sections. If in the middle of the earth are spirits who call the eldest granddaughter, then the deceased waits and depends on the cypress people to cut these spirits into sections. If in the middle of the earth are spirits who call the names of the eldest grandson, the middle grandson, the new daughters-in-law—the middle daughter-in-law and the youngest daughter-in-law—then they should be blocked. If in the middle of the earth are spirits who come to call the names of the daughters—the middle daughter and the youngest daughter—we depend on the cypress people to cut the spirits into sections. If in the middle of the earth are spirits who come to call the name of the elder or the younger son, we depend on the cypress people to cut them into sections. If in the middle of the earth are spirits who call, the evil gods and malevolent ghosts should be decapitated in the middle of the earth. If in the middle of the earth are spirits who call, the elder son. . . . We give one brick copy to the deceased.

This text gives a better sense of what the cypress people can do to prevent summonses to appear in the courts of the underworld. The cypress people are requested variously to block, to cut into sections, even to decapitate any evil spirits or malevolent ghosts who call the names of the deceased's living kin. The text presents a picture of the family by listing the kin in reverse order of their importance to the deceased, or perhaps just in order of their ages: the middle and littlest granddaughters, the littlest grandson, the eldest granddaughter, the eldest and middle grandsons, the middle and youngest daughters-in-law, the middle and youngest daughters, and finally the elder and younger sons. All of these relatives risk being called by evil spirits and malevolent ghosts, and the cypress people have the power to punish any being that issues such a summons to the underworld courts. If the cypress people can prevent such summonses, then the family will be bound to prosper, succeed at farming, make money, and even produce officials.

The final tomb text from Jiangxi confirms the role of the cypress people in resolving underworld suits. This text, found in Pengze county and shown on map 5, is written on the eight-sided body of a cypress figure with a person's head (fig. 10). Oddly sculpted, it does not look at all Chinese and differs markedly from the cypress official of the 890 tomb. Dated 1090, the figure was found in the tomb of the eighth daughter of the Yi family. She was a woman from an important local family, according to her accompanying biography, which is only partially quoted in the excavation report. She was interred in a wooden coffin enclosed in a stone coffin. With her were buried two pottery vases, a pottery figure, her biography carved on a stone plaque, porcelain plates, wooden combs, iron scissors, an iron knife, an iron stick, a copper mirror, a large ax, and some items of relatively high quality: a silver comb, two silver bracelets, and a pair of gold earrings. Clearly, this was a lavish burial.

Unlike the other two Jiangxi tombs, no contract with the lord of the earth lies in this grave. Instead, those who preside over the world of the dead deputize the cypress figure to prevent any lawsuits against the dead woman's and her husband's families. This is what they say:

> On the twenty-second day of the sixth month of the fifth year of the Yuanyou reign (1090), Teacher Qiao Dongbao of the western region association of the Five-Willow district, Pengze county, Jiang prefecture, died and the grave of his late wife, the eighth woman of the Yi family, was relocated. The Elders of the Haoli, the Envoy of the Celestial Emperor, and the Emissary of the First Emperor's True Law, aware that the spirits disturbed by the relocation of the grave might call the living, issued an enlightened decree that one cypress person should cut off all summonses and suits from the middle of the earth.
>
> If the eighth woman's sons and daughters are summoned, the cypress person should block it. If Teacher is summoned by name, the cypress person should block it. If his wife's family is summoned, the cypress person should block it. If the siblings are summoned, the cypress person should block it. If the in-laws are summoned to testify, the cypress person should block it. If pestilence and plague are summoned, the cypress person should block it. If the fields or

Fig. 10. Protecting the Dead from Summonses. This cypress figure was buried with the eighth daughter of the Yi family in 1090 in Pengze, Jiangxi. It has a human head with ears, eyes, mouth, and nose, on an eight-sided torso. The body bears a text in the form of orders from the gods presiding over the underworld, who instruct the cypress figure to prevent anyone from summoning the children of the dead woman, her husband, her family, her siblings, or her in-laws.

This unique figure differs in shape and in content from more typical tomb contracts, but it is the product of the same impulse: to protect one's kin—and oneself—from the dangers of underworld suits. (Photo courtesy of Chen Baiquan.)

silkworms, or the six domestic animals—horses, cattle, sheep, chickens, dogs, and pigs—are summoned, the cypress person should block it. If the first and second trees are summoned, the cypress person should block it. If the summoning does not end, the cypress person should block it. Quickly, quickly in accordance with the statutes and edicts. (*Wenwu* 1980.5:28–31)

The same phrases are repeated over and over in the list of who cannot be summoned or sued by those in the middle of the earth, that is, the spirits of the dead. The text does not say what the result of such a summons would be, but presumably the people mentioned in the text—the dead woman's children, husband, siblings, family, and in-laws—would suffer some kind of misfortune or even death. This text includes more people than the 990 tablet in its list of those to be protected: not just descendants, but also the deceased's in-laws and siblings are named. Furthermore, those in the middle of the earth have the power to bring epidemics. And they can summon fields, silkworms, farm animals, and trees, and so cause havoc on people's farms. Clearly, the cypress figure is the subterranean equivalent of a henchman whose job it is to prevent anyone from serving his mistress with a court summons.

Both pine and cypress trees were traditionally associated with graves in China (de Groot 1892–1907:1.294–300). One Song-dynasty proverb went "Pine lives one thousand years; cypress, ten thousand" in recognition of the longevity of these two trees (*Shilin guangji,* 1699 9:21a). Coffins were frequently made of both types of wood, in the hope of imparting their strength to the dead. Both trees were planted on graves and were viewed as extensions of the dead; in 1152 one such tree spirit appeared in a dream to warn his descendants not to sell the fir tree he inhabited (*Yijianzhi* 4:585–586). A court case from *Clarity and Lucidity* tells of a pitched battle between one hundred tenants of one man and his neighbors over the right to cut down the trees on the neighbors' family graves. The fighting was so fierce that one of the tree-cutting tenants was killed. The judge sympathized with the neighbors, noting that "to love and protect trees on one's ancestors' tombs is to protect one's family line" (*Qingmingji* 9:330–332).

The association of cypress with protection from underworld suits may have derived from an even more ancient belief that government offices in the underworld were constructed of cypress (Yu 1987:391–392). A court jester in Emperor Wu's reign in the Han dynasty (140–86 B.C.) gave part of the answer to a riddle by saying, "Cypress is the government office of ghosts." The commentator Yan Shigu (581–645) explained this comment by remarking, "It is said that ghosts and spirits prefer the dark and shade, hence they make their government office of pine and cypress trees" (*Han shu* 65:2844–45). If, in the world of the living, the government office, or *yamen*, was where the magistrate heard cases, then by extension the ghosts and spirits must have heard cases in their pine and cypress court. Because cypress wood was thought to have properties that would help protect the living in the courts of the dead, documents on cypress could accompany, and sometimes even replace, tomb contracts.

Daoist Versions of the Spirit Code

At the same time that Jiangxi residents placed models of cypress people in their tombs, a new Daoist sect formed in Jiangxi that also addressed the dangers of underworld suits, the Celestial Heart (*Tianxin*) sect. Its founder, Rao Dongtian, was said to have had his first vision in 994 on Huagai Mountain, Chongren county, Fuzhou prefecture (see map 5).[4] Celestial Heart Daoism did not rely on tomb contracts or cedar henchmen for protection from suits. Instead, it postulated a bureaucratically organized heaven, earth, and underworld, all presided over by the Jade Emperor, who could call on the Office for Expelling the Unsanctioned (*Quxieyuan*), Daoist practitioners, and spirit armies to enforce a body of laws designed to control unruly spirits. Standing in opposition to these misbehaving spirits were the sanctioned deities (*zhengshen*), who obeyed these laws and were thus entitled to both recognition from Daoists and worship from the people.

The members of the Celestial Heart sect used the same term for this body of law that the compilers of *The New Book of Earth Patterns* had: the spirit code. Recall that *Earth Patterns* cited only one article of the spirit

4. Scholars debate the dating of three important texts from this sect. One document, *Secret Essentials of the Most High on Assembling the Perfected for the Relief of the State and Deliverance of the People (Taishang zhuguo jiumin zongzhen biyao)*, poses no problems as its preface is dated 1116. The other two, *An Efficacious Spirit Code from the Marrow of Supreme Clarity (Shangqing gusui lingwen guilü)* and *The Correct Rites of the Celestial Heart of Supreme Clarity (Shangqing tianxin zhengfa)*, may also date from the late Northern Song, as Robert Hymes (n.d.) argues, or from the Southern Song, as Judith Boltz (1987:33–35) contends. Because the text of *An Efficacious Spirit Code* appears word for word in *Secret Essentials*, it surely dates from the end of the Northern Song.

code: "To bury without beheading the grass, to buy land without drawing up a contract, these are called wrongful burial and will bring great misfortune" (*Dili xinshu* 14:11b). Most lay people probably thought a spirit code existed, but only a few articles were known to humans. The leaders of the Celestial Heart sect took a different stance, the same as that of the earlier Celestial Master Daoists who had drawn up *The Spirit Code of Nüqing*. They all believed that such a code existed, and its contents could be known in full to Daoist specialists.

Deng Yougong, the author of one text giving the contents of the code, *An Efficacious Spirit Code from the Marrow of Supreme Clarity* (*Shangqing gusui lingwen guilü*), explained in his preface that the contents of the code had been lost over time as practitioners had concentrated on writing talismans and using charms to cure illnesses. *An Efficacious Spirit Code*, Dong claimed, was based on one text revealed to founding immortal Rao Dongtian when he was a clerk in a government office. Rao held, "Although heaven and humankind differ, the principles of law are the same, so one can consult the laws of the country as a reference (*Shangqing gusu lingwen guilü*, preface:2b). And so the founding immortal voiced a concept familiar to everyone but voiced by no one: the netherworld had laws and the principles underlying them were the same as those on earth. The Celestial Heart practitioners did not claim to have originated the laws, merely to have discovered them. Once he had transcribed the 120 articles of *An Efficacious Spirit Code*, Deng burned a copy and asked the Office for Expelling the Unsanctioned and other offices to send a clear sign that his version of the code was complete (*Shangqing gusu lingwen guilü*, preface:3b). We can assume that because he received no negative sign, he was confident that his text was indeed the correct one.

Because the principles underlying the laws of the spirits are the same as those for the laws of man, Deng was able to consult the penal codes in drawing up his *Efficacious Spirit Code*. Their influence is evident. Like *The Tang Code* and its successors, this code is addressed to the bureaucrats who enforce it, not necessarily the beings affected by it. Much of the code concerns bureaucratic infringements such as the failure to draft a memorial properly, or to respond expeditiously to an order from above. The code gives detailed criteria for promotions, and their timing.

The punishments meted out follow the same order of severity as those in the penal code: light beatings, heavy beatings, penal servitude, exile, and death (Johnson 1979:14–15). The crimes, though, are specific to ghosts and spirits. Punishments vary with the crime. So we have: "All ghosts and spirits who improperly take over the souls of people are to be exiled 3,000 third-miles. If violent death occurs because of this, then they are to be executed." And "All ghosts and spirits who steal people's wealth totaling 1,000 cash or more are to be exiled 2,000 third-miles. If the stolen goods do not total 1,000 cash, then hard labor for two years" (*Shangqing gusu lingwen guilü* 1:6a).

One section of the code is addressed to the spirits of the dead. The first article refers to underworld suits:

> If any of the dead who have grievances against the living and are in
> the process of suing them in the subterranean government courts,
> before the suit is resolved, should without authorization bring bizarre
> happenings or excessive harm to people, or take advantage of other
> people's luck to seek positive merits or rewards, even though these
> offenses do not hurt people's lives and only cause trouble, all those
> bringing suits to get revenge on peaceful people should be locked up
> in the subterranean government offices and their forms should be
> obliterated (*Shangqing gusu lingwen guilü* 1:8a; Hymes n.d. II:16).

This article acknowledges that the dead may have good reason to bring suit, but it forbids them to punish the living before their suits have been heard. *An Efficacious Spirit Code* goes on to specify punishments for the souls of the dead who set fire to people's houses, who frighten livestock, who try to stay in the world of the living, who seek offerings, who evade arrest, or who fight with the clerks and soldiers sent to apprehend them. The code threatens with exile or obliteration the masterless souls of the dead who pretend to be the souls of the newly dead in hopes of getting offerings, but allows the souls of the dead to appear to their own families in hope of obtaining food (*Shangqing gusu lingwen guilü* 1:8a–9a). Another text of the school, *The Correct Rites of the Celestial Heart of Supreme Clarity* (*Shangqing tianxin zhengfa* 5:8a–b), instructs officials on how to draw up a talisman (*fu*) to help people who are troubled by an underworld suit.

The author confesses in *An Efficacious Spirit Code* that the punishments are difficult to carry out. "One should thoughtfully study the distinction between light and heavy offenses and follow them to determine punishments. But still, ghosts and spirits give off shadows and cannot be grasped or seen clearly. One has no means of giving lashings as punishment for a crime, and it is difficult to administer punishments" (*Shangqing gusu lingwen guilü*, preface:2b). Still, he does not resolve one of the great mysteries of this text: how could one obliterate the form of a deity? The Chinese did occasionally beat or behead images of deities who failed to perform miracles, but the Celestial Heart practitioners do not advocate such a direct method. They have such confidence in their understanding of the workings of heaven in general, and of the Office for Expelling the Unsanctioned in particular, that they depend on them to administer punishments to unruly spirits in the other world.

A Lay View

Hong Mai (1123–1202), a contemporary of Deng Yougong and also a native of Jiangxi, was an assiduous collector of strange anecdotes, which he published in installments as *The Record of the Listener* (Hansen 1990:17–22). *The Record* contains many accounts of the underworld courts from a lay point of view. Hong came from a family of officials and was himself an official. Because he and his family hired different doctors, monks, and Daoist practitioners whenever they faced an insoluble problem or illness, he is a sympathetic reporter, and his collection gives a sense of the enormous variety of strange tales circulating throughout the empire in his lifetime.

One of his stories illustrates how the punishment of a deity might occur (Hymes n.d. II:19–21; *Yijianzhi* 15:15:1693–94). A rich man in Ningbo died in the prime of life, came back after his death to possess his former concubine, and spoke through her. He explained that a local deity, the God of the Three Chambers, had taken him by force to be his servant. After two years he was given permission to sue in the courts of Mount Tai, where a low official told him to go to the Office for Expelling the Unsanctioned. There the victim made his plaint and watched as a piece of paper circled the god's body, caught on fire, and burned him to ashes. This was just the kind of punishment Deng Yougong must have had in mind when he compiled his penal code: effected in the other world, it did destroy the culprit. The rich man's concubine in this tale appears sufficiently knowledgeable about the teachings of Celestial Heart Daoism to be acquainted with the term for the Office for Expelling the Unsanctioned. Perhaps she actually was, but a more likely explanation is that an unnamed Celestial Heart practitioner was summoned to explain the incident, and Hong Mai gives the practitioner's interpretation of the garbled speech of the concubine.

Because the practitioners of Celestial Heart Daoism thought they had a technique for controlling ghosts and spirits whose marketability hinged on its mystery, they did not want potential customers to know their secrets. Deng did not write down the spirit code for the benefit of lay people. He assumed Daoist practitioners would study the entire body of Celestial Heart ritual, as he himself had done at four Daoist centers (three in Jiangxi and one in Anhui). Daoist ritual was an esoteric tradition whose power hinged on correct transmission by sanctioned masters. The important texts of the Celestial Heart school had to be memorized, because the information they contained about a single ritual was dispersed in several chapters and they could not be consulted while the ritual was being conducted (Hymes n.d. II:5). Some Song officials studied Daoist techniques of exorcism and gained expertise in Daoist rituals (Boltz 1993:256–264). But ordinary people did not have access to these texts—indeed *An Efficacious Spirit Code* instructs the officials of the rites (*faguan*) to keep them secret (*Shangqing gusu lingwen guilü* 2:2b–3a). Lay people had to hire Celestial Heart practitioners to intercede on their behalf in underworld courts.

Lu Shizhong, the author of a Daoist ritual manual that combined Celestial Heart techniques with those of another Daoist sect active in the early twelfth century, was himself an active practitioner who appears in *The Record* (Boltz 1987:36–37; 1993:260–262). In 1125 a man who had been prefect in Shandong fell ill. He asked a friend to write a prayer for him and died soon after a Daoist purification ceremony (*jiao*) was conducted on his behalf. The friend lost consciousness for three days, and when he awoke, reported having gone to a courtroom where he saw the dead prefect in handcuffs and shackles. The prefect said: "Go back and tell my wife to do good deeds quickly to save me. This is because of what happened at Yunzhou [now Dongping county, Shandong]." When his wife heard the contents of the vision, she tearfully explained that the previous year her husband had killed five hundred rebels who had already surrendered. She then hired Daoist Lu Shizhong to conduct another purification ceremony on his behalf (*Yijianzhi* 2:6:232). Lu does not appear in this tale until after the determination of guilt, and he does not challenge that decision.

Hong Mai explains that the literati often consulted Lu in cases involving ghosts, and two years later, in 1127, after the north had fallen to the Jin armies, a district magistrate summoned Lu to help his second daughter, who was possessed. When she saw Lu, she suddenly recovered consciousness, and her elder sister spoke through her. She explained that the second daughter had prevented her from getting married by denying her a gold hairpin, which she needed for her dowry. After listening to her narrative, Lu concluded, "Her case is a strong one." Unable to intervene, he advised the girl's family to pray on her behalf, but she died the next day (*Yijianzhi* 2:7:237–239). For all his reputation, Lu admits that he could not alter a fair decision on the part of the netherworld courts. One cannot help wondering if he was able to save the official who had killed the five hundred surrendering men, but we are never told.

Other Daoist practitioners also were unable to change the verdicts of the netherworld courts, Hong Mai writes. The brother of an examination candidate in Huaizhou (Qinyang county, Henan) sought the help of a Celestial Heart Master when he noticed his brother looking increasingly haggard and after he had heard noises coming from the brother's bedroom. The Master was able to summon the ghost of the woman tormenting the examination candidate, who explained: "I am your former wife of three lives ago. This woman is your daughter. You went to other prefectures as a merchant and fell in love with a prostitute, never to return. I was poor and had no means of survival, so I took our daughter and we jumped to our deaths in a well. I sued you in the court of the emperor." The netherworld emperor ruled that the man's good deeds could not make up for his crime, even if it had occurred in an earlier life, and that he would die ten years later, as indeed he did (*Yijianzhi* 1:13:111–12).

These reports all rely on the device of the underworld judgment to account for the deaths of the man who killed five hundred, of the woman who prevented her sister's wedding, and of the man who had abandoned his family in a previous existence. The justice meted out is not absolute, for good deeds can lessen the punishment for any given offense. Strikingly, the guilty are punished in these underworld courts in a way they do not seem to have been in the real-world courts, and Celestial Heart Masters are unable to overturn the verdicts. Hong Mai's inclusion of these unflattering accounts of the Celestial Heart Masters highlights the importance of *The Record* as a source: unlike earlier sources, *The Record* is nonsectarian and favors neither Buddhist nor Daoist interpretations of the netherworld courts. *The Record* also reveals that common people did not always consult Celestial Heart practitioners. They devised their own solutions to problems with the underworld courts, and when they visited the underworld, whether in their dreams or when unconscious, they often did so alone.

The tales Hong Mai collected indicate that belief in the underworld courts was common throughout his native Jiangxi. One report tells of a magistrate in Guixi county (see map 5), who was sitting with his wife when he saw the ghost of a soldier jailed the previous year whom the magistrate had wrongfully put to death. The magistrate died the next day (*Yijianzhi* 11:3:1244). In a similar case, a woman in Raozhou, also shown on map 5, regularly spotted a ghost. When the woman threatened to summon a Celestial Heart practitioner in order to obtain a judgment from the god of Mount Tai, the ghost identified herself as the spirit of the concubine who had lived next door, who had been driven to hang herself by a jealous wife, and who had yet to be reborn. The woman promised to make an offering in the concubine's name at a rite to give food to hungry ghosts on land and water (*shuiluhui*), to be conducted at a nearby Buddhist monastery. After the woman had made the offering, the ghost appeared in a dream to thank her (*Yijianzhi* 13:9:1456).

Other ghosts sued for different reasons. The ghost of a man's first wife caused his second wife in Changsha to fall ill. They summoned a medium, who diagnosed the source of the problem as the first wife, who must have sued her husband for bigamy in the courts of the dead. The medium urged the official to draw up a bill of divorce, which she then burned with paper money as an offering to the first wife. Hong Mai comments at the end of the tale, "For the living to divorce a dead wife was not heard of in the past" (*Yijianzhi* 4:12:639; de Pee 1991:71–72).

While this ghost wanted a divorce, others were thwarted in their desire to marry. One girl from Fuzhou, Jiangxi, fell ill in the summer of 1196, and lay in bed for two months. Eleven days after she had stopped getting up, she suddenly explained to her astonished parents:

> In the ninth month of last year, Elder Brother Lin 107 passed our gate, saw me and liked me, and returned to tell his elder brother 105 that he wanted to marry me. Then a matchmaker came to discuss the offer, but you refused. Then Gentleman Lin became depressed and fell ill. He died on the nineteenth day of the fifth month. He sued in the underworld court to marry me. Now he has come with me and is waiting by the gate. Remember that when I was alive, I spun 33 bolts of open tabby, 70 bolts of plain silk, and 156 Chinese feet of coarse silk. Hurry and give them back to me.

After her parents prepared the textiles, she bade them goodbye. "Now I am going with Gentleman Lin to western Sichuan to be merchants," and died (*Yijianzhi* 15:10:1642; Sheng 1990:137).

Her parents' offense, like that of the sister who begrudged her elder sister a gold hairpin, was to prevent the marriage. Their punishment was to lose their daughter and the textiles she wove for her dowry, which could be exchanged between this world and the netherworld. The young woman does not say so, but the reader can infer that a subterranean judge ruled that the marriage should take place, that the daughter must join Gentleman Lin in the underworld, that she must pay the same dowry as she would have in the real world, and that the two lovers would be reborn in western Sichuan as merchants.

One of the most informative accounts of the workings of the underworld courts is from a resident of Hong Mai's hometown, Poyang, who lost consciousness for two days, during which he traveled to the underworld. He visited a courtroom, where he saw a neighbor in a scholar's robe and his sister wearing wooden neck braces that restrained their hands and crouching before a kingly figure. Two guards carrying heavy sticks interrogated the two: "When your father was alive, he had paper money with a face value of 170 strings. Where is the money now?" When the king discovered that the narrator had been born in the year of the pig, he berated his clerks: "Wrong! Wrong! This order was to arrest someone in the year of the monkey, so send him back quickly." (This description of a summons issued according to the year of birth tallies with the 890 text from the tomb of the seventeenth woman of the Xiong family.) The narrator was led away and awoke in the world of the living. After several days he called on the family of the examination candidate and was told the brother and sister had been allowed to return to life after swearing that they had never received any of the missing money (*Yijianzhi* 14:9:1540). In this tale the underworld courts appear in an unfavorable light. The netherworld officials erroneously charge the official's children with embezzling money, and they mistakenly summon the narrator.

Preparing Documents for the Courts of the Netherworld

The Record contains one account that so illuminates the relationship between the netherworld and the this-worldly courts that it merits being translated in full.

> Registrar Xia of Ningbo and the wealthy Mr. Lin together bought a concession to sell wine in a government store. They sold the wine wholesale to other stores, who paid their share depending on how much wine they sold. After many years Mr. Lin owed Register Xia 2,000 strings of cash. Registrar Xia realized he would not get the

money back, so he sued Mr. Lin in the prefectural court. The clerks
took a bribe and twisted his words to reverse the story so that
Registrar Xia became the debtor. Prior to this Mr. Lin had ordered
eight of his underlings to change the accounts to show that he was
in the right. Registrar Xia refused to change his story and was put in
jail and beaten. Accordingly he fell ill.

In the prefecture lived a man named Liu Yuan Balang, who was
generous and did not trouble himself over details, and who was upset
by the treatment of Registrar Xia. He proclaimed to the crowd, "My
district has this type of wrongful injustice. Registrar Xia is telling the
truth about the money from the wine, but is miserable in jail. What
is the point of prefectural and county officials? I wish they would
call me as a witness, as I myself could tell the truth, which would
definitely cause someone else to be beaten."

Lin's eight underlings secretly heard what he said and were
afraid it would leak out and harm their case, so they sent two
eloquent men who extended their arms to invite Liu to drink with
them at a flag-decorated pavilion, where they talked about the case
and said: "Why are you concerning yourself with other people's
affairs? Have some more wine." When the wine was done, they
pulled out paper money with a face value of 200 strings and gave it
to Liu saying, "We know that your household is poor, so this is a
little to help you."

Liu furiously replied, "The likes of you start with unrighteous
intent and then bring an unrighteous case. Now you again use
unrighteous wealth to try to corrupt me. I would prefer to die to
hunger. I refuse even one cash of your money. This twisting of the
straight and distortion of the truth is definitely not going to be
resolved in this world. If there is no court in the netherworld, then
let the matter rest. If there is such a court, it must have a place
where wrongs can be righted." Then he called to the bar owner,
"How much was today's bill?"

He said, "1,800 cash."

Liu said, "Three people drank together, so I owe 600." He
suddenly took off his coat and pawned it to pay the bill.

After a while Registar Xia's illness worsened, and he was
released from jail to die. *As he was about to die, he warned his sons:*
"I die a wronged man. Place in my coffin all the previous leases for

the wine concessions and contracts specifying each person's share, so that I can vigorously sue in the underworld."

After just one month Mr. Lin's eight underlings abruptly died, one by one.

After another month Liu was at home when he suddenly felt shaky and everything went dark. He said to his wife: "What I see is not good. It must be that Registrar Xia's case is being heard, and I'm wanted as a witness, so I must die. But since I have led a peaceful life with no other bad deeds, I probably will return to life, so don't bury my corpse for a period of three days. After that you can decide what to do." Late that night he lost consciousness.

After two nights he sat up with a start and said: "Recently two government clerks chased me. We went 100 third-miles and reached the government office. We encountered an official wearing a green robe, who came out from a room in the hall. When I looked at him, I realized it was Registrar Xia. He apologized repeatedly and said: "I am sorry to trouble you to come. All the documents are in good order; we just want you to serve as a witness briefly. It shouldn't be too taxing." Then I saw Lin's eight underlings, all wearing one neck brace that was 15 or 16 Chinese feet long and had eight holes for their heads.

Suddenly we heard that the king was in his palace, and the clerks led us to the court. The king said: "The matter of Xia's family needn't be discussed. Only tell me everything that happened when you drank wine upstairs."

I testified: "These two men sent an invitation. Then we drank five cups of wine and bought three types of soup. They wanted to give me paper money with a face value of 200 strings of cash, but I didn't dare accept it."

The king looked left and right, sighed, and said: "The world still has good people like this. They really are important. We should discuss how to reward him, so let's take a look at his allotted life span."

A clerk went out, and after a moment came back and said, "A total of seventy-nine years."

The king said: "A poor man doesn't accept money—how can we not reward him? Add another decade to his life span." He then ordered the clerk who had brought me to take me to see the jail in the earth. Then I saw many types of people and prisoners in fetters. They were all from the city or the counties of my prefecture. Some bore cangues and some were tied up; some were sentenced to be beaten. When they saw me coming, one by one they cried out and sobbed. They then told me their names and addresses, and asked me to return to the world to tell their families. Some said they had borrowed somebody's money, some said they had borrowed somebody's rent, some said they had borrowed somebody's possessions, and some said they had stolen people's land and harvest. They all asked their families to return their goods so as to lessen the sentences they had to serve in the underworld. Others asked for money and others for merit to be transferred by their relatives. I couldn't bear to look at them and turned away, and I still heard ceaseless sighs.

As I went again to the palace, the king said, "Since you have completed your tour, when you return to life, please tell each detail to the living and teach them about the underworld court." I bowed and took my leave.

As I went out the gate, the clerk seeing me off wanted money, and I steadfastly refused. He berated me. "For two or three days I have served you. How is it that you don't even say thank you. Moreover, give me 10,000 strings." I again refused him saying, "I myself have nothing to eat, so where am I going to get extra money for you?" The clerk then grabbed and knocked off my topknot. He pushed me on the ground, and then I regained consciousness.

He rubbed his head, which was already bald, and his topknot lay between the pillows. Sheriff Wang Yi from Jinan, Shandong, lived in Ningbo at the time and himself saw that it was as told here.

Around 1180, Liu had his eightieth birthday, and he fell ill. Sheriff Wang went to see him and was very concerned. Liu said, "Sheriff, you needn't worry. I haven't died." Afterward he turned out not to be ill. He was probably counting the additional years the king of the netherworld had given him.

When he reached ninety-one, he died. Sheriff Wang is now the Administrator of Public Order in Raozhou, Jiangxi. This story was told by Administrator Wang. (*Yijianzhi* 9:5:1086–88; emphasis added)

The anecdote begins with the facts of the case: how the debtor, Mr. Lin, bribes the clerks in the local court to frame the original lender, Registrar

Xia. The one person willing to speak out on Registrar Xia's behalf is Liu Yuan Balang. In his eloquent refusal to be bought off by Mr. Lin's underlings, he raises the possibility of a court in the underworld where wrongs can be righted. Registrar Xia dies, after instructing his sons to bury with him all the relevant documents concerning Mr. Lin's unpaid debt, so that he can sue in the underworld court. This crucial passage provides the rationale for the burial of tomb contracts. One can submit the same documentary evidence to the court systems both above and below the earth. Placement in the coffin ensures that a given item will arrive in the underworld courts at the same time as the deceased does.

After Mr. Lin's eight underlings die, Liu Yuan Balang has a premonition that he is going to be summoned to testify, and he loses consciousness. The narrative resumes when he wakes up and recounts his experiences. He sees that the eight underlings have been placed in a cangue. Liu visits a kind of purgatory on his way home, where people tell him they "borrowed" money, rent, and possessions. Some ask for money. Others ask their family members to send them merits, as they did in *Records of Miraculous Retribution*. Their requests reflect the Buddhist belief that merits accrued by one person for doing good deeds can be transferred to another, even posthumously. When the runner who has accompanied Liu asks for a bribe, the always righteous Liu refuses, and he wakes up in this world after the clerk pushes him to the ground. The proof that he did indeed journey to the netherworld is twofold—his false topknot lies dislodged on his pillow, and he lives for an extra decade past eighty. The story concludes with Hong Mai's explanation of how he heard it.

The account does not reveal the fate of the real villain of the tale, Mr. Lin. The reader knows only that Registrar Xia succeeded in having the eight underlings punished. Perhaps Mr. Lin has already been punished, but Liu simply does not see him because he was not party to the bribery attempt. Or Mr. Lin's punishment may come later. Or perhaps it will be Mr. Lin's descendants who suffer the consequences of his crime.

This narrative is about justice. Registrar Xia is unable to obtain justice in human courts, but, as Liu Yuan Balang suspects, the underworld does have a court where wrongs can be righted. Many accounts of visits to the netherworld tell of bureaucratic incompetence, but the people summoned by mistake are allowed to return to life. Strikingly, no one is ever punished in the subterranean court for a crime he or she did not commit. Hong Mai seems, like many of his contemporaries, to have believed in the general principle of retribution, that good would be rewarded and evil punished, whether in this life or the next—or even two lives later, as was the case with the man who abandoned his wife and daughter.

Hong Mai tells of a man and his six sons in Fuzhou, Jiangxi, who prospered for twenty years as tenant farmers. Then each member of the family began to have trouble, either falling ill or being arrested for different crimes. The father consulted a local fortune-teller, who said that the previous generation of the family had done something that involved boiling water and fire, and that he could see two ghosts waiting for the family by the doors of the courtroom. The father admitted that his father, who had a kiln in which he smelted metals, had borrowed silk gauze worth 20,000 cash and agreed on a date to repay the loan. When the two merchants came to claim their goods, he pushed them into the kiln and burned them alive. The murder took place forty years before the family began to suffer.

Hong concludes the tale, saying: "People who discuss this said the balance of good and evil went back to the grandfather. He had died well, but the calamities brought by the wronged spirits of the dead waited for the grandchildren. The justice of the underworld can be slow and twisted, but ultimately it catches up with those who have not performed good deeds to offset their crimes. Those families with accumulated wrongs must have extra calamities. Believe this!" (*Yijianzhi* 14:1:1471–72). Hong's tone indicates that he is one of "people who discuss this" and that he has reached this conclusion. The grandfather's crimes are multiple. He reneged on a debt. He killed two innocent men. And he did so in such a gruesome way that both corpses turned to ashes, meaning that the two men could not receive a proper burial, nor could their bodies be reborn in the underworld. It was only right that his descendants should suffer.

The widespread lay belief that dangerous spirits inhabited graves continued into the Yuan dynasty. One writer, Liu Xun (1240–1319), told of two families whose tombs lay on the same forested hill. They had coexisted peacefully for generations, but then, prompted by outsiders, they went to court. The presiding official decided against summoning village officials and neighbors to draw a new border between the two families' plots because he thought it would disrupt the people and the spirits of the dead who lived in the hill. Instead, he drew up the following agreement:

> Party A's tombs are protected by Party B's hill, and Party B's protection is the hill, so their protection is this hill.
>
> Party B's hill is shielded by Party A's graves, and Party A's protection is the hill, so their protection is this hill.

It is forbidden to cut down even one tree.

It is forbidden to trespass.

It is forbidden to have disputes over this land.

If anyone violates this oath, the spirits of the hill will put him to death, cause his family to decline, and prevent the birth of any descendants.

The two parties drank wine, signed the contract, then registered the agreement with the local government office as proof of their sincerity (*Yinju tongyi* 16:5a–6a; reference courtesy of Barend ter Haar). The chilling final clause of the contract credits the spirits of the hill with the power to destroy a family.

The underworld courts admitted evidence and contracts from this world that had been placed in graves to help them better judge the conduct of the dead. Evidence from the underworld was also admitted by this-worldly courts, if a Yuan-dynasty collection of miscellaneous notes is to be believed. In 1343 a resident of a town in northern Shaanxi, near the modern border with Inner Mongolia, accused a fortune-teller of murdering three people. Underlying the standard bureaucratic format of the complaint of sorcery is certainly a grudge: the accuser and the fortune-teller appear to have been enemies of long standing. The accuser cited the testimony of three ghosts and equipment found in his room (including paper models of humans) as evidence against the fortune-teller, and when the investigations confirmed the three people's disappearance, the fortune-teller was sentenced to death by dismemberment and his wife was exiled to Hainan (*Nancun chuogeng lu* 13:155–57; ter Haar n.d.).

The Underworld Courts in Yuan Drama

This real-world case in which the testimony of his deceased victims helped convict a murderer may have been an instance of life imitating art. Several Yuan dramatists wrote courtroom dramas in which the testimony of ghosts enabled magistrates to convict murderers who would otherwise have gone free. Ming-dynasty versions of two plays contain such scenes (Hayden 1978:10). In Guan Hanqing's *Injustice Done to Dou E* (*Dou E yuan*) the spirit of the protagonist, a girl wrongfully executed for poisoning her father-in-law, appears in the courtroom. He sold her as a child before he took the civil service examinations and returns to his home district as an inspector general, whose task it is to review all capital cases. When Dou E's ghost appears in court to help her father identify the real murderer, everyone can see her (*Yuanquxuan* 1514–15; Liu Jung-en 1972:154).

In Zheng Tingyu's *Flower of the Back Courtyard (Houting hua)*, a ghost appears to Judge Bao in the form of a whirlwind that only he can see (*Yuanquxuan* 941; Hayden 1987:158). As discussed in chapter 4, Judge Bao was a real-world official famous for his honesty. The official history of the Song dynasty tells us that the people of Kaifeng even said, "Bribery will get you nowhere, for Old Bao, the king of the underworld, is here" (*Songshi* 316:10317; Hayden 1978:18). In 1180 the famous poet and collector of tales Yuan Haowen (1190–1257) relates that Judge Bao intervened to save a girl kidnapped and brought by troops to just north of the Jin–Southern Song border.

> Because the girl was very attractive, the houses of prostitution
> wanted to buy her at a high price but she refused. When her master
> thrashed her, she fell ill. People in the village sympathized but had
> no way to rescue her. A woman medium was possessed, summoned
> the girl's owner, and scolded him soundly. He asked what he had
> done and to whom he was speaking.
>
> The medium replied: "I am in charge of the office of speedy
> retribution. How dare you take my granddaughter for a prostitute? I
> give you ten days. If you don't marry her off to a good family, I will
> cut off your family line."
>
> The man married her off within a few days. (*Xu Yijianzhi* 1:2–3)

At the time of the tale, Judge Bao, whose voice the medium assumed, had died more than a hundred years earlier. Yuan Haowen comments that all peasants, even those in the hills and remote places, knew that Judge Bao was in charge of speedy retribution (*subaosi*) between earth and the netherworld in the government of Mount Tai, the shadow bureaucracy under the earth (*Xu Yijianzhi* 1:2; Hayden 1987:20–21; Takahashi 1991:44). A 1285 inscription from Mount Tai lists a total of seventy-five underworld offices under three higher supervisors and six courts (*Taishan zhi* 18:27a–28b; Chavannes 1910:364–369). In this hierarchy Judge Bao's position was one of seventy-five; but, like Mercury, his post as a messenger assumed unusual importance. He appears in the same capacity in a Yuan-dynasty play (*Yongle dadian xiwen sanzhong* 317).

The continuities between underworld courts and this-world courts were so notable that playwrights set certain scenes in the courts of the underworld. One play by Zheng Tingyu, *The Wronged Creditor (Yuanjia zhaizhu*), takes up the story of a suit against the local earth god first mentioned in an 1197 temple inscription from a temple to Prefect Cui in Weixian, Shandong (*Weixianzhi* 40:37a–38a; Takahashi 1991:64). Prefect Cui became a popular deity whose temples were built all over northern China in the thirteenth and fourteenth centuries. His jurisdiction was not limited to the human world. One Yuan-dynasty temple inscription from Luzhou (now Changzhi, Shanxi) tells of a woman who came to the prefect because her son, a woodcutter, had been killed by a tiger. Prefect Cui sent a report to the god of walls and moats, the counterpart of the district magistrate among the gods, and the tiger appeared and crouched before him. Prefect Cui ordered him dismembered (*Yishan wenji* 5:1a–2a; Takahashi 1991:58–59).

The Wronged Creditor is set in Fuyang county in Hebei, the purported home of the legendary Prefect Cui, who, like Judge Bao, was credited with being able to go back and forth between the courts of the living and the dead. It was Prefect Cui whom Emperor Taizong encountered in his visit to the underworld earlier in this chapter. The play's protagonist, Zhang Shanyou, goes to the court of Prefect Cui to sue King Yanluo and his messenger, the local earth god, whom he holds responsible for the premature deaths of his two sons and his wife. Zhang believes that the jurisdiction of the courts extends to the gods, but Prefect Cui refuses to hear the case on the grounds that he cannot pass judgment on the gods of the underworld government. He ironically protests: "How can I be compared with Judge Bao, who passed judgment in the world of the living by day and the world of the dead by night? You should go somewhere else to make your plaint" (*Yuanquxuan* 1141). In actuality he does have Judge Bao's ability to travel between the two courts, and he arranges for Zhang to journey to the netherworld. There Zhang meets King Yanluo, who brings his two sons and wife before him. They explain that they have died because of their crimes in this and previous lives (*Yuanquxuan* 1142–44). The playwright does not have to describe the underworld court at length; only a few phrases are required to alert members of the audience that they are in the underworld.

These plays present a different view of the underworld than do other sources. They poke fun at its overly bureaucratic ways, whereas other sources describe the calamities visited upon the living by those same courts. Strikingly, even though the plays are spoofs, justice is done.

Daoist Spirit Codes, Continued

As belief in the underworld courts persisted in the Yuan, so too did the Daoists' urge to draft spirit codes. Sometime after 1356, texts from many different Daoist traditions, each with its own ritual techniques, were gathered into the 268-chapter *Corpus of Daoist Ritual* (*Daofa huiyuan*) (van der Loon 1979:401–405; Boltz 1987:47–49). Two chapters are devoted to a spirit code entitled "The Heavenly Code as Proclaimed by Nüqing in Vermillion from the Mixed Cave on High" (*Taishang hundong chiwen Nüqing zhaoshu tianlü*), which draws on earlier codes including those of the Celestial Heart masters. Much more systematized than theirs, this code is divided into sections for sanctioned gods (*zhengshen*), earth gods, stove gods, ghosts of the dead, unsanctioned gods (*xieshen*), mountain gods, well gods, toilet gods, judges of the underworld, the living, and Daoist officials of rites, among others. Each group is given its own set of statutes. For example, the unsanctioned gods, more mischievous than others, are threatened with having their shapes divided for tossing bricks and throwing tiles at people (*Daofa huiyuan* 251:12b). The code envisions a hierarchy of gods each of whom reports to his superiors, and the Daoist practitioners are divided into nine ranks, just like the officials of the Chinese civil service.

The first article in the code states: "All sanctioned gods are not to accept suits from the people. Those who do will receive nine years of hard labor." Similarly, "All unsanctioned gods who accept suits from the living will have their forms divided." Only officials of rites are permitted to accept the suits of the people, and they are to pass them promptly to the god of Mount Tai. Failure to do so will result in one year of hard labor. When someone dies, the code explains, the sanctioned gods are to send off those who have been called to the world of the dead only after they have received the appropriate documents. If they do not, they will be exiled. The earth gods who are to escort the souls of the dead to the underworld courts will be beheaded if they do not deliver their charges to the correct place, while those who solicit bribes of one coin or more will have their forms divided (*Daofa huiyuan* 251–252).

Once the souls have arrived in the underworld, a host of regulations greets them. They are not to return to the world of the living except on the day of death, they are not to wound or cause the death of any people against whom they bear grudges, and they are not to appear in the dreams of the living. Several of the regulations concern underworld suits. The souls of those who died prematurely and who sue the living will be beheaded. The souls of the dead who have a legitimate grievance against the living are entitled to only one hearing. If the courts find in favor of the complainant, then those deciding questions of rebirth must be informed. If the souls of the dead falsify a complaint, or claim someone as an acquaintance whom they do not know, or call someone a relative who is not related, or accuse someone of having wronged them who has not, the underworld courts will not accept the case (*Daofa huiyuan* 251:8b–11a).

The judges of the subterranean courts (*disiguan*) face even more regulations than do the souls of the dead. Many concern the need to use correct bureaucratic forms and to be prompt in responding to the requests of Daoist practitioners. The regulations stipulating the need for the judges to be honest have broader implications. The judges are threatened with execution for accepting money or goods from the dead, and for twisting the law and not being fair, or for unjustly deciding punishments. Judges who add or deduct from people's life spans will be given nine years of hard labor, and those who do so deliberately will be executed. Judges who do not carry out the law as recorded in the administrative regulations and statutes and who insult their subordinates will be replaced. Judges of the dead who find

> the innocent guilty, those without grievances against them as having grievances against them, those in the wrong in the right, those without grievances to be aggrieved, those without residual karma to have karma, those with good deeds to have none—any judge who does things like this will have his shape divided. And any judge who deliberately detains someone in hope of payment will have the punishment increased one degree.

This list resonates strongly with potential offenses in the real-world courts, as does another article:

> If the judges of the subterranean court take the living into custody for having committed a crime, . . . then they are permitted to keep them only fifty days and nights. Those whose crimes are great should not go past one hundred days and nights. If they should not be released to be reborn into the next life, one should petition one's superiors. Violators, nine years of hard labor. (*Daofa huiyuan* 251:19b–23a)

Was this law code really written with the judges of the subterranean courts in mind? Would its requirements not apply just as well to the judges of the living? Surely real-world judges did not respect a fifty-day or hundred-day limit on detention of suspects. Surely the system of judicial review did not ensure that all judges were always punished for finding the innocent guilty or the guilty innocent. These rules have a wistful, idealistic quality to them. It is as if the compilers wanted things in the underworld to function the way they wished their own court system would—even though they knew it did not.

Conclusion

As early as the Six Dynasties, if not before, underworld courts provided those who had not obtained justice in the real-world courts with a second chance. Although underworld suits were a legal option open only to the dead, tales about them must have offered a curious satisfaction to those who suffered in the earthly courts. Strikingly, the dead never give up their grievances. The murder victims who return to the world of the living to accuse their killers are still hungry for justice. The man whose fields were taken by his neighbor may already be dead, but he persists in suing so that his neighbor can be punished. The five hundred soldiers who were killed after their surrender continue to seek justice in the underworld courts as did the women whose engagements were blocked. When the dying Registrar Xia instructs his sons to put all his receipts in his grave, he still has the will to go after his debtor, Mr. Lin, until justice is done. None of the dead in these accounts ever decries underworld justice as too little, too late. They, like their readers, want to see justice done, regardless of the fact the underworld courts are the only place where it can be done. The courts provided a forum in which justice can be (but is not always) carried out, even if it is after the fact and even if it is in the underworld.

8

The Courts of the Living and the Courts of the Dead

Anyone reading these pages will recognize how strongly ordinary people's understanding of tomb contracts and the subterranean legal system derived from their experiences with this-worldly counterparts. The same problems that plague earthly contracts appear in the netherworld, as do many of the same solutions. People tried, and often failed, to make the signing of a contract coincide with the time of payment, because they hoped to lessen the possibility of suits. For once, their interests coincided with those of government officials who hoped more definitive contracts would lead to fewer suits and a lighter workload.

Everyone struggled, too, to understand transactions in which all the correct procedures had been followed but a deeper law had been violated. The judges writing in *Clarity and Lucidity* called such transactions wrongful sales and overturned them; funeral manuals such as *Earth Patterns* referred to them as wrongful burials and proposed preventive measures drawn from a spirit code. Spirit codes surviving in the Daoist canon drew extensively on real-world codes to formulate a law for the spirits of the dead, and the regulations they proposed to control the bureaucratic abuses of the subterranean courts would have applied just as well to the courts of the real world. The living could draw up tomb contracts confident that the courts of the living and the dead were so similar that they accepted the same types of documentary evidence.

As a result, this-worldly contracts and tomb contracts share many formal characteristics. Recall the description, cited in the first chapter, of a contract by Sulaiman, the anonymous Arab merchant who visited China in 851. Two copies are drawn up, finger joints are sketched, and then some characters (probably those for "contract") are drawn on the seam. The ceremonial signing of the tomb contract described in *Earth Patterns* fits Sulaiman's description perfectly. Ritual officials act as proxies to perform the signing of the contract between the deceased and the god(s) selling the funeral plot, by writing the characters for "contract" (*hetong*) on the seam of the two contracts. If the pair of *Earth Patterns* contracts surviving from 1568 (shown in fig. 9) is typical, then the contract for the gods is a mirror image of the deceased's copy. Tomb contracts resemble real-world contracts in other ways. Like surviving contracts from Turfan and Dunhuang, the tomb contract in *Earth Patterns* does not name the seller, because the seller was superior to the buyer.

Tomb contracts, like real-world contracts, specify the timing of payment. The *Earth Patterns* model says, "When the money and land have been exchanged, the order will be given to the workers and carpenters to construct the tomb." The phrasing implies that the moment of sale is not when the character *hetong* is drawn on the two contracts, but at the end of the ceremony when the paper offerings to the gods are burned.

This problem of timing is one we first glimpsed at Turfan. When does a transaction occur—when the contract is drafted or when payment is received? The first contract in this book to mention the moment when ownership shifts dates to 638, just before the Tang-dynasty conquest of Turfan. It specifically links payment with the transfer of property: "When the money is all paid up, ownership of the field will change hands." A contract for the sale of a camel in 673 says, "Once the camel and the cloth are exchanged, the transaction shall be complete," but it does not specify whether the money changes hands before or after a three-day trial period. Contracts from Dunhuang during the period of Tibetan rule are also worded to prevent partial payment and say "with nothing left hanging."

Although all of these clauses were intended to prevent subsequent disputes claiming insufficient payment, the evidence from the Tang dynasty gives little indication that officials were overly concerned about the large number of law suits. *The Tang Code* voices the government's reluctance to interfere in private transactions, and contracts from the seventh and eighth centuries reveal a body of practices that developed independently of laws issued by the imperial court. They use the word "agreement" (*yue*) to describe the terms that people have arrived at themselves, and they contrast those terms with "official law" (*zhengfa*), the law of government officials. Even at the peak of government authority, people did not always register their contracts with local officials, and their contracts regularly denied the applicability of imperial amnesties.

Sources from the Song describe the perennial difficulty sellers had in collecting full price at the time of sale. One unusual dispute involved a man who sold his wife for 300 strings but received only 100. Rather than pay the remaining amount, the new husband kept the woman prisoner. This dispute ended in the courts, and we know about it only because the decision was reprinted in *Clarity and Lucidity*.

The Song government took more active steps to reduce suits in the hope of achieving a more harmonious Confucian society while lightening the workload of its officials. In 983 one official urged the adoption of regional models for contracts that would specify borders accurately. Suits would also be reduced, he argued, if neighbors, who enjoyed the right of first refusal, were consulted before the sale. The anonymous author of *Self-Admonitions* warned his readers about people who paid for something but did not use a contract, and also about people who used a contract but did not pay the full price. Both practices were the cause of lawsuits. The sale of livestock was particularly vexatious, he explained, because local custom was to make a small deposit on the price of an animal and wait three days to see if the animal was in good health. Only then did the buyer pay the full price, and only then did the two parties draw up a contract. He was concerned because officials had to hear the case if the animal fell ill, and they had no documentary proof to consult in the case of a dispute. His comments were farsighted.

The contract in *Old China Hand* eliminated the unworkable three-day waiting period and linked the sale of the animal with receipt of payment. The buyer was responsible for detecting any flaws or illness at the time of sale. When the buyer discovered that one of the Korean horses had a runny nose, the fault was his, and he had to pay the penalty for canceling the transaction. Officials during the Mongol era continued to complain about the wiliness of the population and the excessive number of suits they brought. A model contract from an almanac tried to prevent suits by describing unambiguous borders, by specifying that the price was to be paid in full at the time of sale, and by saying that the sale had not been coerced. It also gave the seller only three years in which to exercise the buyback option.

The residents of Huizhou came up with an elegant solution to the problem of timing. They recognized that a contract had to be drafted before payment was made, so they added a final note. The first contract extant from Huizhou, dating to 1215, contained an addendum: the seller and the guarantor recorded that they had received payment in full. The seller, who received the money, made his mark a second time after this clause. The same solution extended to the underworld as well. A 1454 *Earth Patterns* contract, buried in the tomb of a member of the ceremonial guard, was modified so that it ended with an unusual statement: "Today at this time we willingly hand over the price of the land. The dragon deity guards the tomb, and the earth receives the money and serves as a witness that 6 strings of 1,000 cash have been paid, with nothing owing." The earth (*tudi*) served both as the seller and as the witness verifying receipt of the money. There was an odd discrepancy in the amount paid. The body of the contract said the price to be paid was 6 ounces of silver, but this final note said 6 strings of 1,000 cash had been paid. The contract was drawn up with one type of spirit money in mind, facsimile ounces of silver; but another type, facsimile strings of cash, was actually burned.

This attempt to pin down the relationship between the contract and the moment of sale shaped later contracts as well. Contracts drawn up in the Ming and Qing were very much the descendants of those used in earlier periods: many of the same clauses occur in contracts for purchasing, renting, and mortgaging. Writing about the commercial contracts in Taiwan at the end of the nineteenth century, Rosser H. Brockman (1980:128) argues that people tried to avoid the courts by drawing up simple self-enforced contracts. Payment was made at the same time as delivery.

If, as Ramon H. Myers (1982:296–298) has proposed, the ubiquity of contracts underlay China's economic growth in the late imperial period, it must also have contributed to the dramatic economic growth of the twelfth and thirteenth centuries. Still, Peter Perdue (1987:136–150) cautions against exaggerating the rationalization of property rights during the eighteenth and nineteenth centuries. Problems with contracts for conditional sales persisted. Even in the case of so-called final sales, the original owners persisted in asking the purchasers for supplementary payments long after a plot of land had changed hands. Land was not a commodity whose value could be expressed simply in money. Like First-Victory, people felt connected to their land even when they did not hold legal title to it.

In southeast China during the Ming and Qing dynasties, a more flexible system of land tenure evolved, in which multiple ownership of the same plot was common. It was referred to as "one field, two owners" (*yitian liangzhu*). One family would retain rights to the surface, or the skin of the land (*tianpi*), while another kept rights to the subsoil, or the bones of the land (*tiangu*) (Myers and Chen 1976; Myers 1982:291; Kroker 1959:127; Wiens 1982:5).

Tomb contracts also presupposed dual ownership, with the deceased retaining surface rights and the gods holding subsoil rights. This view of divided ownership had a potentially treasonous interpretation: how could the emperor claim to own all the land in the empire if the gods owned the subsoil rights? Was the emperor's claim in fact a claim to the surface rights only? These are questions so legalistic that no one may have asked them at the time.

The use of tomb contracts did not die out completely after 1400. Nora Waln, a young American Quaker, lived in the 1920s with an irrigation official's family somewhere along the Yellow River. In *House of Exile* she describes all stages of a funeral, including the modern equivalent of buying land from the gods of the earth: "The males of the House of Wong dressed in gowns and head fillets of coarse white cloth, put on straw sandals and walked to the Temple of Agriculture to announce to the Lord of the Soil that their ancestor now had need of a place in the earth for his body" (Waln [1933] 1986:63). Tomb contracts occasionally recorded the purchase of land from earth gods, although under regional variants of their names.

Tomb contracts were used in other parts of China as well. A Chinese scholar transcribed a woodblock-printed contract in use in 1941 in Sichuan and noted that it was burned during the funeral (Tai 1950:9–10). David Crockett Graham, who lived in Sichuan as a missionary, provides a rough translation of the same text, suggesting that it enjoyed wide circulation, and comments that such tomb contracts were "printed and sold in Chinese shops" (Graham 1961:44–45; Asim 1993:232–233). Modern Daoist funerals in Taiwan include a step in which money to purchase land, a model of a house, and a contract showing ownership are all burned so that the deceased can demonstrate ownership in the underworld (Lagerwey 1987:185–188; Schipper 1989:132). The contract is read aloud during the ceremony, as *Earth Patterns* instructed, and family members confirm the accuracy of its contents (Hou 1975:51, 66). A shift to paper contracts, of course, would generate no lasting evidence and would account for the infrequent survival of tomb contracts in later periods.

Contracts on the *Earth Patterns* model have been found all over China in tombs of both the poor and the rich, in the tombs of both those who did not hold government position and those who did, and even in the tomb of one grand councillor, Zhou Bida. In Jiangxi the kin of the dead, in further measures to protect their dead, buried cypress figures who were charged with preventing any subterranean suits against the deceased.

Even those who did not bury tomb contracts believed in underworld courts—perhaps in Buddhist judges determining the workings of karma, or perhaps in Daoist judges enforcing *The Spirit Code,* or perhaps in a more eclectic judge dispensing popular concepts of justice. Western scholars, most notably Joseph Needham, have argued that the Chinese had no conception of a higher, or divine, law: "There was no confidence that the code of Nature's laws could be unveiled and read, because there was no assurance that a divine being, even more rational than ourselves, had ever formulated such a code capable of being read" (1969:327).

The widespread belief in the netherworld courts and in a spirit code belies this view. Some people, like the author of *Earth Patterns,* claimed to know only one or two articles of the spirit code. Others, like the Celestial Heart Daoists, claimed knowledge of the entire code. Both groups agreed that a code for spirits existed, and they envisioned a court system that enforced that code. Since the realm of the spirits was thought to be below the ground, we may conclude that the Chinese conceived of a divine subterranean law.

Earth Patterns warned readers that failure to build a luminous hall, to behead the grass, or to bury a tomb contract were all causes of wrongful burial. The idea of wrongful burial mirrored the concept of wrongful sale, so often cited by the judges of *Clarity and Lucidity.* To the judges, a wrongful sale was one that violated some fundamental principle of the law, usually having to do with keeping family property together, regardless of whether the correct procedures had been carried out. Remember the woman who married her deceased husband's brother and sold off the land of her late husband's children. The court ordered all the land returned, even though all the sales had been recorded by contract. A contract offered no protection in such a case to the person buying land. Wrongful burial, by extension, rendered purchase of a tomb plot uncertain. In using the term "wrongful burial" the manual's authors are presuming a high level of legal knowledge among their readership—a level that the evidence indicates was just as high as they assumed.

Similarly, those drawing up spirit codes assumed familiarity with this-worldly suits. As innocent people could be penalized under the provisions of mutual responsibility for crimes not of their own doing, so too could they be punished by the courts of the underworld—simply because a relative had done something so heinous that they were implicated. The relative might have knowingly committed a crime during his or her lifetime, as Xu Mi's uncle did when he murdered his subordinate. Or the crimes could occur inadvertently after their deaths, as they would if they were buried on top of someone who had a prior claim to their plot. The people of Jiangxi buried cypress people in the hope they could block such claims.

The punishments in the spirit code (beheading, exile, tattooing) were all based on those in *The Tang Code*, and were specified even when certain incongruities, like the beheading of a deity, arose. The author of one spirit code, Rao Dongtian, is quoted as saying that he consulted the human law code when compiling his spirit code. As well he might, given the similarities between people and spirits! We have seen one spirit who demanded a divorce from her still-living husband, who had remarried and whom she considered guilty of bigamy.

The tone of the Daoist code drafted at the end of the Mongol era echoes that of a law code promulgated in 1291 (*Zhiyuan xinge*; Ch'en, Paul 1979). *The New Code of the Zhiyuan Era* captures the desire of the Chinese advisers to the Mongols, who wanted an orderly society to be restored. One article reads:

> Among all matters concerning civil administration, to prohibit [the officials] from disturbing the common people is the most urgent. . . . Only those who are scrupulous and without negligence shall be retained, and all extra members shall be dismissed. [Moreover,] each matter shall, by establishment of rules, still be examined and checked so that [the officials] may not, as before, oppress the common people. (Ch'en, Paul 1979:120–121, 161)

Compare this with the regulations for the judges of the dead from "The Heavenly Code as Proclaimed by Nüqing." If they find

> the innocent guilty, those without grievances against them as having grievances against them, those in the wrong in the right, those without grievances to be aggrieved, those without residual karma to have karma, those with good deeds to have none—any judge who does things like this will have his form divided. And any judge who deliberately detains someone in hope of payment will have the punishment increased one degree.

The enumeration of offenses in the human code and in the spirit code is wistful. The well-connected Daoists who drew up this spirit code were familiar with bureaucratic abuses under the Mongols. And they would have shared the conviction of their official acquaintances that the judicial system needed reform.

What was the relationship between earthly and subterranean courts? Hong Mai's twelfth-century *Record of the Listener* gives one answer. A corrupt official frames Registrar Xia, whose innocence is asserted by only one man, a believer in the netherworld court "where wrongs can be righted." Registrar Xia also believes in this court, because as he lies dying, he tells his sons to "place in my coffin all the previous leases for the wine concessions and contracts specifying each person's share so that I can vigorously sue in the underworld." The same evidence one uses in this-world courts can be submitted to the underworld courts.

This belief explains, I think, why fifteen intact contracts were buried in 673 with Moneylender Zuo in his tomb at Astana. The contracts all predate his death by as much as thirteen or as little as three years. Why bury these contracts? Because Moneylender Zuo had never managed to collect on them in this world, and he hoped to do so in the next. His relative who wrote a letter denying responsibility for the theft of 500 silver coins shared the same faith in the subterranean courts. Because he did not want to be found guilty of robbery, he placed the letter in his potential accuser's tomb to head off such a charge.

When the real-world courts failed to dispense justice, the underworld courts offered another hearing. Even today people often end an unresolved argument saying, "When the time comes, we will settle accounts before King Yanluo," the judge who presides over the court of the underworld. The protagonists in all the tales about the netherworld courts had such a strong sense of justice that they were willing to fight long after they had died. They believed it was wrong to kill and go unpunished, to encroach on a neighbor's land, to kill troops who had already surrendered, or to prevent someone's engagement. Surprisingly, the failure of the earthly courts to enforce these ideals of justice did not weaken them, for the courts of the dead kept them very much alive.

Appendix A

Known Tomb

Contracts

Date	Place (Province, County)	Source
76	Zhejiang, Kuaiji	Ikeda 1981:213–214
82	Shanxi, Yizhou	Ikeda 1981:214
85	Shandong, Juxian	Ikeda 1981:214
100–200	—	Ikeda 1981:274
100–200	—	Ikeda 1981:224
100–200	Shaanxi, Baoji	Ikeda 1981:275
100–200	Henan, Lingbao	Ikeda 1981:275–276
100–200	Henan, Luoyang	Ikeda 1981:223–224
133	Shaanxi, Huxian	Ikeda 1981:270
147	Shaanxi, Xian	Ikeda 1981:270–271
150–200	Henan, Luoyang	Ikeda 1981:223
151	Shandong, Cangshan	Ikeda 1981:214–215
156	—	Ikeda 1981:271
156	Shaanxi, Xian	Ikeda 1981:271–272
161	Henan, Mengjin	Ikeda 1981:215–216
162	Sichuan, Wanzhou	Ikeda 1981:216
163	Shandong, Yixian	Ikeda 1981:216–217
168	Zhejiang, Xiaoshan	Ikeda 1981:217–219
169	Henan, Luoyang	Ikeda 1981:219
171	Henan, Luoyang	Ikeda 1981:219–220
172	Shaanxi, Xian	Ikeda 1981:272
173	Jiangsu, Nanjing	Ikeda 1981:273; *Wenwu* 1965.6:22
174	Jiangsu, Changzhou	Ikeda 1981:261
175	—	Ikeda 1981:273–274
176	Jiangsu, Yangzhou	Ikeda 1981:220
177	—	Ikeda 1981:220
178	Shanxi, Linfen	Ikeda 1981:220–221
179	Henan, Luoyang	Ikeda 1981:221
182	Hebei, Wangdu	Ikeda 1981:221–222

Date	Place (Province, County)	Source
188	Henan, Luoyang	Ikeda 1981:270
188	Henan, Luoyang	Ikeda 1981:222–223
193	Shaanxi, Xian	Ikeda 1981:274
200–400	Gansu, Dunhuang	Ikeda 1981:276–277
226	Jiangxi, Nanchang	Ikeda 1981:224
227	Hubei, Wuhan	Ikeda 1981:225
245	Anhui, Nanling	*Kaogu* 1984.11:975
252	Zhejiang, Hangzhou	Ikeda 1981:225
254	Jiangsu, Nanjing	*Wenwu ziliao congkan* 1980.8:3, 5
262	Hubei, Wuhan	Ikeda 1981:225
274	Anhui, Dangyu	*Wenwu* 1987.4:92
284	Zhejiang, Kuaiji	Ikeda 1981:226
297	—	Ikeda 1981:227
300	Jiangsu, Zhenjiang	*Kaogu* 1984.6:540–541
300–400	—	Ikeda 1981:228–229
302	Jiangsu, Nanjing	Ikeda 1981:227
337	Jiangsu, Dantu	*Wenwu* 1965.6:48
337	Zhejiang, Pingyang	*Wenwu* 1965.6:48–49
369	Dunhuang	Ikeda 1981:277
408	Korea	Ikeda 1981:263
424	—	Ikeda 1981:229
432	Jiangsu, Xuzhou	Ikeda 1981:229
472	Shanxi, Datong	Ikeda 1981:229–230
477	Shaanxi, Changwu	*Wenwu* 1983.8:94
481	Guangdong, Guangzhou	Ikeda 1981:230
485	Henan, Nanyang	Ikeda 1981:230–231
485	Hubei, Wuchang	*Kaogu* 65.4:182–183
487	Guangxi, Guilin	Ikeda 1981:231–232
499	Model text	*Zhengao* 10:17a–b

Date	Place (Province, County)	Source
506	Hunan, Zixing	*Kaogu xuebao* 1984.3:355
507	Hebei, Zhuoxian	*Taozhai cangshiji* 6:11a–b
514	Guangxi, Rongan	*Kaogu* 1983.9:790–791
520	Hunan, Zixing	*Kaogu xuebao* 1984.3:354
520	Hunan, Zixing	*Kaogu xuebao* 1984.3:355
525	Korea	Ikeda 1981:263–264
525	Hebei, Wuji	*Wenwu* 1959.1:44–45
552	—	Ikeda 1981:532
610	Hunan, Changsha	*Wenwu* 1981.4:43
618–910	Model text	*Yaoxiu keyi jielü chao* 15:14a
618–910	Henan, —	Ikeda 1981:237–238
694	Jiangsu, Zhenjiang	*Wenwu* 1965.8:53–54
700–800	Henan, Fugou	*Kaogu* 1965.8:388
763	Japan	Ikeda 1981:265
769	Xinjiang, Astana	Ikeda 1981:278; *Wenwu* 1975.7:12, 24
800–900	Japan	Ikeda 1981:265–266
814	Henan, Zhuoxian	Ikeda 1981:234
835	Jiangsu, Jiangdu	Ikeda 1981:234–235
837	Jiangxi, Yiyang	*Kaogu* 1987.3:223, Chen Baiquan 1991:549
847	Hebei, Dingxian	*Taozhai cangshiji* 33:1b–2a
883	Jiangsu, Huating	Ikeda 1981:235–236
890	Jiangxi, Nanchang	*Kaogu* 1977.6:402
900	Zhejiang, Shanglinhu	*Wenwu* 1988.12:90
939	Jiangsu, Yangzhou	*Wenwu* 1964.12:61–62
946	Anhui, Hefei	*Wenwu cankao ziliao* 1958.3:66
953	Anhui, Hefei	*Kaogu tongxun* 1958.7:57
955	Sichuan, Pengshan	*Kaogu tongxun* 1958.5:18–26
960–1000	Henan, Huixian	Ikeda 1981:241–242
960–1127	Henan, Fangcheng	*Wenwu* 1959.6:77

Date	Place (Province, County)	Source
960–1260	Shaanxi, Lüeyang	*Wenwu cankao ziliao* 1956.8:71
962	Guangdong, Guangzhou	Ikeda 1981:240–241
984	Hebei, Dingxian	Ikeda 1981:241
995	Jiangxi	Beijing Library, Muzhi 3712
1025	Jiangxi, Ruichang	*Wenwu* 1986.1:71
1032	Shanxi, Taiyuan	*Kaogu* 1963.5:252–253
1033	Shanxi, Taiyuan	*Kaogu* 1963.5:260
1035	Jiangxi, Ruichang	*Wenwu* 1986.1:72
1055	Jiangsu, Jiangyin	*Wenwu* 1982.12:29
1056	Henan, Zhengzhou	*Wenwu cankao ziliao* 1958.5:54
1057	Jiangxi, Nancheng	*Kaogu* 1965.11:572; Chen 1991:551
1062	Jiangsu, Wuxi	*Kaogu* 1986.12:1140
1069	Sichuan, Huayang	*Wenwu cankao ziliao* 1956.12:42
1072	Sichuan, Pujiang	*Kaogu yu wenwu* 1986.3:45–46
1072	Sichuan, Pujiang	*Kaogu yu wenwu* 1986.3:46
1075	Jiangxi, Jishui	*Kaogu* 1987.3:224
1080	Sichuan, Hongya	*Kaogu* 1982.1:38–39
1086	Jiangxi, Xinyu	Chen 1991:553
1090	Jiangxi, Pengze	*Wenwu* 1980.5:30
1093	Shanxi, Datong	*Kaogu* 1963.8:435
1099	Shaanxi, Lantian	*Wenwu* 1965.5:57–58
1099	Hebei, Baisha shuiku	Su Bai 1957:44–45
1099	Jiangxi, Pengze	*Kaogu* 1987.3:230
1104	Hubei, Niangyang	*Jiang Han Kaogu* 1985.3:29
1105	Jiangxi, Wuning	*Kaogu* 1987.3:230
1107	Shanxi, Datong	*Kaogu tongxun* 1958.6:32–33
1118	Jiangxi, Jinxian	*Kaogu* 1987.3:225; Chen 1991:555–556
1119–1123	Jiangsu, Jiangdu	*Taozhai cangshiji* 40:15a–16a; Beijing Library, Muzhi 5082

Date	Place (Province, County)	Source
1121	Jiangxi, Dexing	*Kaogu* 1987.3:230–231
1124	Hebei, Baisha shuiku	Su Bai 1957:3, 83; *Kaogu* 1963.2:100
1126	Hubei, Xiaogan	*Wenwu* 1989.5:70
1128	Gansu, Longxi	*Wenwu cankao ziliao* 1955.9:90–92
1132	Sichuan, Chengdu	Ikeda 1981:246
1132	Sichuan, Chengdu	Ikeda 1981:246
1133	Jiangxi, Ruichang	Chen 1991:558
1138	Henan, Jiaozuo	Yang 1985:440–441
1139	Shaanxi, Baoji	Beijing Library, Muzhi 5079
1141	Korea	Ikeda 1981:264
1162	Shaanxi, Hanzhong	*Kaogu yu wenwu* 1984.5:61–62
1175	Jiangxi, Linchuan	Chen 1991:559
1183	Neimeng, Dongsheng	*Beitu taben* 46:163 (Muzhi 4911)
1183	Shanxi, Yuanqu	*Kaogu tongxun* 1956.1:48
1185	Jiangxi, Jinxi	Chen 1991:560
1186	Fujian, Nan'an	*Wenwu* 1975.3:78
1188	Jiangxi, Xingan	*Kaogu* 1987.3:231
1190	Jiangxi, Fengcheng	*Kaogu* 1987.3:225; Chen 1991:562
1190	Jiangxi, Qingjiang	Chen 1991:562–563
1191	Henan, Loyang	Ikeda 1981:248–249
1198	Jiangxi, Linchuan	Chen 1991:563–564
1199	Jiangxi, Fenyi	*Kaogu* 1964.2:72, 85; Chen 1991: 564–565
1201	Jiangxi, Yihuang	*Kaogu* 1987.3:226; Chen 1991:565–566
1204	Jiangxi, Ji'an	Chen 1991:566–567
1204	Sichuan, Guangyuan	*Wenwu* 1986.12:25
1204	Sichuan, Guangyuan	*Wenwu* 1986.12:27
1208–1224	Sichuan, Mianyang	*Kaogu tongxun* 1959.8:448

Date	Place (Province, County)	Source
1210	Shanxi, Houma	Liu Nianzi 1986:54; *Kaogu* 1959.5:227; *Wenwu* 1959.3:71; 1959.6:51; 1959.10:50
1210	Shanxi, Houma	Liu Nianzi 1986:54
1211	Jiangxi, Qingjiang	*Kaogu* 1965.11:574; Chen 1991: 567–568
1224	Jiangxi, Qingjiang	Chen 1991:568–569
1226	Zhejiang, Wenzhou	Ikeda 1981:250
1227	Jiangxi, Qingjiang	*Kaogu* 1965.11:573
1229	Jiangxi, Jinxian	Chen 1991:570–571, 199–200
1232	Jiangxi, Jinxian	Chen 1991:571–572
1233	Jiangsu, Jiangdu	Ikeda 1981:251–252
1237	Jiangxi, Yugan	*Kaogu* 1987.3:231
1243	Fujian, Fuzhou	*Wenwu* 1977.7:1, 14
1250	Jiangxi, Qingjiang	*Beitu taben* 46:163
1252	Jiangxi, Jingdezhen	*Wenwu* 1979.4:23
1252	Jiangxi, Nanchang	*Kaogu* 1987.3:231
1254	Jiangxi, Jishui	*Wenwu* 1987.2:68
1257	Fujian, Jinmen	Fang 1974:187–188
1260	Jiangxi, Xiajiang	Chen 1991:575–576
1261	Shanxi, Datong	*Wenwu* 1987.6:88
1265	Shanxi, Datong	*Wenwu* 1962.10:40
1272	Jiangxi, Ruichang	Chen 1991:577; *Kaogu* 1986.11
1272	Jiangxi, Ruichang	*Kaogu* 1986.11:1053
1288	Henan, Jixian	Ikeda 1981:254
1293	Jiangxi, Nanchang	*Kaogu* 1963.10:572; Chen 1991: 578
1296	Henan, Sanmenxia	*Kaogu* 1985.11:1054–55
1297	Shanxi, Xiaoyi	*Kaogu* 1960.7:60
1298	Hebei, Weixian	*Kaogu* 1983.3:284
1301	Jiangxi, Nanchang	Chen 1991:579

Date	Place (Province, County)	Source
1303	Shanxi, Fencheng	*Wenwu cankao ziliao* 1952.1:35
1314	Shanxi, Houma	*Wenwu* 1959.12:48, 49
1319	Jiangxi, Yongfeng	*Wenwu* 1987.7:85–86; Chen 1991: 580–581
1321	Jiangxi, Jinxian	Chen 1991:581
1325	Jiangxi, Nanchang	*Kaogu* 1987.3:231, 219
1339	Jiangxi, Jinxian	Chen 1991:582–583
1344	Jiangxi, Nanchang	Chen 1991:583–584
1368–1644	Jiangsu, Yangzhou	*Taozhai cangshiji* 44:23b
1446	Jiangxi, Nanchang	*Kaogu* 1987.3:229
1454	Jiangxi, Poyang	Chen 1991:585–587
1457	Shandong, Penglai	Ikeda 1981:255
1457	Jiangsu, Jiangning	Ikeda 1981:255–256
1476	Jiangxi, Xinjian	*Kaogu* 1987.3:219
1513	Jiangsu, Tongshan	Ikeda 1981:256
1515	Beijing	*Wenwu* 1964.11:47
1533	Jiangsu, Taizhou	*Wenwu* 1986.9:1–2
1542	Shanghai	*Kaogu* 1985.6:544
1547	—	*Beitu taben* 56:130
1549	Jiangsu, Yangzhou	Ikeda 1981:256–257
1553	Hunan, Fenghuang	*Wenwu* 1962.1:58
1553	Jiangsu, Jiangdu	Ikeda 1981:257
1555	Sichuan, Huayang	Ikeda 1981:257–258
1559	Sichuan, Yuechi	Ikeda 1981:258
1568	Jiangsu, Yangzhou	*Taozhai cangshiji* 44:15b–17a
1598	Sichuan, Chengdu	*Beitu taben* 58:86
1622	Jiangsu, Taicang	*Wenwu* 1987.3:19
1627	Zhejiang, Hangzhou	Ikeda 1961:259–260
1631	Jiangsu, Taicang	*Wenwu* 1987.3:20

Date	Place (Province, County)	Source
1643	Jiangsu, Songjiang	*Wenwu* 1964.12:63
1714	Jiangsu, Suzhou	Ikeda 1981:261; *Wenwu* 64.12:63
1759	Jiangsu, Shuyang	Jiangsu Provincial Museum, Nanjing
1941	Sichuan, Jiangjin	Ikeda 1961:262–263

Appendix B

Deities Named

as Sellers in

Tomb Contracts

Year	Place (Province, County)	Deity
168	Zhejiang, Xiaoshan	Lord of the Hill (*Shangong*)
226	Jiangxi, Nanchang	King Father of the East (*Dongwanggong*) Queen Mother of the West (*Xiwangmu*)
252	Zhejiang, Hangzhou	Lord of the Earth (*Tugong*)
254	Jiangsu, Nanjing	Celestial [Emperor] (*Tiandi*) [Earl] of the Earth (*Tubo*)[1]
262	Hubei, Wuhan	[Name of first deity is missing] Father of the Grave Mound (*Qiufu*) King of the Earth (*Tuwang*)
284	Zhejiang, Kuaiji	Lord of the Earth
300	Jiangsu, Zhenjiang	Celestial [Emperor] [Earl] of the Earth
337	Zhejiang, Pingyang	Celestial [Emperor] [Earl] of the Earth
337	Jiangsu, Dantu	Celestial [Emperor] [Earl] of the Earth
485	Henan, Nanyang	God of the Earth (*Tushen*)
485	Hubei, Wuchang	God of the Earth
694	Jiangsu, Zhenjiang	Elder of Haoli[2] (*Haoli fulao*) Deputies of Left and Right (*Zuoyoucheng*) Earl of the Tomb (*mubo*) Netherworld 2,000-bushel officials (*tuxia erqian dan*)[3]

Year	Place (Province, County)	Deity
		Wuyi King (*Wuyi wang*)
		Andu King (*Andu wang*)[4]
837	Jiangxi, Yiyang	Zhang Jiangu[5]
890	Jiangxi, Nanchang	Elder of Haoli
		Deputy of Andu
		Wuyi King
962	Guangdong, Guangzhou	Wuyi King
995	Jiangxi, —	King Father of the East
		Queen Mother of the West
1025	Jiangxi, Ruichang	[Earl] of the Earth
1033	Shanxi, Taiyuan	King Father of the East
		Queen Mother of the West
1062	Jiangsu, Wuxi	King Father of the East
		Queen Mother of the West
1075	Jiangxi, Jishui	Opening Emperor Master of the Earth (*Kaihuang dizhu*)
1099	Jiangxi, Pengze	Wuyi King
1118	Jiangxi, Jinxian	[Wu]yi King
1139	Shaanxi, Baoji	Father Emperor of the Heavens (*Huangtian*)
		Mother Empress of the Earth[6] (*Houtu*)
		Twelve harvest altars (*Sheji shier bian*)
1185	Jiangxi, Jinxi	Opening Emperor Master of the Earth
1199	Jiangxi, Fenyi	Zhang Jiangu
1201	Jiangxi, Yihuang	Opening Emperor Master of the Earth
1204	Jiangxi, Ji'an	Shadow officers of the Empress of the Earth (*Houtu yinguan*)
1204	Sichuan, Guangyuan	Opening Emperor Father
		Mother Empress of the Earth
		Harvest altars
1229	Jiangxi, Jinxian	Goddess of the Earth, Houtu (*Houtu fuao*)
1232	Jiangxi, Jinxian	Goddess of the Earth, Houtu

Year	Place (Province, County)	Deity
1233	Jiangsu, Jiangdu	Opening Emperor Father Mother Empress of the Earth Thirty-eight generals Efficacious spirits and company (*lingshi*)
1252	Jiangxi, Jingdezhen	Opening Emperor Father Mother Empress of the Earth Harvest altars
1257	Fujian, Jinmen	Zhang Jiangu Li Dingdu
1260	Jiangxi, Xiajiang	Shadow officers of the Empress of the Earth
1293	Jiangxi, Nanchang	Empress of the Earth, Houtu
1319	Jiangxi, Yongfeng	Opening Emperor Master of the Land (*Kaihuang tuzhu*)
1344	Jiangxi, Nanchang	Opening Emperor True Master (*Kaihuang zhenzhu*)
1446	Jiangxi, Nanchang	Shadow officers of the Empress of the Earth
1476	Jiangxi, Xinjiang	King Father of the East Queen Mother of the West
1553	Hunan, Fenghuang	Opening Emperor Father
1627	Zhejiang, Hangzhou	Opening Emperor Empress of the Earth, Houtu Green dragon (*qinglong*)

1. Some of the residents of Jiangsu and Zhejiang purchased their land from the Celestial Emperor, and their house (or tomb structure) from the Earl of the Earth.

2. Haoli was a district of the underworld near Mount Tai, where one of two souls was thought to go after death (Yü 1987:392).

3. The deputies, the tomb earls, and the 2,000-bushel officials all appear in the earliest tomb ordinances from the Han dynasty as gods associated with tombs.

4. The Wuyi King was the lord of the earth, according to a 962 contract from Guangzhou. The Andu King may simply have been his counterpart.

5. Zhang Jiangu and his counterpart, Li Dingdu, appear as witnesses as early as 487 in a tomb contract from Guangxi and Guilin. These names are too perfect as names for witnesses to be real; they rhyme, and their meanings are similar. "Jiangu" means to uphold the certain, and "Dingdu" means to fix an amount. The two names appear frequently as witnesses to contracts with or grave lists for the

gods, and occasionally in other roles as well: guarantor, scribe, and even seller (*Tulufan chutu wenshu* 2:62–63; 3:21; Kleeman 1984:25–26). Ye Changchi ([1909] 1980:182) quotes from one tomb contract that identifies both Li and Zhang as divine immortals (*shenxian*).

6. Houtu, Empress of the Earth, an ancient earth god, is often paired with her mate, Huangtian, Father Emperor of the Heavens. Sheji is the ancient god of the crops.

Glossary

Terms that are not translated are names of people or gods.

Andu wang (Andu king) 安都王

ba (measure of land) 把

bai (white) 白

bai (cypress) 柏

bairen (cypress figure) 柏人

baixing (commoner) 百姓

baoren (guarantor) 保人

bu (step) 步

buluo (settlement) 部落

canzheng (assistant grand councilor) 參政

Cengyi (First-Ever) 曾一

chi (foot) 尺

chi (edict, celestial ordinance) 敕

chu (produce) 出

ci (this) 茲

Cui fujun (Prefect Cui) 崔府君

cun (inch) 寸

dan (picul) 石

daomai (wrongful sale) 盜賣

daozang (wrongful burial) 盜葬

didang (collateral loan) 抵當

difu (subterranean bureaucracy) 地府

difu zhi shen (gods of the subterranean bureaucracy) 地府之神

disiguan (judges of the subterranean courts) 地司官

dixia erqian dan (netherworld 2,000-bushel officials) 地下二千石

diyu (subterranean prison) 地獄

Dongtanglao (Elder of the Eastern Studio) 東堂老

Dongwanggong (King Father of the East) 東王公

dou (peck) 斗

Dou E yuan (Dou E's revenge) 竇娥冤

dusi panguan (deciding official from the office manager's office) 都司判官

duyaya (clerk) 都押衙

duyuhou (inspector-in-chief) 都虞候

erbi (those with brushes inserted in their hats) 珥筆

fa (law) 法

faguan (officials of the rites) 法官

fayi (intent of the law) 法意

Foshuo beidou qixing yanming jing (sutra of extending life in conformity with the seven stars of the Big Dipper, according to the Buddha) 佛説北斗七星延命經

fu (talisman) 符

fujun (prefect) 府君

fuzu koufendi (personal share land of a son's father and ancestors) 父祖口分地

ganlin (encroach) 忓惏

Gao Dafu 高大夫

ge (regulations) 格

gong (duke) 公

gongju, first occurrence; erroneous characters 功局

gongju, second occurrence (official receipt) 公據

guilü (spirit code) 鬼律

Guiyijun (Returning-to-Righteousness Army) 歸義軍

Haoli fulao (Elder of Haoli) 蒿里父老

he (agreement) 和

hetong (contract) 合同

Hetong wenzi (The contract) 合同文字

hou (marquis) 侯

Houtu (Empress of the Earth) 后土

Houtu fuao (Goddess of the Earth) 后土富媪

Houtu yinguan (shadow officers of the Empress of the Earth) 后土陰官

Houtumu (Mother Empress of the Earth) 后土母

hu (picul) 斛

hua (change) 化

Huang Tingjian (1045–1105) 黃庭堅

Huangdi (Yellow Emperor) 黃帝

Huangtianfu (Father Emperor of the Heavens) 皇天父

huaya (personal mark) 花押

Huiyuan (344–416) 慧遠

huolangdan (singing technique used by peddlers) 貨郎旦

huozhou (prefecture of fire) 火州

huzhu (household head) 戶主

ji (a type of contract) 劑

Jia Gongyan 賈公彥

jianmin (inferior classes) 賤民

jianren (witness) 見人

jiansong (those who encourage suits) 健訟

jiao (Daoist purification ceremony) 醮

jin (catty) 斤

jingjie (border survey) 經界

Jingshi dadian (Great compendium spanning generations) 經世大典

jiu (long-lasting) 久

jiu (nine) 九

Kaihuang dizhu (Opening Emperor Master of the Earth) 開皇地主

Kaihuang tuzhu (Opening Emperor Master of the Earth) 開皇土主

Kaihuang zhenzhu (Opening Emperor True Master) 開皇真主

Kanqiannu (The moneywatcher) 看錢奴

koufen (personal share) 口分

leishu (almanac) 類書

li (third-mile) 里

Li Dingdu 李定度

liang (ounce) 兩

likuang taishen (great deity who erects the tomb) 立壙太神

ling (statutes) 令

lingzhi (efficacious spirits and company) 靈祇

linjianren (secondary witness) 臨見人

linzuo (other witness) 臨坐

liu (six) 六

mai (buy) 買

mai (sell) 賣

maidiquan (contracts to buy land, tomb contracts) 買地券

meng (blood covenant) 盟

mie 乜; copyist's error for "hua"

mou (certain) 某,厶

mu (sixth-acre) 畝

mubo (Earl of the Tomb) 墓伯

mumeng (wood covenant) 木盟

panguan (deciding official) 判官

pijia (approve the price) 批價

pingzhang (midlevel official in the Secretariat) 平章

pitui (refuse the price) 批退

qi (contract) 契

qi Heduan shen (Wife Kotoun's body) 妻合端身

qianshu (scribe) 倩書

qichu (seven outs) 七出

Qin Jianfu (fl. 1330–1333) 秦簡夫

qinglong (green dragon) 青龍

qiucheng (deputy of the grave mound) 丘丞

Qiuci (alternative name for Kucha) 龜茲

qiufu (father of the grave mound) 丘父

Qu (family name) 麴

quan (contract) 券

Quxieyuan (Office for Expelling the Unsanctioned) 驅邪院

renqing (human feeling) 人情

san (three) 三

Shangong (Lord of the Hill) 山公

sheji shier bian (twelve harvest altars) 社稷十二邊

sheng (pint) 升

Shengyi (First-Victory) 勝一

shenxian (divine immortals) 神仙

shi (ordinances) 式

shi (ten) 十

shijian (chief witness) 時見

shiquan (market certificate) 市券

shizhishen 氏之神

Shouwu (Fifth-Longevity) 壽五

shuiluhui (rite to give food to hungry ghosts on land and water) 水陸會

si (die, faint) 死

sihu (monastic household) 寺戶

sikong (official in charge of digging canals) 司空

siqi (private contract) 私契

subaosi (office of speedy retribution) 速報司

Taishang hundong chiwen nüqing zhaoshu tianlü (Heavenly code as proclaimed by nüqing in vermillion from the mixed cave on high) 太上混洞赤文女青詔書天律

Taishang laojun (Lord Lao the Most High) 太上老君

Taishang laojun shuo changqing jingjing (Lord Lao the Most High explains how to obtain the Dao eternally) 太上老君說常清靜經

taizi xima (attendant and mentor to the heir apparent) 太子洗馬

Tang Quenei 唐雀內

tiancao (heavenly section) 天曹

Tiandi (Celestial Emperor) 天帝

tiangu (bones of the land) 田骨

tianpi (skin of the land) 田皮

Tianxin (Celestial Heart) 天心

tiji (one's own land) 梯己

tiling hubu (director of revenue ministry) 提領戶部

tongyuanren (neighbors) 同院人

Tubo (Earl of the Earth) 土伯

tufu jiangjun (generals of underworld bureaucracy) 土府將軍

Tugong (Lord of the Earth) 土公

Tujue (Turkic) 突厥

Tushen (God of the Earth) 土神

Tuwang (King of the Earth) 土王

tuxia erqian dan (netherworld 2,000-bushel officials) 土下二千石

Wang Qi 王氣

Wanqi (Ten-Thousand Seven) 萬七

wuxing (five names) 五姓

Wuyi wang (Wuyi king) 武夷王

xiangyuan tili (local precedent) 鄉原體例

Xianwu (Fifth-Wisdom) 賢五

Xiao Hong 蕭宏

xiashoushu (lower-the-hand contracts) 下手書

xieshen (unsanctioned deities) 邪神

Xiwangmu (Queen Mother of the West) 西王母

ya (to sign) 押

yahui (broker) 押會

Yan Shigu (581–645) 顏師古

yang (masculine active cosmological principle) 陽

yaya (clerk) 押衙

yazi (broker) 押子

yikan dali (follow the precedent for big change) 壹看大例

yin (female passive cosmological principle) 陰

yitian liangzhu (one field, two owners) 一田兩主

yongye (permanent holdings) 永業

youquan (contract to the right) 右券

youshou zhongzhi jie (joint of middle finger of right hand) 右手中指節

yuanjia zhaizhu (wronged creditor) 冤家債主

yue (agreement) 約

zanglu (record of burial) 葬錄

zhang (decafoot) 丈

Zhang Jiangu 張堅固

Zhao Gongming 趙公明

zhe (punish, blame) 讁

zhe (convert) 折

Zheng Xuan (127–200) 鄭玄

zhengdian (buyback loan) 正典

zhengfa (law of officials) 政法

zhengshen (sanctioned deities) 正神

zhi (type of contract) 質

zhi (know, understand) 知

zhi (possessive particle) 之

zhijianren (witness) 知見人

zhiqi (guarantor) 知契

zhongshen (gods of the tomb) 冢神

zhuyaqi ren (cosigner, guarantor) 助押契人

Zuo Chongxi 左憧憙

zuoshou zhongzhi jie (joint of middle finger of left hand) 左手中指節

Zuoyoucheng (Deputies of Left and Right) 左右丞

Bibliography

Primary Sources

Because the primary sources are in a confusing variety of formats, the entries here give different publication information as appropriate. Each entry gives the title of the book, romanized, and the title in Chinese characters, then a translation of the title into English. The date of composition, when known, follows. The author's name, and dates when known, are next. For books published in modern editions, the entry gives the city of publication, publisher, and date. For books appearing in collectanea, the entry gives the name of the collectanea edition. Entries that are books from the Daoist canon give Daozang volume number, followed by the number in the Harvard-Yenching index (HY). For manuscripts and rare books, the name of the library housing the copy is shown. For archeological journals, the city and publishing organization are given.

Baqiong shi jinshi buzheng 八瓊室金石補正 (Supplement to inscriptions from the Eight Treasure Room). Lu Zengxiang 陸增祥 (1816–1882). *Shike shiliao xinbian* edition.

Beishan wenji 北山文集 (Collected papers of Zheng Gangzhong). Zheng Gangzhong 鄭剛中 (1088–1154). *Congshu jicheng* edition.

Beitu taben: Beijing tushuguan cang Zhongguo lidai shike taben huibian 北京圖書館藏中國歷代石刻拓本匯編 (A collection of Chinese historical rubbings from stone stored in the Beijing Library). Ed. Beijing tushuguan jinshi zu 北京圖書館金石組. Zhengzhou: Zhongzhou guji chubanshe, 1990.

Changbian: Xu zizhi tongjian 續資治通鑑長編 (A continuation of the comprehensive mirror for aid in government). Li Tao 李燾 (1115–1184). Beijing: Zhonghua shuju, 1979.

Changli xiansheng quanwenji: Zhu Wengong jiao 朱文公校昌黎先生全文集 (The complete collected papers of Han Yu, annotated by Zhu Xi). Han Yu 韓愈 (768–824). *Sibu congkan* edition.

Chaoye qianzai: Sui Tang jiahua 朝野僉載隋唐嘉話 (Complete record of the government and the people: Fine words of the Sui and Tang dynasties). Zhang Zhuo 張鷟 (c. 680–740). Beijing: Zhonghua shuju, 1979.

Chi Songzi zhangli 赤松子章歷 (Petition almanac of Master Red Pine). *Daozang* 315 (HY 615).

Chuijianlu quanbian 吹劍錄全編 (Records of sounds made breathing into a sword). 1249. Yu Wenbao 俞文豹 (?–after 1250). Beijing: Zhonghua shuju, 1958.

Daofa huiyuan 道法會元 (Corpus of Daoist ritual). 1356. Daozang 884–941 (HY 1220).

Daomen dingzhi 道門定制 (Prescribed practices from the gate of the Dao). Lü Yuansu 呂元素 and Hu Xianglong 胡湘龍 (1188). *Daozang* 973–975 (HY 1214).

Da Tang Xinyu 大唐新語 (New stories from the great Tang dynasty). Liu Su 劉肅 (Tang dynasty). Beijing: Zhonghua shuju, 1984.

Dili xinshu: Chong jiaozheng 重校正地理新書 (The revised new book of the ways of the earth). 1070. Wang Zhu 王洙. 1192. Zhang Qian 張謙 revised. Qing photolithograph of 1192 edition held in the Beijing Library.

Dili xinshu: tujie jiaozheng 圖解校正地理新書 (The revised new book of the ways of the earth). 1070. Wang Zhu 王洙. 1192. Zhang Qian 張謙 revised. Reprint of 1192 edition held in the Taibei Central Library. Taibei: Jiwen shuju, 1985.

Diquan zhengcun 地券徵存 (A collection of surviving tomb contracts). Luo Zhenyu 羅振玉. In *Luo Xuetang xiansheng quanji* 羅雪堂先生全集 (volume 83). Taibei: Datong shuju, 1976.

Dong Jieyuan Xixiangji 董解元西廂記 (Master Dong's Western chamber romance). c. 1200. Anon. Ed. Ling Jingyan 凌景埏. Beijing: Renmin wenxue chubanshe, 1962.

Dongjing menghualu 東京夢華錄 (Reveries of the splendor of Kaifeng). 1147. Meng Yuanlao 孟元老 (c. 1090–1150). Beijing: Zhongguo shangye chubanshe, 1982.

Dunhuang bianwenji 敦煌變文集 (Collected popular narratives from Dunhuang). Ed. Wang Zhongmin 王重民 et al. Beijing: Renmin chubanshe, 1957.

Dunhuang shehui jingji wenxian zhenji shilu 敦煌社會經濟文獻真蹟釋錄 (An annotated catalogue of photographs of social and economic documents from Dunhuang). Ed. Tang Geng'ou 唐耕耦. Beijing: Quanguo tushuguan wenxian suowei fuzhi zhongxin, 1990.

Guixin zashi 癸辛雜識 (Miscellaneous notes from the Guixin quarter, Hangzhou). c. 1298. Zhou Mi 周密 (1232–1308). Xuejin taoyuan edition.

Hanmo quanshu: Xinbian shiwen leiju 新編事文類聚翰墨全書 (A new collection of topically ordered letters written with brush and ink). 1307. Liu Yingli 劉應李 (d. 1311). Yonezawa Municipal Library copy.

Han shu 漢書 (A history of the Han dynasty). Ban Gu 班固 (A.D. 32–92). Beijing: Zhonghua shuju, 1962.

Haoli yiwen 蒿里遺文 (Surviving writings from the netherworld). Luo Zhenyu 羅振

玉 In *Luo Xuetang xiansheng quanji* 羅雪堂先生全集 (volume 4). Taibei: Datong shuju, 1976.

Hebi shilei beiyao: Gujin 古今合璧事類備要 (A topical encyclopedia of old and new well-matched objects placed side by side). Xie Weixin 謝維新 and Yu Zai 虞載 Taibei: Xinxing shuju, 1969.

Houcun xiansheng daquanji 後村先生大全集 (The complete writings of Liu Kezhuang). Liu Kezhuang 劉克莊 (1187-1269). *Sibu congkan* edition.

Houde lu 厚德錄 (A record of great virtue). Li Yuangang 李元綱 (fl. 1170). In *Biji xiaoshuo daguan* 筆記小説大觀 Taibei: Xinxing shuju, 1962.

Huang Shangu xiansheng quanshu: Song 宋黃山谷先生全書 (Complete collected works of Huang Tingjian). Huang Tingjian 黃庭堅 (1045-1105). 1785 edition.

Huizhou qiannian qiyue wenshu 徽州千年契約文書 (Contract documents from one thousand years of Huizhou history). Ed. History Institute of the Chinese Academy of Social Sciences. Shijiazhuang: Huashan wenyi chubanshe, 1991.

Jiang Han Kaogu 江漢考古 (Jianghan archeology). Wuhan: Archeological Association of Hubei Province.

Jiangsu jinshizhi 江蘇金石志 (A collection of inscriptions from Jiangsu). 1927. Compiled by Jiangsu Tongzhi ju 江蘇通志局 (Bureau for Compiling the Union Gazetteer for Jiangsu). *Shike shiliao xinbian* edition.

Jianjielu 鑑誡錄 (A record of instructions and warnings). He Guangyuan 何光遠 (c. 910–960). *Xuejin taoyuan* edition.

Jie jiangwang: Xinbian tongyong qizha 新編通用啟劄截江網 (A new edition of a broad selection of commonly used letters). Xiong Huizhong 熊晦仲. Seikadō copy.

JingChu suishi ji 荊楚歲時記 (A record of the annual festivals in Jing and Chu). Zong Lin 宗懍. *Sibu beiyao* edition.

Jinshi cuibian 金石萃編 (Collected inscriptions). Wang Chang 王昶 (1725–1807). *Shike shiliao xinbian* edition.

Jinshu 晉書 (A history of the Jin dynasty). Fang Xuanling 房玄齡 (578–648). Beijing: Zhonghua shuju, 1974.

Jiuhuang huomin shu 救荒活民書 (A book for alleviating famine and enabling the people to live). Dong Wei 董煟 (advanced degree 1194). *Shoushange congshu* edition.

Jiu Tangshu 舊唐書 (The old history of the Tang). Liu Xu 劉昫 (887–946). Beijing: Zhonghua shuju, 1975.

Jiu Wudai shi 舊五代史 (The old history of the Five Dynasties). Xue Juzheng 薛居正 (912–981). Beijing: Zhonghua shuju, 1976.

Kaogu 考古 (Archeology). Beijing: Chinese Academy of Sciences, Institute of Archeology.

Kaogu tongxun 考古通訊 (Archeological reports). Beijing: Chinese Academy of Sciences, Institute of Archeology.

Kaogu xuebao 考古學報 (Archeological reports). Beijing: Chinese Academy of Sciences, Institute of Archeology.

Kaogu yu wenwu 考古與文物 (Archeology and artifacts). Xian: Archeological Research Institute of Shaanxi Province.

Lao Qida yanjie 老乞大諺解 (Old China Hand explained). c. 1400. Keishōkaku sōsho edition. Reprinted in Svetlana Rimsky-Korsakoff Dyer, *Grammatical Analysis of the Lao Ch'i-ta with an English Translation of the Chinese Text* (Canberra: Faculty of Asian Studies, Australian National University, 1983).

Laoxue an biji 老學庵筆記 (Notes from the Laoxue Cloister). Lu You 陸游 (1125–1210). Beijing: Zhonghua shuju, 1979.

Lingwen guilü: shangqing gusui 上清骨髓靈文鬼律 (An efficacious spirit code from the marrow of supreme clarity). Deng Yougong 鄧有功. *Daozang* 203 (HY 461).

Liu Zongyuan ji 柳宗元集 (Collected papers of Liu Zongyuan). Liu Zongyuan 柳宗元 (773–819). Beijing: Zhonghua shuju, 1979.

Lizhi pu 荔枝譜 (A study of lichees). Cai Xiang 蔡襄 (1012–1067). *Baichuan xuehai* edition.

Luguipu san zhong: Jiaoding 校訂錄鬼簿三種 (*Register of ghosts, Three editions, edited and punctuated*). Zhong Sicheng 鍾嗣成 (Yuan dynasty). Ed. Wang Gang 王鋼. Zhengzhou: Zhongzhou guji chubanshe, 1991.

Lunheng 論衡. (Discussing the unusual). c. A.D. 50 Wang Chong 王充 (27–97). *Sibu beiyao* edition.

Luoyang mudan ji 洛陽牡丹記 (A record of peonies in Luoyang). Ouyang Xiu 歐陽修 (1007–1072). *Baichuan xuehai* edition.

Mengxi bitan: Xin jiaozheng 新校正夢溪筆談 (A newly annotated and corrected edition of *Dream Brook Notes*). Shen Gua 沈括 (1030–1095). Ed. Hu Daojing 胡道靜. Hong Kong: Zhonghua shuju, 1975.

Mingbaoji 冥報記 (Records of miraculous retribution). Tang Lin 唐臨 (seventh century). *Taishō shinshū daizōkyō* 大正新修大藏經 50:787–803.

MingQing Huizhou shehui jingji ziliao congbian, di er ji 明清徽州社會經濟資料叢編 第二輯 (Collected materials concerning economy and society from Huizhou during the Ming and Qing dynasties, volume 2). Ed. Huizhou wenqi zhengli zu 徽州文契整理組 (Group in charge of editing contracts from Huizhou). Beijing: Zhongguo shehui kexue chubanshe, 1990.

Mizang jing: Da Han yuanling 大漢原陵秘葬經 (The great Han's secret burial manual for plains and hills). Zhang Jingwen 張景文. *In Yongle dadian* edition (8199).

Muan ji 牧庵集 (Collected papers of Yao Sui). Yao Sui 姚燧 (Yuan dynasty). *Sibu congkan* edition.

Nancun chuogeng lu 南村輟耕錄 (A record of the southern village after having stopped plowing). Tao Zongyi 陶宗儀 (fl. 1360–1368). Beijing: Zhonghua shuju, 1980.

Nan shi 南史 (A history of the southern dynasties). Li Yanshou 李延壽 (c. 629). Beijing: Zhonghua shuju, 1975.

Nenggai zhai manlu 能改齋漫錄 (Free recollections from the can-change studio). 1157. Wu Zeng 吳曾. Shanghai: Shanghai guji chubanshe, 1960.

Nüqing guilü 女青鬼律 (Spirit code of Nüqing). *Daozang* 565 (HY 789).

Ouyang Wenzhong Gongji 歐陽文忠公集 (The collected papers of Ouyang Xiu). Ouyang Xiu 歐陽修 (1007–1072). *Sibu congkan* edition.

Panzhou wenji 盤洲文集 (The collected works of Hong Gua). Hong Gua 洪适 (1117–1184). *Sibu congkan* edition.

Pu Tongshi yanjie 朴通事諺解 (Interpreter Pak explained). c. 1400. Anon. *Keishō-kaku sōsho* edition.

Qidong yeyu 齊東野語 (Scattered talk from east of Qi). Zhou Mi 周密 (1232–1298). Beijing: Zhonghua shuju, 1983.

Qingmingji: Minggong shupan 名公書判清明集 (Collected models of clarity and lucidity by famous judges). c. 1250. Anon. Ed. History Institute of the Chinese Academy of Social Sciences. Beijing: Zhonghua shuju, 1987.

Qingyi lu 清異錄 (Strange tales). c. 960. Tao Gu 陶穀 (903–970). *Xiyin xuan congshu* edition.

Qingyuan tiaofei shilei 慶元條法事類 (The laws of the Qingyuan era [1195–1200] divided by category). Xie Shenfu 謝深甫. Beijing: Zhongguo shudian, 1981.

Qizha qingqian: Xinbian shiwen leiyao, fu qingming ji 新編事文類要啟劄青錢附清明集 (A new collection of topically ordered documents, letters, and essential texts, with *Collected models of clarity and lucidity* appended). 1324. Anon. Taibei: Dahua shuju, 1980.

Quan Yuan xiqu 全元戲曲 (The complete plays of the Yuan dynasty). Ed. Wang Jisi 王季思. Beijing: Renmin wenxue chubanshe, 1990.

Rongzhai suibi 容齋隨筆 (Notes from my studio). 1162–1202. Hong Mai 洪邁. Shanghai: Shanghai guji chubanshe, 1978.

Santian neijie jing 三天內戒經 (The internal proscriptions of the three heavens). Anon. *Daozang* 876 (HY 1196).

Shangqing tianxin zhengfa 上清天心正法 (Correct rites of the celestial heart of supreme clarity). Deng Yougong 鄧有功. *Daozang 318, 319 (HY 566)*.

Shijiazhai yangxinlu 十駕齋養新錄 (A new record from the Shijia studio). 1799. Qian Daxin 錢大昕 (1728–1804). *Sibu beiyao* edition.

Shilin guangji 事林廣記 (Wide-ranging notes from the forest of life). Chen Yuanjing 陳元靚 (fl. thirteenth century). Kyoto: Chūbun shuppansha, 1988 photolithograph of Zhishun (1330–1332) edition.

———. Japanese imperial library copy of Zhiyuan (1335–1340) edition.

———. 1699 Japanese reprint held in Komazawa City Library.

Shisanjing zhushu 十三經註疏 (An annotated edition of the thirteen classics). Ed. Ruan Yuan 阮元. Beijing shuju, 1980.

Shuihu quanzhuan 水滸全传 (The complete water margin). Shi Naian 施耐菴 and Luo Guanzhong 羅貫中. Shanghai: Shanghai guji chubanshe, 1984.

Shushu zhinan: Chongkan 重刊書敍指南 (A reprinted guide to writing letters). Ren Guang 任廣 (fl. 1102–1106). 1649 Japanese reprint.

Song huiyao jigao 宋會要輯稿 (A draft version of the important documents of the Song). Ed. Xu Song 徐松 (1781–1848). Taibei: Xinwenfeng chubanshe, 1962.

Songshi 宋史 (A history of the Song). Tuo Tuo 脱脱 (1313–1355) et al. Beijing: Zhonghua shuju, 1977.

Song xingtong 宋刑統 (The penal code of the Song dynasty). Dou Yi 竇儀 (914–966). Ed. Wu Yiru 吳翊如. Beijing: Zhonghua shuju, 1984.

SongYuan diqi jicun 宋元地契集存 (Collected extant land contracts from the Song and the Yuan dynasties). Beijing Library microfilm.

Soushen ji 搜神記 (Investigations into the divine). Gan Bao 干寶. Beijing: Zhonghua shuju, 1979.

Soushui jiwen 涑水紀聞 (A record of what I heard at Sou stream). Sima Guang 司馬光 (1019–1086). Ed. Deng Guangming 鄧廣銘 and Zhang Xiqing 張希清. Beijing: Zhonghua shuju, 1989.

Sui shu 隋書 (A history of the Sui dynasty). Wei Zheng 魏徵 (580–643). Beijing: Zhonghua shuju, 1973.

Taiping guangji 太平廣記 (Wide-ranging notes from the Taiping era). Ed. Li Fang 李昉 (925–996). Beijing: Zhonghua shuju, 1961.

Taiping yulan 太平御覽 (Imperially reviewed encyclopedia of the Taiping era). Ed. Li Fang 李昉 (925–996). Beijing: Zhonghua shuju, 1966.

Taishang zhuguo jiumin zongzhen biyao 太上助國救民總真祕要 (Secret essentials of the most high on assembling the perfected for the relief of the state and deliverance of the people). Yuan Miaozong 元妙宗 (fl. 1086–1116). *Daozang* 986–987 (HY 1217).

Taishan zhi 泰山志 (A record of Mount Tai). Jin Qi 金棨. 1801, 1810 reprint.

Tang dazhao lingji 唐大詔令集 (Collected edicts of the Tang). 1070. Song Minqiu 宋敏求. *Siku quanshu* edition.

Tang huiyao 唐會要 (Important documents of the Tang). Wang Pu 王溥 (922–982). Beijing: Zhonghua shuju, 1955.

Tang liudian: Da 大唐六典 (The compendium of administrative law of the six divisions of the Tang bureaucracy). 738. Zhang Jiuling 張九齡. *Siku quanshu* edition.

Tanglü shuyi 唐律疏議 (The Tang code explained). 737 (compiled 653). Zhangsun wu-ji 長孫無忌 (?–659). Ed. and punct. Liu Junwen 劉俊文. Beijing: Zhonghua shuju, 1983.

Tangren xiaoshuo 唐人小説 (Stories from the Tang dynasty). Ed. Wang Bijiang 汪辟疆. Hong Kong: Zhonghua shuju, 1987.

Tangyin bishi 棠陰比事 (Parallel cases under the pear tree). Gui Wanrong 桂萬榮. *Siming congshu* edition.

Taozhai cangshiji 匋齋藏石記 (A record of rubbings kept at the Tao studio). Duan Fang 端方. *Shike shiliao xinbian* edition.

Tieanji 鐵菴集 (Collected papers from the iron cloister). Fang Dacong 方大琮 (1183–1247). *Siku quanshu* edition.

Tongdian 通典 (Encyclopedic history of institutions). 801. Duyou 杜佑. Beijing: Zhonghua shuju, 1984.

Tongzhi tiaoge 通制條格 (Comprehensive regulations and statutes of the Yuan). Anon. Ed. and punct. Huang Shijian 黃時鑑. Hangzhou: Zhejiang guji chubanshe, 1986.

Tulufan chutu wenshu 吐魯番出土文書 (Excavated documents from Turfan). Guojia wenwuju gu wenxian yanjiushi 國家文物局古文獻研究室, volumes 1–10. Beijing: Wenwu chubanshe, 1981–1991.

Weixianzhi 濰縣志 (A gazetteer of Wei county [Shandong]). 1941. Chen Hechai 陳鶴儕 et al. Taibei: Xuesheng shuju, 1968.

Wenwu 文物 (Artifacts). Beijing: Wenwu chubanshe.

Wenwu cankao ziliao 文物參考資料 (Materials concerning artifacts). Beijing: Wenwu chubanshe.

Wenwu ziliao congkan 文物資料叢刊 (Collected materials concerning artifacts). Beijing: Wenwu chubanshe.

Wenxian tongkao 文獻通考 (General history of institutions and critical examination of documents). 1224. Ma Duanlin 馬端臨. Beijing: Zhonghua shuju, 1986.

Wenyuan yinghua 文苑英華 (Beautiful flowers from the garden of literature). 987. Ed. Li Fang 李昉 (925–996). Taibei: Hualian chubanshe, 1965.

Wudai huiyao 五代會要 (The important documents of the Five Dynasties). Wang Pu 王溥 (922–982). Shanghai: Shanghai guji chubanshe, 1978.

Xiangshan ji 相山集 (Collected papers of Wang Zhidao). Wang Zhidao 王之道 (1093–1169). *Siku quanshu* edition.

Xin Tangshu 新唐書 (A new history of the Tang). Ouyang Xiu 歐陽修 (1007–1072). Beijing: Zhonghua shuju, 1975.

Xiyuan jilu 洗冤集錄 (Collected writings on the washing away of wrongs). 1247. Song Ci 宋慈. Beijing: Qunzhong chubanshe, 1988.

Xu Yijianzhi: Huhai xinwen Yijian xuzhi 續夷堅志：湖海新聞夷堅續志 (The record of the listener continued, and The newly heard record of the listener from Huhai). Yuan Haowen 元好問 (Jin dynasty). Beijing: Zhonghua shuju, 1986.

Yanfanlu 演繁露 (Extended commentaries). Cheng Dachang 程大昌 (1123–1195). *Xuejin taoyuan* edition.

Yaoxiu keyi jielu chao 要修科儀戒律鈔 (A digest copy of the revised regulations, rituals, prohibitions, and laws). *Daozang* 205 (HY 463).

Yijianzhi 夷堅志 (The record of the listener). 1161–1202. Hong Mai 洪邁. Ed. He Zhuo何卓. Beijing: Zhonghua shuju, 1981.

Yingyuan zonglu 塋原總錄 (A general record of graves). Anon. Beijing Library, Yuan dynasty copy.

Yinju tongyi 隱居通議 (Collected opinions while in seclusion). Liu Xun 劉壎 (1240–1319). *Siku quanshu* edition.

Yishan wenji 一山文集 (Collected papers of Li Jiben). Li Jiben 李繼本 (Yuan dynasty). Siku quanshu edition.

Yiyuji 疑獄集 (Collection of difficult cases). He Ning 和凝 (early tenth century) and He Meng 和㠓 (951–995). Taibei: Shangwu yinshuguan, 1974.

Yongle dadian xiwen sanzhong jiaozhu 永樂大典戲文三種校肴 (Three plays from the Yongle Dadian Encyclopedia, punctuated and annotated). Ed. Qian Nanyang 錢南揚. Beijing: Zhonghua shuju, 1979.

Yuandai falu ziliao jicun 元代法律資料輯存 (Collected remnants of legal materials from the Yuan dynasty). Ed. Huang Shijian 黃時鑑. Hangzhou: Zhejiang guji chubanshe, 1988.

Yuan dianzhang (Da Yuan Shengzheng guochao dianzhang) 大元聖政國朝典章 (Institutions of the great Yuan sacred government). 1320–1322. Taibei: Wenhai chubanshe, 1974.

Yuankan zaju sanshi zhong xinjiao 元刊雜劇三十種新校 (A newly punctuated edition of thirty Yuan editions of plays). Ed. Ning Xiyuan 宁希元. Lanzhou: Lanzhou daxue chubanshe, 1988.

Yuanqu xuan 元曲選 (A selection of plays from the Yuan dynasty). 1615–1616. Zang Mouxun 藏懋椒. Beijing: Zhonghua shuju, 1958, 1989.

Yuanshi 元史 (The official history of the Yuan dynasty). Song Lian 宋濂. Beijing: Zhonghua shuju, 1976.

Yuanshi Changqing ji 元氏長慶集 (Collected writings of Mr. Yuan from the Changqing reign period [821–824]). Yuan Zhen 元稹 (779–831). Sibu congkan edition.

Yuanshi shifan 袁氏世範 (Mr. Yuan's principles of family behavior). 1179. Yuan Cai 袁采 (1140–1190). *Siku quanshu* edition.

Yuzhao xinzhi: Touxia lu 投轄錄：玉照新志 (A record of governing: New notes from the residence of the old mirror). 1198. Wang Mingqing 王明清 (1127–after 1214). Shanghai: Shanghai guji chubanshe, 1991.

Zangjing 葬經 (The classic of burial). Qing Wuzi 青烏子. Ed. Wu Qinze 兀欽仄 (Jin dynasty). Xuejin taoyuan edition.

Zhengao 真誥 (Declarations of the perfected). 499. Tao Hongjing 陶弘景 (456–536). *Daozang* 637–640 (HY 1010).

Zheyu guijian yizhu 折獄龜鑑譯註 (An annotated edition of the mirror for deciding law suits). Zheng Ke 鄭克 (?–after 1133). Ed. Liu Junwen 劉俊文. Shanghai: Shanghai guji chubanshe, 1988.

Zhou Bida wenji: Zhou Yiguo wenzhong gong wenji 周益國文忠公文集 (Collected papers of Zhou Bida). Zhou Bida 周必大 (1126–1204). *Siku quanshu* edition.

Zhouxian tigang 州縣提綱 (Suggested policies for local administration). c. 1158. Anon. *Sibu congkan* edition.

Zhu Wengong wenji: Huian xiansheng 晦庵先生朱文公文集 (The collected works of Zhu Xi). Zhu Xi 朱熹 (1130–1200). *Sibu congkan* edition.

Zhu Wengong zhengxun 朱文公政訓 (Zhu Xi's teachings on government). Zhu Xi 朱熹 (1130–1200). *Congshu jicheng* edition.

Zuoyi zizhen 作邑自箴 (Self-admonitions for local administrators). 1117. Li Yuanbi 李元弼. Sibu congkan edition.

Secondary Sources

Abe Ryūichi 阿部隆一. 1976. *Chūgoku hōshoshi* 中國訪書志 (A record of visiting books in China). Tokyo: Kyūko shoin.

Akagi Ryūji 赤城隆治. 1985. "NanSōki no soshō ni tsuite—'kenshō' to chihōkan" 南宋期の訴訟について一"健訟"と地方官 (About law suits in the Southern Song period: "Jiansong" and local officials). *Shichō* 史潮 16:4–25.

Asim, Ina. 1993. *Religiöse Landverträge aus der Song-Zeit*. Heidelberg: Edition Forum.

———. 1994. "Status Symbol and Insurance Policy: Song Land Deeds for the Afterlife." In *Burial in Song China*, ed. Dieter Kuhn, 307–370. Heidelberg: Edition Forum.

Atiyah, P. S. 1971. *An Introduction to the Law of Contract.* Oxford: Clarendon Press.

Baker, J. H. 1990. *An Introduction to English Legal History.* London: Butterworth.

Balazs, Etienne. 1954. *Le traité juridique de "Souei-chou."* Leiden: E. J. Brill.

Beckwith, Christopher I. 1987. *The Tibetan Empire in Central Asia: A History of the Struggle for Great Power among Tibetans, Turks, Arabs, and Chinese during the Early Middle Ages.* Princeton: Princeton University Press.

Birge, Bettine. 1992. "Women and Property in Sung Dynasty China (960–1279): Neo-Confucianism and Social Change in Chien-chou, Fukien." Doctoral dissertation, Columbia University.

Bol, Peter. 1977. "The *Tso-i tzu-chen*: A Twelfth-Century Guide for Subprefects." Unpublished.

Boltz, Judith Magee. 1987. *A Survey of Taoist Literature, Tenth to Seventeenth Centuries.* Berkeley: Institute of East Asian Studies.

———. 1993. "Not by the Seal of Office Alone: New Weapons in Battles with the Supernatural." In *Religion and Society in T'ang and Sung China,* ed. Patricia Buckley Ebrey and Peter N. Gregory, 241–306. Honolulu: University of Hawaii Press.

Bray, Francesca. 1984. *Science and Civilization in China.* Volume 6, *Biology and Biological Technology.* Part II: Agriculture. New York: Cambridge University Press.

Brockman, Rosser H. 1980. "Commercial Contract Law in Late Nineteenth-Century Taiwan." In *Essays on China's Legal Traditions,* ed. Jerome Alan Cohen, R. Randle Edwards, and Fu-mei Chang Chen, 76–136. Princeton: Princeton University Press.

Cable, Mildred, and Francesca French. 1987. *The Gobi Desert.* Boston: Beacon Press.

Cartier, Michel. 1988. "Dette et propriété en Chine." In *Lien de vie, noeud mortel: Les représentations de la dette en Chine, au Japon, et dans le monde indien,* ed. Charles Malamoud, 17–30. Paris: Editions de l'Ecole des Hautes Etudes en Sciences Sociales.

Chavannes, Edouard. 1910. *Le T'ai Chan: Essai de monographie d'un culte chinois.* Paris: Ernest Leroux.

Chen Baiquan 陳柏泉. 1987. "Jiangxi chutu diquan zongshu" 江西出土地券綜述 (A survey of land deeds excavated in Jiangxi). *Kaogu* 3:223.

———. 1991. *Jiangxi chutu muzhi xuanbian* 江西出土墓志選編 (A selection of funerary texts excavated in Jiangxi). Nanchang: Jiangxi jiaoyu chubanshe.

Chen Gaohua 陳高華. 1988. "Yuandai tudi dianmai de guocheng he wenqi" 元代土
地典賣的過程和文契 (The process of and contracts from buying and mortgaging
land in the Yuan dynasty). *Zhongguo shi yanjiu* 1988. 4:35–48.

Chen Guocan 陳國燦. 1983a. "Cong Tulufan chutu de 'zhikuzhang' kan Tangdai de
zhiku zhidu 從吐魯番出土的質庫帳看唐代的質庫制度 (An examination of the
pawnshops of the Tang dynasty based on pawn tickets from Turfan). In
Dunhuang Tulufan wenshu chutan 敦煌吐魯番文書初探 (A beginning exploration
of documents from Dunhuang and Turfan), 316–343. Wuhan: Wuhan daxue
chubanshe.

———. 1983b. "Tangdai de minjian jiedai—Tulufan Dunhuang deng di suochu
Tangdai jiedai chiquan chutan" 唐代的民間借貸—吐魯番敦煌等地所出唐代借貸契
券初探 (Borrowing and lending among the people of the Tang dynasty: A
preliminary examination of contracts for borrowing and lending from Turfan,
Dunhuang, and other places). In *Dunhuang Tulufan wenshu chutan* 敦煌吐魯番
文書初探 (A beginning exploration of documents from Dunhuang and Turfan),
217–44. Wuhan: Wuhan daxue chubanshe.

Ch'en Li-li, trans. 1976. *Master Tung's Western Chamber Romance (Tung Hsi-
hsiang chu-kung-tiao)*. New York: Cambridge University Press.

Chen Mengjia 陳蒙家. 1966. "DongZhou mengshi yu chutu zaishu" 東周盟誓于出土
載書 (Oaths of the Eastern Zhou and excavated records of them). Kaogu 5:271–
279.

Ch'en, Paul Heng-chao. 1979. *Chinese Legal Tradition under the Mongols: The
Code of 1291 as Reconstructed*. Princeton: Princeton University Press.

Chen Zhichao 陳智超. 1987. "Songshi yanjiu de zhengui shiliao—ming keben
'Minggong shupan qingmingji'" 宋史研究的珍貴史料—明刻本名公書判清明集 (A
valuable source for the study of Song history: The Ming edition of *Collected
models of clarity and lucidity by famous judges*). In *Minggong shupan
qingming ji* 名公書判清明集 (Collected models of clarity and lucidity by famous
judges), ed. History Institute of the Chinese Academy of Social Sciences, 645–
686. Beijing: Zhonghua shuju, 1987.

Chikusa Masaaki 竺沙雅章. 1973. "Kanseki shihai monjo no kenkyū" 漢籍紙背文書
の研究 (A study of documents on the backs of the pages of Chinese books).
Kyōto daigaku bungakubu kenkyū kiyō 14:1–54.

Chu Ron-Guey. 1989. "Chu Hsi and Public Instruction." In *Neo-Confucian
Education: The Formative Stage*, ed. Wm. Theodore de Bary and John W.
Chaffee, 252–273. Berkeley: University of California Press.

Clanchy, M. T. 1979. *From Memory to Written Record: England, 1066–1307*.
Cambridge, Mass.: Harvard University Press.

Cleaves, Francis Woodman. 1955. "An Early Mongolian Loan Contract from Qara
Qoto." *Harvard Journal of Asiatic Studies* 18:1–49.

Dobson, W. A. C. H. 1968. "Some Legal Instruments of Ancient China, *ming* and *meng*." In *Wen-lin: Studies in the Chinese Humanities*, ed. Chow Ts'e-tsung, 269–282. Madison: University of Wisconsin Press.

Dong Guodong 凍國棟. 1990. *Tangdai de shangpin jingji yu jingying guanli* 唐代的商品經濟與經營管理 (The commercial economy of the Tang dynasty and its management and control). Wuhan: Wuhan daxue chubanshe.

Doré, Henri. 1911–34. *Recherches sur les superstitions en Chine*. Paris: Librairie Orientale et Americaine.

Dudbridge, Glen. 1970. *The Hsi-yu chi: A Study of Antecedents to the Sixteenth-Century Chinese Novel*. New York: Cambridge University Press.

Dyer, Svetlana Rimsky-Korsakoff. 1983. *Grammatical Analysis of the Lao Ch'i-ta with an English Translation of the Chinese Text*. Canberra: Faculty of Asian Studies, Australian National University.

Ebrey, Patricia Buckley. 1984. *Family and Property in Sung China: Yuan Ts'ai's Precepts for Social Life*. Princeton: Princeton University Press.

———. 1990. "Cremation in Sung China." *American Historical Review* 95. 2:406–428.

———. 1993. *The Inner Quarters: Marriage and the Lives of Chinese Women in the Sung Period*. University of California Press: Berkeley.

Elvin, Mark. 1973. *The Pattern of the Chinese Past: A Social and Economic Interpretation*. Stanford: Stanford University Press.

Fan Sheng-chih. 1994. "Fan Sheng-chih's Book." In *The Columbia Anthology of Traditional Chinese Literature*, ed. Victor H. Mair, 626–627. New York: Columbia University Press.

Fang Chaoying. 1969. *The Asami Library: A Descriptive Catalogue*. Berkeley: University of California Press.

Fang Hao 方豪. 1974. "Jinmen chutu Songmu maidiquan kaoshi" 金門出土宋墓買地券考釋 (A study of a tomb contract excavated from a Song tomb in Jinmen). In *Liushi zhi liushisi zixuan teding gao* 六十至六十四自選特定稿 (A special self-selected collection of writings from 1970 to 1974), 187–202. Taibei: Xuesheng shuju.

Fang Shiming 方詩銘. 1973. "Cong Xu Sheng diquan lun Handai diquan zhi jianbie" 從徐勝地券論漢代地券之鑒別 (A discussion of how to evaluate Han dynasty tomb contracts on the basis of Xu Sheng's tomb contract). *Wenwu* 5: 52–55.

Fong, Wen C. 1992. *Beyond Representation: Chinese Painting and Calligraphy 8th–14th Centuries*. New Haven: Yale University Press.

Forke, Alfred. 1908. "Lun-Heng. Selected Essays of the Philosopher Wang Ch'ung." *Mitteilungen des Seminars für orientalische Sprachen an der königlichen Friedrich-Wilhelms-Universität zu Berlin* 11: 1–188.

Franke, Herbert. 1981. "Jurchen Customary Law and the Chinese Law of the Chin Dynasty." In *State and Law in East Asia: Festschrift Karl Bünger*, ed. Dieter Eikemeier and Herbert Franke, 214–233. Wiesbaden: Otto Harrasowitz.

Fujieda Akira 藤枝晃. 1942. "Sashū kigigun setsudoshi shimatsu" 沙州歸義軍節度使始末 (A history of rule by the Return-to-Righteousness Army). *Tōhōgakuhō* (Kyōto) 12:494–527.

———. 1961. "Toban shihaiki no Tonkō" 吐蕃支配期の敦煌 (Dunhuang under Tibetan rule). *Tōhōgakuhō* (Kyōto) 31:199–292.

Gates, Hill. 1987. "Money for the Gods: The Commoditization of the Spirit." *Modern China* 13:259–77.

Gernet, Jacques. 1957. "La vente en Chine d'après les contrats de Touen-houang (IXe—Xe siècles)." *T'oung Pao* 45: 295–391.

———. 1966. "Location de chameaux pour des voyages à Touen-houang." In *Mélanges de sinologie offerts à Monsieur Paul Demiéville*. Paris: Presses Universitaires de France.

Gjertson, Donald E. 1989. *Miraculous Retribution: A Study and Translation of T'ang Lin's Ming-pao chi*. Berkeley: Berkeley Buddhist Studies Series, University of California.

Golas, Peter J. 1980. "Rural China in the Song." *Journal of Asian Studies* 39: 291–325.

de Groot, J. J. M. 1892–1907. *The Religious System of China: Its Ancient Forms, Evolution, History and Present Aspect, Manners, Customs, and Social Institutions Connected Therewith*. Volumes 1–6. Leiden: E. J. Brill.

Graham, David Crockett. 1961. *Folk Religion in Southwest China*. Washington: Smithsonian Miscellaneous Collections.

Guo Dongxu 郭東旭. 1990. "Songdai zhi songxue" 宋代之訟學 (The study of suing in the Song dynasty). In *Songshi yanjiu luncong* 宋史研究論叢 (Collected essays in Song studies), ed. Qi Xia 漆俠, 133–147. Baoding: Hebei daxue chubanshe.

Han Guopan 韓國磐 1986. "Zai lun Tangdai Xizhou de tianzhi" 再論唐代西州的田制 (Reconsidering the land system in Xizhou during the Tang dynasty). In *Dunhuang Tulufan chutu jingji wenshu yanjiu* 敦煌吐魯番出土經濟文書研究 (Studies of economic documents excavated at Dunhuang and Turfan), ed. Han Guopan, 1–38. Xiamen: Xiamen daxue chubanshe.

Hanan, Patrick. 1973. *The Chinese Short Story: Studies in Dating, Authorship, and Composition*. Cambridge, Mass.: Harvard University Press.

Hansen, Valerie. 1990. *Changing Gods in Medieval China, 1127–1276*. Princeton: Princeton University Press.

———. 1992. "Songdai de maidiquan" 宋代的買地券 (Tomb contracts in the Song dynasty). In *Guoji Songshi taolunhui lunwen xuanji* 國際宋史討論會論文選集

(Selected papers from the international Song studies conference), ed. Deng Guangming 鄧廣銘 and Qi Xia 漆俠, 133–149. Baoding: Hebei daxue chubanshe.

Harada Masami 原田正己 1967. "Bokenbun ni mirareru meikai no kami to sono saishi" 墓券文に見られる冥界の神とその祭祀 (The gods of the otherworld and their liturgical celebrations as seen in *muquan* manuscripts). *Tōhō shūkyō* 29: 17–35.

Hartwell, Robert M. 1978. "Regional Economic Development and the Transformation of Chinese Society, 750–1250 A.D." Paper presented at Conference on Regionalism and Economic Development in China, Subcommittee for Research on the Chinese Economy, Philadelphia.

Hayden, George A. 1978. *Crime and Punishment in Medieval Chinese Drama: Three Judge Bao Plays*. Cambridge, Mass.: Harvard University Press.

Hori Toshikazu 堀敏一 1980. "Tōdai ni okeru dendo no chintaishaku to teitō shichiire to no kankei—soden keiyaku kara tenchi keiyaku ni itaru made no shokeitai" 唐代における田土の賃貸借と低当質人との関係—租佃契約から典地契約にいたるまでの諸形態 (The relationship between mortgaging and renting land in the Tang dynasty: The different types, from rental contracts to mortgage contracts). *Tōyōshi kenkyū* 39. 3:34–64.

———. 1983. "Tangdai tiandi de zulin he diya de guanxi—cong zudian qiyue dao diandiqi de zhu xingtai" 唐代田地的租賃和抵押的關係拳—租佃契約到典地契的諸形態 (The relationship between mortgaging and renting land in the Tang dynasty: The different types, from rental contracts to mortgage contracts). *Zhongguo shehui jingji shi yanjiu* 4:76–87.

Hou Can 侯燦 1982. "Kaiping shiyi nian Wang Nian maituoqi ji qi shuoming de lishi wenti" 開平十一年王念賣駝契及其說明的歷史問題 (Wang Nian's 367 contract to buy a camel and the historical problems it illuminates). *Kaogu yu wenwu* 5:104, 101.

Hou Ching-lang. 1975. *Monnaies d'offrande et la notion de trésorerie dans la religion chinoise*. Paris: Presses Universitaries de France.

Hu Ji 胡戟 et al. 1987. *Tulufan* 吐魯番 (Turfan). Xian: Santai chubanshe.

Hu Liuyuan and Feng Zhuohui 胡留元，馮桌慧 1983. "Cong Shaanxi jinwen kan XiZhou minfa guifan ji minshi susong zhidu" 從陝西金文看西周民法規范及民事訴訟制度 (A view based on inscriptions from Shaanxi of the norms of civil law extending to the system of civil suits in the Western Zhou). *Kaogu yu wenwu* 6:72–78, 63.

Hucker, Charles O. 1985. *A Dictionary of Official Titles in Imperial China*. Stanford: Stanford University Press.

Hulsewé, Anton F. P. 1978. "'Contracts' of the Han Period." In *Il Diritto in Cina*, ed. Lionello Lanciotti, 11–38. Florence: Editore Leo S. Olschki.

Hymes, Robert. 1986. *Statesmen and Gentlemen: The Elite of Fu-chou, Chiang-hsi, in Northern and Southern Song.* New York: Cambridge University Press.

———. n. d. "Way and Byway: Taoist Saints' Cults and Exorcist Masters in Sung and Yuan China." Unpublished.

Idema, Wilt. *The Dramatic Œuvre of Chu Yu-tun (1379–1439).* Leiden: E. J. Brill.

Idema, Wilt, and Stephen H. West. 1982. *Chinese Theater, 1100–1450: A Source Book.* Wiesbaden: Franz Steiner Verlag.

Ikeda On 池田温 1973a. "Chūgoku kodai no sodenkei" 中国古代の租田契 (Contracts for renting land in ancient China," part 1). *Tōyō bunka kenkyūjo kiyō* 60:1–112.

———. 1973b. "T'ang Household Registers and Related Documents." In *Perspectives on the T'ang,* ed. Arthur F. Wright and Denis Twitchett, 121–150. New Haven: Yale University Press.

———. 1975. "Chūgoku kodai no sodenkei" 中国古代の租田契 (Contracts for renting land in ancient China," part 2). *Tōyō bunka kenkyūjo kiyō* 65:1–112.

———. 1979. *Chūgoku kodai sekichō kenkyū—gaikan rokubun* 中國古代籍帳研究概觀錄文 (A study of household registers in ancient China: Overall view and texts). Tokyo: Tōkyo Daigaku Tōyō Bunka Kenkyūjo.

———. 1981. "Chūgoku rekidai boken ryakkō" 中國歷代墓券略考 (A study of Chinese tomb deeds through the ages). *Tōyō bunka kenkyūjo kiyō* 86:193–278.

———. 1986. "Tulufan, Dunhuang qiquan gaiguan" 吐魯番，敦煌契券概觀 (An introduction to the contracts of Turfan and Dunhuang). *Hanxue yanjiu* 4:9–40.

Ikeda On, Yamamoto Tatsuro, and Okano Makoto. 1980. *Tun-huang and Turfan Documents Concerning Social and Economic History.* Volume 1, *Legal Texts: (A) Introduction and Texts.* Tokyo: Toyo Bunko.

Inagaki Hisao and P. G. O'Neill. 1988. *A Dictionary of Japanese Buddhist Terms: Based on References in Japanese Literature.* Union City: Heian International.

Iwaki Hideo 岩城秀夫 [1959] 1972. "Gen no saiban geki ni okeru Hō Jō no tokuisei" 元の裁判劇における包拯の特異性 (The special characteristics of Judge Bao as he appears in Yuan courtroom drama). In *Chūgoku gikyoku engeki kenkyū* 中國戲曲演劇研究 (A study of Chinese drama), 452–481. Tokyo: Sōbunsha.

Jiang Xidong 姜錫東. 1991. "Songdai maimai qiyue chutan" 宋代買賣契約初探 (A preliminary study of Song dynasty contracts for buying and selling). In *ZhongRi Songshi yantaohui: Zhongfang lunwen xuanbian* 中日宋史研討會：中方論文選編 (The Sino-Japanese conference on Song history: Selected papers from the Chinese side), ed. Deng Guangming 鄧廣銘 and Qi Xia 漆俠, 91–106. Baoding: Hebei daxue chubanshe.

Jin Weinuo 金維諾 and Wei Bian 衞邊 1975. "Tangdai Xizhou muzhong de juanhua" 唐代西州墓中的絹畫 (Tang paintings on silk from the tombs of Xizhou). *Wenwu* 1975. 10:36–43.

Johnson, Wallace. 1979. *The T'ang Code*. Volume 1, *General Principles*. Princeton: Princeton University Press.

Jun Wenren and James M. Hargett. 1989. "The Measures Li and Mou during the Song, Liao, and Jin Dynasties." *Bulletin of Sung-Yuan Studies* 21:8–30.

Kaltenmark, M. 1960. "Ling-pao: Note sur un terme du taoïsme religieux." In *Mélanges publiés par l'Institut des Hautes Etudes Chinoises*, volume 2, 559–588. Paris: Presses Universitaires de France.

Kang Shizhen 康實鎮 1985. *Laoqida Putongshi yanjiu: zhushu zhi zhucheng ji qi shuzhong hanyu yuyin yufa zhi fenxilun* 老乞大朴通事研究—諸書之著成及其書中漢語語音語法之分析論 (A discussion and analysis of the Chinese phonetics and grammar and authorship of the two books *Old China Hand and Interpreter Pak*). Taibei: Xuesheng shuju.

Katō Shigeshi 加藤繁 1953. *Shina keizaishi kōshō* 支那經濟史考證 (Studies in Chinese economic history). Volume 2. Tokyo: Tōyō bunko.

Kleeman, Terry. 1984. "Land Contracts and Related Documents." In *Chūgoku no shūkyō: shisō to kagaku* 中国の宗教：思想と科学 (Religion, thought, and science in China: A festschrift in honor of Professor Ryōkai Makio on his seventieth birthday), 1–34. Tokyo: Kokusho kankōkai.

Kong Xiangxing 孔祥星 1983. "Tangdai qianqi de tudi zudian guanxi—Tulufan wenshu yanjiu" 唐代前期的土地租佃關系—吐魯番文書研究 (Tenant relations on the land in the early years of the Tang dynasty: A study of Turfan documents). In *Dunhuang Tulufan wenshu yanjiu* 敦煌吐魯番文書研究, ed. Sha Zhi 沙知 and Kong Xiangxing 孔祥星, 236–276. Lanzhou: Ganshu renmin chubanshe.

Kroker, Edward. 1959. "The Concept of Property in Chinese Customary Law." *Transactions of the Asiatic Society of Japan*, series 3, 7:123–146.

Kuhn, Dieter. 1990. *The Mute Witnesses: Tombs Contribute to Studies in the History of China, Two Essais*. Heidelberg: Wüzburger Sinologische Schriften.

Lagerwey, John. 1987. *Taoist Ritual in Chinese Society and History*. New York: Macmillan Publishing Company.

Langlois, J. D. 1981. " 'Living Law' in Sung and Yuan Jurisprudence." *Harvard Journal of Asiatic Studies* 41:165–217.

Li Gan 李幹 1985. *Yuandai shehui jingji shigao* 元代社會經濟史稿 (A draft social and economic history of the Yuan dynasty). Wuhan: Hubei renmin chubanshe.

Li Jiaju 酈家駒. 1988. "LiangSong shiqi tudi suoyouquan de zhuanyi" 兩宋時期土地所有權的轉移 (Changes in the land tenure system of the Northern and Southern Song). *Zhonguo shi yanjiu* 4:25–34.

Li Shougang 李壽岡 1978. "Ye tan 'diquan' de jianbie" 也談〈地券〉的鑒別 (A further discussion evaluating tomb contracts). *Wenwu* 7:79–80.

Li Zheng 李征 1973. "Tulufan xian Asitana—Helahezhuo gumuqun fajue jianbao"

吐魯番縣阿斯塔那—哈拉和卓古墓羣發覺簡報 (A preliminary site report of the ancient graveyards of Astana and Helahuzhuo in Turfan county). *Wenwu* 10:7–27.

Lin Ganquan 林甘泉 1989. "Hanjian suojian Xibei biansai de shangpin jiaohuan he maimai qiyue" 漢簡所見西北邊塞的商品交換和買賣契約 (Contracts for the sale and exchange of commodities on the northwest border region, as seen in Han bamboo records). *Wenwu* 9:25–33.

Liu Fu 劉復 [1934] 1957. *Dunhuang duosuo* 燉煌掇瑣 (Selected trifles from Dunhuang). Reprint. Beijing: Zhongguo kexueyuan kaogu yanjiusuo.

Liu Hehui 劉和惠 1984. "Yuandai Huizhou diqi 元代徽州地契 (Land contracts from Huizhou during the Yuan dynasty). *Yuanshi ji beifang minzushi yanjiu jikan* 8:28–34.

Liu Jung-en, trans. 1972. *Six Yuan Plays*. Baltimore: Penguin Books.

Liu Junwen 劉俊文. 1989. *Dunhuang Tulufan Tangdai fazhi wenshu kaoshi* 敦煌吐魯番唐代法制文書考釋 (A study of Tang-dynasty legal documents from Turfan and Dunhuang). Beijing: Zhonghua shuju.

Liu Nianzi 劉念茲 1986. *Xiqu wenwu congkao* 戲曲文物叢考 (An examination of material relics from dramatic performances). Beijing: Zhongguo xiju chubanshe.

Liu Qingzhu 劉慶柱 1983. "Shaanxi Changwuxian chutu Taihe yuannian diquan" 陝西長武縣出土太和元年地券 (A tomb contract dated the first year of the Taihe reign [477], excavated in Changwu county, Shaanxi). *Wenwu* 8:94.

Liu Xinru. 1988. *Ancient India and Ancient China: Trade and Religious Exchanges, A.D. 1–600*. Delhi: Oxford University Press.

Loewe, Michael, ed. 1993. *Early Chinese Texts: A Bibliographical Guide*. Berkeley: Institute of East Asian Studies.

Ma Shichang 馬世長 1978. "Guanyu Dunhuang cangjingdong de jige wenti" 關於敦煌藏經洞的幾個問題 (A few questions about the sealed library at Dunhuang). *Wenwu* 12:21–33.

MacCormack, Geoffrey. 1985. "The Law of Contract in China under the T'ang and Sung Dynasties." *Revue Internationale des Droits de L'Antiquité* 32:17–68.

———. 1990. *Traditional Chinese Penal Law*. Edinburgh: Edinburgh University Press.

Maine, Sir Henry Sumner. 1861. *Ancient Law: Its Connection with the Early History of Society, and Its Relation to Modern Ideas*. London: John Murray.

Mair, Victor. 1981. "Lay Students and the Making of Written Vernacular Narrative: An Inventory of Tun-huang Manuscripts." *Chinoperl Papers* 10:5–96.

———. 1983. *Tun-huang Popular Narratives*. New York: Cambridge University Press.

———. 1990. "*Tufan* and *Tulufan*: The Origins of the Old Chinese Names for Tibet and Turfan." *Central and Inner Asian Studies* 4: 14–70.

———. 1991. "Reflections on the Origins of the Modern Standard Mandarin Place-Name 'Dunhuang'—With an Added Note on the Identity of the Modern Uighur Place-Name 'Turpan.'" In *Papers in Honour of Professor Dr. Ji Xianlin on the Occasion of his 80th Birthday (II)*, ed. Li Zheng and Jiang Zhongxin, 901–954. Nanchang: Jiangxi renmin chubanshe.

Maruyama Hiroshi 丸山宏 1986. "Seiichi Dōkyō no jōshō girei ni tsuite: 'chōshō shō' o chūshin to shite" 正一道教の上章儀禮について："冢訟章"を中心として (On the Taoist rituals of submitting petitions to settle complaints from ancestral tombs: A study of the Zhongsong zhang). *Tōhō shūkyō* 68:44–64.

Maspero, Henri. 1934–35. "Le serment dans la procédure judiciare de la Chine antique." *Mélanges Chinois et Bouddhiques* 3: 257–317.

———. 1953. *Les documents chinois de la troisième expédition de Sir Aurel Stein en Asie centrale*. London: Trustees of the British Museum.

McDermott, Joseph. 1984. "Charting Blank Spaces and Disputed Regions: The Problem of Sung Land Tenure." *Journal of Asian Studies* 44:13–41.

McKnight, Brian, trans. 1981. *The Washing Away of Wrongs: Forensic Medicine in Thirteenth-Century China*. Ann Arbor: Center for Chinese Studies.

———. 1987. "From Statute to Precedent: An Introduction to Sung Law and Its Transformation." In *Law and the State in Traditional East Asia: Six Studies on the Sources of East Asian Law*, ed. Brian McKnight, 111–131. Honolulu: University of Hawaii Press.

———. 1989. "Mandarins as Legal Experts: Professional Learning in Sung China." In *Neo-Confucian Education: The Formative Stage*, ed. Wm. Theodore de Bary and John W. Chaffee, 493–516. Berkeley: University of California Press.

Miyazaki Ichisada 宮崎市定 1964. "Sō Gen jidai no hōsei to saiban kikō" 宋元時代の法制と裁判機構 (The legal system and the judicial structure in the Song and Yuan periods). In *Ajiashi kenkyū* アジア史研究 (Studies in Asian history), volume 4, 179–305. Kyoto: Dōbōsha. Originally in *Tōhō gakuhō* 24 (1954):115–225.

———. 1980. "The Administration of Justice during the Sung Dynasty." In *Essays on China's Legal Traditions*, ed. Jerome Alan Cohen, R. Randle Edwards, and Fu-mei Chang Chen, 56–75. Princeton: Princeton University Press.

Morgan, Carole. 1990–91. "T'ang Geomancy: The Wu-hsing ('Five Names') Theory and Its Legacy." *T'ang Studies* 8–9: 45–76.

Morita Kenji 森田憲司 1991. "Guanyu zai Riben de Shilin guangji zhuben" 關於在日本的《事林廣記》諸本 (About the different editions in Japan of *Wide-ranging notes from the forest of life*). In *Guoji Songshi taolunhui lunwen xuanji* 國際宋

史討論會論文選集 (Selected papers from the international Song studies conference), ed. Deng Guangming 鄧廣銘 and Qi Xia 漆俠, 266–280. Baoding: Hebei daxue chubanshe.

Mullie, Jos. 1947. "Les formules du serment dans le Tso-Tchouan." *T'oung Pao* 38. 1:43–74.

Myers, Ramon H. 1982. "Customary Law, Markets, and Resource Transactions in Late Imperial China." In *Explorations in the New Economic History: Essays in Honor of Douglass C. North*, ed. Roger L. Ransom, Richard Sutch, and Gary M. Walton, 273–298. New York: Academic Press.

Myers, Ramon H., and Fu-mei Chang Chen. 1976. "Customary Law and the Economic Growth of China during the Ch'ing Period." *Ch'ing-shih wen-t'i* 3. 5: 1–32.

Needham, Joseph. 1969. "Human Law and the Laws of Nature." In *The Grand Titration: Science and Society in East and West*, 299–331. London: George Allen & Unwin.

Niida Noboru 仁井田陞 [1937] 1983. *Tōsō hōritsu monjo no kenkyū* 唐宋法律文書 の研究 (A study of legal documents of the Tang and Song eras). Reprint. Tokyo: Tōkyō daigaku shuppankai.

———. 1937. "Shina kinsei no gikyoku shōsetsu ni mietaru shihō" 支那近世の戯曲 小説に見えたる私法 (Chinese civil law as reflected in early modern plays and novels). In *Nakada sensei kanreki shukuga hōseishi ronshū* 中田先生還曆祝賀法 制史論集, ed. Ishii Ryōsuke 石井良助, 315–517. Tokyo: Iwanami shoten.

———. 1938. "Kan Gi Rikuchō no tochi baibai monjo" 漢魏六朝の土地賣買文書 (Documents for the sale and purchase of land during the Han, Wei, and Six Dynasties periods). *Tōhō gakuhō* (Tokyo) 8:33–101.

———. 1939. "A Study of Simplified Seal Marks and Finger-Seals in Chinese Documents." *Memoirs of the Research Department of the Toyo Bunko* 11:79–131.

———. 1960a. *Chūgoku hōseishi kenkyū: tochihō, torihikihō* 中國法制史研究：土地 法，取引法 (A study of Chinese legal history: Land law and transactional law). Tokyo: Tōkyō daigaku shuppankai.

———. 1960b. "Toroban shutsudo no Tōdai torihikihō kankei monjo" 吐魯番出土 の唐代取引法関系文書 (A study of documents related to transactional law excavated at Turfan). In *Saiiki bunka kenkyū (Monumenta Serindica)*, volume 3, 189–223. Kyoto: Hōzōkan.

———. 1962. *Chūgoku hōseishi kenkyū: dorei nōdo hō, kazoku sonraku hō* 中國法 制史研究：奴隷農奴法，家族村落法 (A study of Chinese legal history: Slave and serf law, family and village law). Tokyo: Tōkyō daigaku shuppankai.

———. 1964. *Chūgoku hōseishi kenkyū: hō to kanshū, hō to dōtoku* 中國法制史 研究：法と慣習、法と道徳 (A study of Chinese legal history, law and custom, law and morality). Tokyo: Tōkyō daigaku shuppankai.

Nishijima Sadao 西島定生 1959. "Toroban shutsudo monjo yori mitaru kindensei no shikō jōtai: kyūden monjo, taiden monjo o chūshin to shite" 吐魯番出土文書より見たる均田制の施行状態…給田文書・退田文書を中心として (An examination of the enforcement of the equal-field system based on documents excavated at Turfan: Focusing on documents giving out land and documents returning land). In *Saiiki bunka kenkyū (Monumenta Serindica)* volume 2, 151–291.

Oda Yoshihisa 小田義久 1984. *Ōtani monjo shūsei* 大谷文書集成 (The complete Otani documents), volume 1. Kyoto: Hōzōkan.

———. 1990. *Ōtani monjo shūsei* 大谷文書集成 (The complete Otani documents), volume 2. Kyoto: Ryūkoku daigaku (Zenpon sōsho 10).

Ogawa Tamaki 小川環樹 et al. 1968. *Shinjigen* 新字源 (A new source of characters). Tokyo: Kadokawa shoten.

de Pee, Christian. 1991. "Women in the *Yi Jian Zhi*: A Socio-Historical Study Based on Fiction." Master's thesis, University of Leiden.

Perdue, Peter. 1987. *Exhausting the Earth: State and Peasant in Hunan, 1500–1850.* Cambridge, Mass.: Harvard University Press.

Perng Ching-hsi. 1978. *Double Jeopardy: A Critique of Seven Yüan Courtroom Dramas.* Ann Arbor: Center for Chinese Studies, University of Michigan.

Qi Xia 漆俠 1987a. *Songdai jingji shi, shangce* 宋代經濟史上冊 (An economic history of the Song dynasty, volume 1). Shanghai: Shanghai renmin chubanshe.

———. 1987b. *Songdai jingji shi, xiace* 宋代經濟史下冊 (An economic history of the Song dynasty, volume 2). Shanghai: Shanghai renmin chubanshe.

Qu Chaoli 屈超立 1991. "Cong Songdai hunyin fagui yu sifa shijian kan Songdai funü de shehui diwei" 從宋代婚姻法規與司法實踐看宋代婦女的社會地位 (A look at the social position of women during the Song dynasty on the basis of Song marriage law and its enforcement). *Sichuan daxue xuebao* 53: 97–107.

———. n.d. "Songdai tiandi jiaoyi fagui ji sifa shijian" 宋代田地交易法規及司法實踐 (Laws governing the sale of land in the Song dynasty and their enforcement). Unpublished.

Ratchnevsky, Paul. 1937. *Un code des Yuan.* Paris: Librarie Ernest Leroux.

———. 1972. *Un code des Yuan.* Volume 2. Paris: Presses Universitaires de France.

———, with Françoise Aubin. 1977. *Un code des Yuan.* Volume 3, index. Paris: Presses Universitaires de France.

———. 1985. *Un code des Yuan.* Volume 4. Paris: Presses Universitaires de France.

Reinaud, Joseph Toussant. 1845. *Relations des voyages par les Arabes and les Persans dans l'Inde et à la Chine.* Paris: Imprimerie Royale.

Sauvaget, Jean. 1948. *Relation de la Chine et de l'Inde.* Paris: Association

Guillaume Budé.

Schipper, Kristofer. 1974. "The Written Memorial in Taoist Ceremonies." In *Religion and Ritual in Chinese Society*, ed. Arthur P. Wolf, pp. 309–324. Stanford: Stanford University Press.

———. 1989. "Mu-lien Plays in Taoist Liturgical Context." In *Ritual Opera, Operatic Ritual: "Mu-lien Rescues his Mother" in Chinese Popular Culture*, ed. David Johnson, 126–154. Berkeley: Chinese Popular Culture Project.

Schurmann, Franz H. 1956a. *Economic Structure of the Yüan Dynasty: Translation of Chapters 93 and 94 of the Yuan shih*. Cambridge, Mass.: Harvard University Press.

———. 1956b. "Traditional Property Concepts in China." *Far Eastern Quarterly* 15. 4: 507–516.

Scogin, Hugh T. 1990. "Between Heaven and Man: Contract and the State in Han Dynasty China." *Southern California Law Review* 63.5: 1325–1404.

———. 1994. "Civil 'Law' in Traditional China: History and Theory." In *Civil Justice in Qing and Republican China*, ed. Kathryn Bernhardt and Philip Huang, 13–41. Stanford: Stanford University Press.

Seidel, Anna. 1978. "Buying One's Way to Heaven: The Celestial Treasury in Chinese Religions." *History of Religions* 17.3–4: 419–432.

———. 1983. "Imperial Treasures and Taoist Sacraments—Taoist Roots in the Apocrypha." In *Tantric and Taoist Studies in Honour of R. A. Stein*, ed. Michel Strickmann, volume 2, 291–371. Brussels: Institut Belge des Hautes Etudes Chinoises.

———. 1987. "Traces of Han Religion in Funeral Texts Found in Tombs." In *Dōkyō to shūkyō bunka* 道教と宗教文化 (Daoism and Religious Culture), ed. Akitsuki Kan'ei 秋月觀映, 21–57. Tokyo: Hirakawa shuppansha.

———. 1989–90. "Chronicle of Taoist Studies in the West, 1950–1990." *Cahiers d'Extrême-Asie* 5: 223–347.

Shapiro, Sidney, trans. 1980. *Outlaws of the Marsh*. Beijing: Foreign Languages Press.

Sheng, Angela. 1990. "Textile Use, Technology, and Change in Rural Textile Production in Song China (960–1279)." Doctoral dissertation, University of Pennsylvania.

Shi Pingting 施萍婷 1972. "Cong yijian nubi maimai wenshu kan Tangdai de jieji yapo" 從一件奴婢買賣文書看唐代的階級壓迫 (What one document for the sale of a slave reveals about class oppression in the Tang dynasty). *Wenwu* 12: 68–71.

Shi Yikui 施一揆 1957. "Yuandai diqi" 元代地契 (Land contracts of the Yuan dynasty). *Lishi yanjiu* 9: 79–84.

Shiba Yoshinobu 斯波義信 1968. *Sōdai shōgyōshi kenkyū* 宋代商業史研究

(Commercial activities during the Song dynasty). Tokyo: Kazama shobō.

——. 1970. *Commerce and Society in Sung China*, trans. Mark Elvin. Ann Arbor: Center for Chinese Studies, University of Michigan.

Simpson, A. W. B. 1987. *A History of the Common Law of Contract: The Rise of the Action of Assumpsit*. New York: Oxford University Press.

Smith, Paul J. 1991. *Taxing Heaven's Storehouse: Horses, Bureaucrats, and the Destruction of the Sichuan Tea Industry, 1074–1224*. Cambridge, Mass.: Harvard University Press.

Stein, R. A. 1979. "Religious Taoism and Popular Religion from the Second to Seventh Centuries." In *Facets of Taoism: Essays in Chinese Religion*, ed. Anna Seidel and Holmes Welch, 53–81. New Haven: Yale University Press.

——. 1988. "Les serments des traités Sino-tibetains (8e–9e siècles)." *T'oung Pao* 74: 119–138.

Strickmann, Michel. 1979. "On the Alchemy of T'ao Hung-ching." In *Facets of Taoism: Essays in Chinese Religion*, ed. Anna Seidel and Holmes Welch, 123–192. New Haven: Yale University Press.

——. 1981. *Le taoïsme du Mao Chan: Chronique d'une révélation*. Paris: Presses Universitaires de France.

Su Bai 宿白 1957. *Baisha Songmu* 白沙宋墓 (The Song tomb at Baisha). Beijing: Wenwu chubanshe.

Tai Jingnong 臺靜農 1950. "Ji Sichuan Jiangjin xian diquan" 記四川江津縣地券 (A record of a tomb contract in Jiangjin county, Sichuan). *Dalu zazhi* 1.3: 9–10.

Takahashi Bunji 高橋文治 1989. "Kin-Genbo no kōshizu to Genkyoku" 金元墓の孝子図と元曲 (Pictures of filial children from Jin and Yuan tombs and Yuan drama). *Mimei* 8: 29–61.

——. 1991. "Sai Fukun o megutte—Gendai no byō to densetsu to bungaku" 崔府君をめぐって―元代の廟と伝説と文学 (A look at Cui Fujun: In Yuan-dynasty temples, legends, and literature). In *Tanaka Kenji hakase shōju kinen Chūgoku koten gikyoku ronshū* 田中謙二博士頌壽記念中國古典戲曲論集 (A collection of essays on Chinese classical drama in memory of Dr. Tanaka Kenji), 35–81. Tokyo: Kyūko shoyin.

Tao Xisheng 陶希聖 [1937] 1982. *Tangdai jingji shiliao congbian: di er zhong, tudi wenti* 唐代經濟史料叢編：第二種，土地問題 (A collection of materials on the economic history of the Tang dynasty: the second type, land questions). Taibei: Shihuo chubanshe.

Teiser, Stephen F. 1988. "'Having Once Died and Returned to Life': Representations of Hell in Medieval China." *Harvard Journal of Asiatic Studies* 48.2: 433–464.

——. 1993. "The Growth of Purgatory." In *Religion and Society in T'ang and*

Sung China, ed. Patricia Buckley Ebrey and Peter N. Gregory, 115–146. Honolulu: University of Hawaii Press.

ter Haar, Barend. 1992. *The White Lotus Teachings in Chinese Religious History*. New York: E. J. Brill.

———. n. d. "Images of Outsiders: The Fear of Death by Mutilation." Unpublished.

Tohi Yoshikazu 土肥義和. 1980. "Kigigun (Tō kōki·Godai·Sōsho) jidai" 歸義軍（唐後期・五代・宋初）時代 (The Returning-to-Righteousness Army in the late Tang, Five Dynasties, and Song periods). In *Tonkō kōza: Tonkō no rekishi* 敦煌講座：敦煌の歷史 (Discussing Dunhuang: The history of Dunhuang), ed. Enoki Kazuo 榎一雄, 233–296. Tokyo: Daitō shuppansha.

Turner, Karen. 1990. "Sage Kings and Laws in the Chinese and Greek Traditions." In *Heritage of China: Contemporary Perspectives on Chinese Civilization*, ed. Paul S. Ropp, 86–111. Berkeley: University of California Press.

Twitchett, Denis C. 1957–58. "The Fragment of the Tang Ordinances." *Asia Major* n.s. 6: 3–79.

———. [1963] 1970. *Financial Administration under the T'ang Dynasty*. New York: Cambridge University Press.

———. 1966. "The T'ang Market System." *Asia Major* n. s. 12: 202–248.

———. 1968. "Merchant, Trade, and Government in Late T'ang." *Asia Major* 14:3–95.

———. 1978. "The Implementation of Law in Early T'ang China." In *Il Diritto in Cina*, ed. Lionello Lanciotti, 57–84. Florence: Editore Leo S. Olschki.

———. 1979. "Hsüan-tsung (Reign 712–756)." In *The Cambridge History of China*. Volume 3, *Sui and T'ang China, 589–906, Part I*, ed. Denis C. Twitchett, 433–463. New York: Cambridge University Press.

Unger, Roberto M. 1976. *Law in Modern Society: Toward a Criticism of Social Theory*. New York: Free Press.

van der Loon, Piet. 1979. "A Taoist Collection of the Fourteenth-Century." In *Studia Sino-Mongolica Festschrift für Herbert Franke*, ed. Wolfgang Bauer, 401–405. Wiesbaden: Franz Steiner Verlag.

van Gulik, R. H., trans. 1956. *T'ang-yin-pi-shih "Parallel Cases from Under the Pear Tree": A 13th-Century Manual of Jurisprudence and Detection*. Leiden: E. J. Brill.

Vandermeersch, Léon. 1978. "Le statut des terres en Chine à l'époque des Han." In *Il Diritto in Cina*, ed. Lionello Lanciotti, 39–56. Florence: Editore Leo S. Olschki.

———. 1985. "An Enquiry in the Chinese Conception of the Law." In *The Scope of State Power in China*, ed. S. R. Schram, 3–25. London: School of African and Oriental Studies.

Waley, Arthur, trans. 1938. *The Analects of Confucius*. London: George Allen and Unwin.

———. 1960. *Ballads and Stories from Tun-huang*. London: George Allen and Unwin.

Waln, Nora. [1933] 1986. *The House of Exile: An Intimate Domestic and Social Record of Everyday Life in Pre-Revolutionary China*. New York: Penguin Books.

Wang Deyi 王德毅 1974. "Li Chunnian yu NanSong tudi jingjie" 李椿年與南宋土地經界 (Li Chunnian and the cadastral survey of the Southern Song). In *Songshi yanjiu ji* 宋史研究集 (Studies in Song history), 441–480. Taibei: Taiwan shuju.

Wang Tse-sin. 1932. *Le divorce en Chine*. Paris: Editions Domat-Montchrestien.

Wechsler, Howard J. 1979. "T'ai-tsung (Reign 626–649) the Consolidator." In *The Cambridge History of China*. Volume 3, *Sui and T'ang China, 589–906, Part I*, ed. Denis Twitchett, 188–241. New York: Cambridge University Press.

Werblowsky, R. J. Zwi. 1988. "On Mortuary Symbolism and a Chinese Hell Picture." In *Funerary Symbols and Religion: Essays Dedicated to Professor M. S. H. G. Heerma van Voss on the Occasion of His Retirement from the Chair of the History of Ancient Religions at the University of Amsterdam*, ed. J. H. Kamstra, H. Milde, and K. Wagtendock, 154–164. Kampen: J. H. Kok.

Wiens, Mi Chu. 1988. "Property Rights in High Tenancy Regions during the Ch'ing Period." Paper presented at the annual meeting of the American Association for Chinese Studies, Stanford, October 21–23.

Wilbur, C. Martin. 1943. *Slavery in China during the Former Han Dynasty*. Chicago: Field Museum of Natural History.

Xie Xigong 解希恭 1963. "Taiyuan Xiaojingyu Song, Ming mu diyici fajue ji" 太原小井峪宋明墓第一次發掘記 (The first report on excavations of Song and Ming tombs at Xiaojinggu, Taiyuan). *Kaogu* 5: 250–258.

Xinjiang Museum. Xinjiang zizhiqu bowuguan 新疆自治區博物館 1975a. *Xinjiang chutu wenwu* 新疆出土文物 (Excavated artifacts from Xinjiang). Shanghai: Wenwu chubanshe.

———, with Archeology Section of History Department, Xibei University. 1975b. "1973 nian Tulufan Asitana gumuqun fajue jianbao" 1973年吐魯番阿斯塔那古墓羣發掘簡報 (A short report on the excavation of the group of ancient tombs at Astana, Turfan, in 1973). *Wenwu* 1975.7: 8–26.

Xinjiang Uighur Autonomous District Museum, ed. 1987. *Shinkō uiguru jijiku hakubutsukan* 新疆ウイグル自治區博物館 (Xinjiang Uighur Autonomous District Museum). Tokyo: Kodansha-Bunbutsu shuppansha.

Xu Pingfang 徐苹芳. 1963. "TangSong muzang zhong de 'mingqi shensha' yu 'muyi' zhidu—du *DaHan yuanling mizang jing zhaji*" 唐宋墓葬中的 "明器神煞" 與 "墓儀" 制度—讀《大漢原陵秘葬經》札記 (The system of grave goods and funeral rituals in Tang and Song burials: Notes on reading *The great Han's secret burial manual for plains and hills*). *Kaogu* 2: 87–106.

Yamamoto Tatsuro and Ikeda On, eds. 1986. *Tun-huang and Turfan Documents Concerning Social and Economic History*. Volume 3, *Contracts: B, Plates*. Tokyo: Toyo Bunko.

———. 1987. *Tun-huang and Turfan Documents Concerning Social and Economic History*. Volume 3, *Contracts: A, Introduction and Texts*. Tokyo: Toyo Bunko.

Yang Lien-sheng 楊聯陞 1957. "Lao Qida Pu Tongshi li de yufa yuhui" 老乞大朴通事里的語法語彙 (The vocabulary and grammar of *Old China Hand* and *Interpreter Pak*). *Bulletin of the Institute of History and Philology, Academia Sinica* 29:197–208.

Yang Xianyi and Gladys Yang. 1979. *Selected Plays of Guan Hanqing*. Beijing: Foreign Languages Press.

Yang Yubin 楊育彬 1985. *Henan kaogu* 河南考古 (Henan archeology). Zhengzhou: Zhongzhou guji chubanshe.

Ye Changchi 葉昌熾 [1909] 1980. *Yushi* 語石 (Epigraphical notes). Taibei: Shangwu yinshuguan.

Yoshikawa Kōjirō 吉川幸次郎 1954. "*Gentenshō* ni mieta kanbun ritoku no buntai" 元典章に見えた漢文吏牘の文體 (The style of Chinese official documents as seen in *Yuan dianzhang*). *Tōhō gakukō* (Kyoto) 24: 367–396.

Yu, Anthony C. 1977. *The Journey to the West*. Volume 1. Chicago: University of Chicago Press.

Yü Ying-shih. 1987. " 'O Soul, Come Back!' A Study in Changing Conceptions of the Soul and Afterlife in Pre-Buddhist China." *Harvard Journal of Asiatic Studies* 47.2: 363–396.

Yuan Shishi 袁世碩 et al. 1989. *Yuanqu baike cidian* 元曲百科辭典 (Encylopedia of Yuan drama). Jinan: Shandong jiaoyu chubanshe.

Yule, Henry. [1914] 1966. *Cathay and the Way Thither, Being a Collection of Medieval Notices of China*. Volume 3. New York: Paragon Book Gallery.

Zhang Chuanxi 張傳璽 1982. "Zhongguo gudai qiyue xingshi de yuan he liu" 中國古代契約形式的源和流 (The origin and development of the format of ancient Chinese contracts). *Wenshi* 16: 21–33.

Zhang Guangda 張廣達 1988. "Tang mie Gaochangguo hou de Xizhou xingshi" 唐滅高昌國後的西州形勢 (The situation of Xizhou after the Tang destruction of the Gaochang kingdom). *Tōyō bunka* 68: 69–107.

Zhang Yincai 張蔭才 1973. "Tulufan Asitana Zuo Chongxi mu chutu de jijian Tangdai wenshu" 吐魯番阿斯塔那左憧憙墓出土的几件唐代文書 (Several Tang-dynasty documents excavated from the tomb of Zuo Chongxi in Astana, Turfan). *Wenwu* 10: 73–80.

Zhongguo Xinjiang-Tulufan huace bian weihu 中國新疆吐魯番畫冊編委會 1989. *Zhongguo Xinjiang-Tulufan (Han-Wei)* (Turfan, Xinjiang, China, in Chinese and Uighur) 中國新疆吐魯番（漢維）. Urumqi: Xinjiang renmin chubanshe.

Zhu Lei 朱雷 1983. "Dunhuang suochu 'Tang Shazhou moushi shijiabu koumahang shigu' kao" 敦煌所出〝唐沙州某市時價簿口馬行時沽〞考 (A study of "A price list for horses and slaves from a market in Shazhou" excavated at Dunhuang). In *Dunhuang Tulufan wenshu chutan* 敦煌吐魯番文書初探 (A beginning exploration of documents from Dunhuang and Turfan), 500–518. Wuhan: Wuhan daxue chubanshe.

Zurndorfer, Harriet. 1989. *Change and Continuity in Chinese Local History: The Development of Hui-chou Prefecture, 800 to 1800.* Leiden: E. J. Brill.

Index

Actors, model of, 178
Adoption, 104, 118
Aladdin (Alaoding), 137–38
Almanacs, 113, 125–28, 178, 224
Along, Widow, 68–74
Amnesty, imperial, 35, 56, 58–63, 68, 77, 223
An Lushan Rebellion, 22, 45, 57, 60
Analects, The, 24, 39
Andu, King, 240, 241n4; deputy, 240
Anhui, 195; Huizhou, contracts from, 3, 79, 109–11, 109n7, 120–21, 120n2, 224–25; Hefei, 166, 177
Animals of zodiac, 164–65, 179
Arabs, 8–9, 136–38, 222–83
Artists, 99
Asim, Ina, 149n1, 150
Astana. *See* Turfan

Backward writing, 183, 186–88
Bai Xingzhen, 6
Bao Cheng, 82, 131n6, 132, 217, 218
Barnhart, Richard, 195n3
Beheading the grass, 180–81, 183, 227; spirits, 183
Beijing, 114, 142, 179
Big Dipper, 178
Blood covenants, 7
Blue-Green Crow, 180
Bodies, intact needed for underworld, 215
Boltz, Judith, 203n4
Book of Songs, The, 24
Booklets at Dunhuang, 65–66
Books, 96, 178, 188
Bribes, 193, 211, 213
Brockman, Rosser H., 225
Brokers, 75–76, 117, 126, 144; of slaves, 52, 87–88; problems with, 78, 84–85; role of, 80–81; of women, 83, 84, 87–88; of livestock, 85–86, 142–45; of land, 86; of grain, 111; fee for, 144–45
Brushes inserted in their hats, those with, 97, 192
Buddha, 38, 53
Buddhism, 51–53, 178, 192–94
Burial objects, 160–64, 175–79, 196, 200
Buyback contracts. *See* Conditional sales

Cable, Mildred, 50
Calendar, 170
Camels, 24, 40, 62, 144
Carriers for funeral, 176–77, 182
Cave 17. *See* Library cave at Dunhuang

Celestial Emperor, 152, 156–57, 200, 239, 241n1
Celestial Heart Daoism, 203–9, 227
Celestial Masters, 154, 204
Celestial ordinances, 153–54, 157, 182
Central Asians, 115
Changan. *See* Shanxi, Xian
Chen Baiquan, 149n2
Chen Gaohua, 137n7
Chi Songzi zhangli, 190–92
Chief mourner, 176–77, 182
Chikusa Masaaki, 121, 122n3
Civil service examinations, 1, 2, 5, 102, 113; candidates for, 130, 132, 135, 162, 208, 210, 216
Clarity and Lucidity, Collected Models of, 95–109, 117, 179, 202, 222, 224, 227
Classic of Burials, The, 180
Classic of Filial Piety, The, 24
Cleaves, Francis, 138
Clerks in subterranean bureaucracy, 172
Codes for gods. *See* Spirit code
Coffins, 202
Collection of Difficult Cases, The, 89
Community head, 131–32
Concubines, 78, 82–83, 87, 206, 209; tomb contract for, 150n3, 161, 177. *See also* Women
Conditional sales, 98, 99, 118–19, 123, 125, 224
Confucius, 5, 107. See also *Analects, The*
Consideration, 6, 100
Contract, The (a play), 131–32
Contracts: use of, among families, 5, 26; dictation of, 6, 134, 136; earliest surviving, 7; *ji*-type and *zhi*-type, 8; changes between Gaochang and Tang periods, 33; differences between Turfan and Dunhuang, 47–48, 56–57; in booklets, 65; government-drafted models, 80; stamped and unstamped, 88–89, 120; almanac models, 125–29; similarities to tomb contracts, 222–23
    Type: sale of camels, 24, 40, 62; sale of land, 24–29, 32–33, 55–56, 57–58, 61–62, 109–11, 120–24, 125–27, 137–38; loans, 33–34, 36, 37, 58–59, 138–39, 140; rental of land, 36, 67; sale of slave, 50, 52, 63; sale of livestock, 54–55, 142–44; sale of house, 63, 65–66; exchange of land, 66–67; the loan of land, 69; sale of

tomb land, 81, 94, 115–16; sale of wife, 83; sale of milknurse, 84; for occupancy rights, 124; for engagement, 124–25; safeguarding of money, 130; division of property, 131–32; sale of a child, 132–33, 140–41; adoption, 134–35; rental of a house, 140
    Year: dated *367*, 24; dated *477*, 26; dated *507*, 26–27; dated *541*, 25; dated *616*, 27–28; dated *638*, 28–29, 223; dated *643*, 32; dated *659*, 32–33; dated *666*, 34–35; dated *673*, 40–41, 223; dated *815* or *827*, 55; dated *822*, 54–55; dated *835*, 57; dated *852*, 66–67; dated *900*, 58; dated *904*, 67–68; dated *909*, 61–62; dated *934*, 69; dated *984*, 81; dated *1215*, 109; dated *1234*, 115–16. *See also* Tomb contracts
Copying exercises, 61, 63, 64
Corpse clauses, 151–52
Corpus of Daoist Ritual, 219–21
Correct Rites of Celestial Heart, 203n4, 205
Courts for the dead, 3, 13, 185, 188, 189–90, 227–29; similarities to courts for the living, 167–69, 222; plaints in, 178; suits in, 185, 191–92, 195–96, 197–98, 205–6, 218, 221; Daoist views of, 190–92, 203–6, 219–21; judges of, 192, 219, 220; Buddhist views of, 192–94; summonses to, 199, 210
Courts for the living, 5; dispute over non-payment of debt in, 44; at Dunhuang, 66–74; land disputes in, 121–24; forms for plaints in, 128; similarities to courts for the dead, 222
Cremation, 150, 150n3
Cui fujun, 194–95, 218
Currency, 11, 99–100; paper, 102, 109, 133, 137, 210–14; silver, 143, 159; facsimile money, 153, 164–65, 185, 191, 198–99, 225; conversion between this-world and netherworld, 169–70
Cypress figures, 196–203, 228; texts on, dated *899*, 196–98; dated *995*, 198–200; dated *1090*, 200–202
Cypress trees, 202–3

Daodejing, 154, 178n12
Daofa huiyuan, 219–21
Daoism, 115, 154–57, 190–92, 203–6,

219–21; texts of, 173, 178, 189; purification ceremony, 207

Daomai. See Wrongful sale

Daozang. See Wrongful burial

Declarations of the Perfected, The, 156, 190

Delhi Museum, 20

Deng Yougong, 204–6

Depth of burial, 158

Deputies of Left and Right, 239, 241n3

Deputy of the grave mound, 152, 154, 170, 172, 182–83

Diamond Sutra, The, 178

Dictionary, 178

Dictionary of Official titles in Imperial China, xii

Difu. See Subterranean bureaucracy

Digging into earth, danger of, 152, 155–57, 182

Dili xinshu. See Earth Patterns

Disputes. *See* Courts for the dead; Courts for the living

Divination, 174–75

Divorce, 63–64, 90, 101–3, 117–18, 135–36; posthumous, 209

Dixia erqian dan. See Netherworld 2,000-bushel officials

Dizang, 195

Dong Jieyuan xixiang ji, 101

Dongtanglao, 129–31

Dongwanggong. See King Father of the East

Dou E's Revenge (Dou E Yuan), 135, 216–17

Dou Yi, 45

Dowry, 90, 102, 106, 208, 209–10

Drama. *See* Plays

Duke of Zhou, 180

Dunhuang, Gansu: contracts from, 3, 47–48, 139, 172; history, 50; Tibetan rule, 54–56; Chinese rule after *848*, 60

Dyer, Svetlana Rimsky-Korsakoff, 142n9

Earl of rivers, 172

Earl of the Earth, 239, 241n1

Earl of the Tomb, 153–54, 170, 172, 182, 239, 241n3

Earth banquets, 150

Earth gods, 51, 158, 218, 219, 226, 239

Earth Patterns, The New Book of, 173n11, 175, 180–84, 203, 222, 225, 226, 227

Edsen-gol, 138

Education. *See* Literacy

Efficacious Spirit Code, 203n4, 204–6

Elder Brother Lin 107, 209–10

Elder of the Eastern Studio, The, 129–31

Emissary of the First Emperor's True Law, 200

Empress of the Earth, 182

Encyclopedias. *See* Almanacs

Engagements, 100–101, 117–18, 124, 135; blocked, 207–8, 209–10

Epidemic. *See* Plague

Equal-field system, 10–11, 29–31; decline of, 45, 47

Eunuchs, 177

Families, changes in, 12, 104–7; conception of, 199, 202

Famine, 88, 111

Fang Yue, 97

Father Emperor of the Heavens, 240, 242n6

Father of the Grave Mound, 239

Finger joints, drawing, 9–10, 35, 37, 55, 56, 70, 72

First-Victory. *See* Zheng First-Victory

Five Directions, 156; Emperors of, 166, 173, 179, 182

Five Dynasties, 61

Five-colored silk, 166, 170

Five-names school, 174, 184

Food offerings for dead, 166, 172, 181, 188

Forgeries, 97–98, 111–12, 117, 118

Fortune-teller, 216

Fujian, 88, 93, 95, 179; Quanzhou, 136–38

Funeral house competition, 6

Funerals, 150–54, 159, 164–65, 176–77, 179–84, 191

Gansu, Juyan, 138; Lingtai, 25 *See also* Dunhuang

Gao Dafu, 99

Gaochang Kingdom. *See* Turfan

General Record of Graves, 184–85

Generals of underworld, 166–67, 172, 182

Gernet, Jacques, 62, 67

Glanvill, 44

Go-between, 85, 133, 137, 141. *See also* Brokers

God of the Three Chambers, 206

Goddess of the Earth, 240

Golden Splendor Sutra, 178

Graham, David Crockett, 226

Grass, 150–51, 159. *See also* Beheading the grass
Grave inventories, 38
Graves. *See* Tomb land
Grave-siting, 174–75
Guan Hanqing, 135, 216–17
Guarantor, 10, 166, 224; as signatory, 30, 50, 55, 58, 59, 67, 76, 110, 126–27, 139; obligations of, 32, 34, 40–42, 43, 44, 59, 61, 67, 68, 84; term for, 33, 127, 139; in previous life, 51; disappearance or death of, 60, 98; payment to, 125; time-limit on, 141; in tomb contracts, 166, 172
Guardians of four directions, animal, 166, 170, 241
Guilü. See Spirit code
Guiyijun. *See* Returning-to-Righteousness Army

Han Gaozu, 7
Han Yü, 42
Handwriting, analysis of, 100–101. *See also* Literacy
Haoli, 184, 241n2; Elder of, 196, 200, 239–40
Harvest altars, 240–41, 242n6
Heart Sutra, 178
Heavenly Code as Proclaimed by Nüqing, 219, 228
Heavenly Masters, 154
Heavenly section, 181, 193
Hebei, Anxi, 81; Cangzhou, 135; Jiumen, 75; Zhuoxian, 25–26, 158
Heduan, 36
Henan: Luoyang, 44, 45; Kaifeng, 82–84, 100, 131–32, 217; Suixian, 88; Tangzhou, 90; Fugou, 157; Zhengzhou, 177; Huaizhou, 208
Hetong wenzi, 131–32
Higher law, 227
Hill, Lord of, 154
Hill spirits, 182, 215–16, 219
Hong Mai, 78–79, 83, 87–88, 92, 206–15, 229
Horses, 142–44, 159
Houdelu. See Records of Great Virtue
House construction, 152
House of Exile, 226
Household registers, 68, 71, 82. *See also* Equal-field system
Houtu. *See* Mother Empress of the Earth
Hu Ying, 95, 104–5, 107
Huang Chao, 159
Huang Gan, 93–95

Huang Tingjian, 8
Huangdi. *See* Yellow Emperor
Hucker, Charles, xii
Huiyuan, 48, 51–53, 143
Huizhou. *See* Anhui
Human feeling, 104–5, 108
Hunan, 89, 95; Yongzhou, 57; Shaoyang, 97; Changsha, 109, 209; Tanzhou, 118; Mawangdui, 178n12
Hungry ghosts on land and water, rite for, 209
Huolangdan, 134–35
Hymes, Robert, 203n4

Ikeda On, xi, 4, 33, 33n4
Imperial amnesty. *See* Amnesty, imperial
Imperial Secretariat, 119
Incense, 164, 181–82
Intent of the law, 104–5
Interest, rates of, 35, 43, 59
Interpreter Pak, 140–41
Iron, 150–51, 154, 158, 159, 164, 169, 181

Jade Emperor, 203
Japan, 19, 72
Jia Gongyan, 8
Jiang Tong, 155–57
Jiangsu, 95, 178; Jiangdu, 57, 184; Yangzhou, 124, 185; Jiangyin, 178
Jiangxi, 88, 93, 95, 96, 198–200; Yuanzhou, 42, 97; Nanchang, 88, 196–98; Xingan, 93–95; Ruizhou, 118; Maoshan, 156–57, 189–92; Fenyi, 184; Poyang, 185, 210; Pengze, 200–202; Huagai Mountain, 203; Guixi, 208–9; Raozhou, 209; Fuzhou, 209, 215
Jiao, 207
Jin Dynasty. *See* Jurchens
Journey to the West, The, 140
Judge Bao. *See* Bao Cheng
Judges. *See* Courts for the dead
Jurchens, 86, 112, 134–35
Justice, concepts of, 190–92, 195, 208, 214, 218, 221, 229

Kaifeng. *See* Henan
Kanqiannu, 132–33
Karakhoja. *See* Turfan
Karma mirror, 195
King Father of the East, 158, 167, 198, 239–41
King of the Earth, 239
King of underworld, 212–13
Kleeman, Terry, 151, 154, 157n6

Korea, 19, 72, 114
Koreans, 140–45
Kozlov, Piotr, 138
Ksitigarbha, 195
Kuhn, Dieter, 149*n*1

Land contracts. *See* Contracts
Land disputes. *See* Courts for the living
Land survey, 88, 122
Land tenure, 4, 5, 158
Lao Qida. See *Old China Hand*
Laozi, 154. *See also* Lord Lao the Most
  High
Latter Jin dynasty, 61, 75
Law code for gods. *See* Spirit code
Li Dingdu, 241, 242*n*5
Li Wa, 6
Li Yuangang, 90
Liao Dynasty, 86
Library cave at Dunhuang, 48–49
Lice, 152
Lichees, 111
Lin 107, 209–10
Lin, Mr., 210–14
Lin Chong, 135–36
Literacy, 11–12, 47, 49, 56, 63, 65, 67,
  113; linked to handwriting, 67, 110,
  121, 169, 198; of women, 97, 134
Litigation, 80, 96–97, 113. *See also*
  Courts for the dead; Courts for the
  living
Liu Kezhuang, 100–103, 108
Liu Xun, 215–16
Liu Yuan Balang, 210–14
Liu Zongyuan, 57
Lord Lao the Most High, 184, 198
*Lord Lao the Most High Explains How
  to Obtain the Dao Eternally*, 178
Lord of the Earth, 239
Lord of the Hill, 154, 239
Lord of the Soil, 226
Lu Shizhong, 207–8
Lu You, 102
Luguipu. See *Roster of Dead Souls*
Luminous hall, 179–83, 227

Maidiquan. See Tomb contracts
Maine, Sir Henry, 7
Manumission, 90–91
Maoshan school, 156–57, 189–92
Market certificate, 39–40, 41–42
Marks, personal, 71, 110, 121, 129, 131,
  134, 138–39
McDermott, Joseph, 120
Meat, 192
Medieval transformation, changes of,

1–3, 10–13, 108, 111–12, 145–46
Medium. *See* Spirit medium
Meng. See Blood covenants
Middleman. *See* Go-between
Milknurses, 84, 134–35, 162
Ming baoji, 192–94
Mirror for Deciding Lawsuits, The, 89
Miyazaki Ichisada, 4
Money. *See* Currency
Moneylender Zuo, 33–39, 229
Moneywatcher, The, 132–33
Mongols, 92, 112, 113–18; language of,
  138–40
Mortuary objects. *See* Burial objects
Mother Empress of the Earth, 240–41,
  242*n*6
Mount Emei, Sichuan, 74–75
Mount Tai, 184, 206, 217; god of, 132,
  209, 219
Mountain gods. *See* Hill spirits
Mubo. *See* Earl of the Tomb
Muhammed (Mahemo), 137
Murder, 121–23, 190, 193, 194–95, 207,
  209, 215–16, 227
Mutual liability, 196
Myers, Ramon H., 225

Naming practices, 123
Needham, Joseph, 227
Neighborhood heads, 166, 172, 183
Neo-Confucianism, 95
Netherworld, contracts for. *See* Tomb
  contracts
Netherworld 2,000-bushel officials,
  153–54, 191, 239, 241*n*3
New Code of the Zhiyuan Era, The,
  228
*New Collection of Topically Ordered
  Documents, A*, 125–27
Nickerson, Peter, 155*n*5
Niida Noboru, ix, 4, 18, 69
99,999 strings, 151, 152, 159, 166–70,
  196
Ningzong, Song, 165
Nirvana Sutra, The, 51
Nüqing, 166, 173, 185, 191
Nüqing guilü, 173

Offer, making an, 6, 53
Office for Expelling the Unsanctioned,
  203, 204, 206
Officials of rites, 219
Officials of the underworld. *See*
  Subterranean bureaucracy
Old China Hand, 7, 140–45, 224
One field, two owners, 225–26

Opening Emperor, 240–41
Oral agreements, 6, 53, 85–86,
    100–101, 104, 144
Otani Kozui, 20
Ougong benmo, 121
Ouyang Xiu, A Short History of, 121
Ownership of land, 152

P3155, 67–68
P3257, 68–74
P3331, 63
P3394, 66–67
P3649, 63
P4017, 65
Paintings, 21, 99–100
Paper goods, 22, 38, 150–51; painting,
    21; coffin, 159; cloth, 181; people, 216
Paths through the fields, gods of. *See*
    Generals of underworld
Pawnshops, 22, 99, 104, 130
Penal code, 204
Penal Code of the Song, 19
Peonies, 111
Perdue, Peter, 225
Personal marks. *See* Marks, personal
*Petition Almanac of the Red Pine
    Master, The*, 190–92
Pijia, 137
Pine trees, 202–3
Pitui, 137
Plague, 170, 191, 200, 202
Plays, 3, 114, 129–36, 216–18
Pottery-making, 90, 94
Prefect Cui. *See* Cui fujun
Pu tongshi. See Interpreter Pak
Puayou, 138
Punishments for spirits, 205–6, 219,
    228

Qiao Dongbao, 200
Qing Wuzi, 180
*Qingmingji. See Clarity and Lucidity,
    Collected Models of*
Qiucheng. *See* Deputy of the grave
    mound
Qizha qingqian, 125–27
Qu family, 24, 29
Qubilai Qan, 116
Queen Mother of the West, 158, 167,
    198, 239–41
Quxieyuan. *See* Office for Expelling the
    Unsanctioned

Rao Dongtian, 203–4, 228
Rashod al-Don, 9
Reader of the prayer, 176–77, 182

Record of Burial, 174, 180
Record of the Listener, The, 78–79,
    206–15, 229. *See also* Hong Mai
Records of Great Virtue, 90, 91
*Records of Miraculous Retribution,
    The*, 192–94, 214
Red contracts. *See* Contracts, stamped
    and unstamped
Registrar Xia, 210–14, 229
Religious practitioners, 175
Remarriage, 101–3
Renzong, Ming, 185
Renzong, Song, 174
Restaurants, 169
Retribution. *See* Justice, concepts of
Returning-to-Righteousness Army, 60,
    62
Right of refusal, 58, 75, 79–80, 107–8,
    116, 118, 127, 224
Rites, Ministry of, 118–19
Rites of Zhou, The, 8
Ritual officials, 176–77, 182
River spirits, 182
*Romance of the Western Chamber,
    The*, 101
Roster of Dead Souls, 129

S1285, 63
S1473, 58–59
S1475, 54–55
S1946, 63
S2263, 174, 180
S3877, 61–62
S5280, 55
S5583, 65
S5647, 65
S5700, 65–66
S5826, 55
Sanctioned deities, 203, 219
Scribes, 28, 75, 136, 137, 140–41,
    169; knowledge of, 24, 31, 34, 39, 49,
    57; as signatory, 25, 32, 69; term for,
    33
*Secret Burial Manual for Plains and
    Hills, The Great Han's*, 180, 182n14
Secret Essentials, 203n4. *See also* Tax
    on contracts; Tomb contracts
Seidel, Anna, 153, 154
Selections from Yuan Drama, 129
Self-Admonitions, 84–86, 144, 224
Seven outs, 64, 101, 117
Shaanxi, 216
Shadow officers, 240–41
Shan Gong. *See* Lord of the Hill
Shandong, 134; Yunzhou, 207; Weixian,
    218

Shangqing gusui lingwen guilü. See
  Efficacious Spirit Code
Shangqing tianxin zhengfa. See *Correct*
  Rites of Celestial Heart
Shanxi: Xian, 45, 134, 167n9; Datong,
  115; Taiyuan, 150, 167–70; Houma,
  178
Shaozong, Tang, 42
Sheji. *See* Harvest altars
Shen Gua, 96
Sheng, 25, 63
Sheriff Wang, 213
Shilin guangji, 127–29
Shoes, paper, for the dead, 22
Shuihu zhuan. See *Water Margin*
Shuiluhui, 209
Sichuan, 87, 92; Mount Emei, 74–75;
  Yazhou, 74–75; Pengshan, 170
Slavery, 41, 42, 51–52, 90–91, 117
Sogdians, 23, 40, 45
Song dynasty, 78–79, 111–12, 151, 164
Song Xingtong. See *Penal Code of the*
  Song, 19
Sources for the study of contracts,
  1–3, 78–79
Speedy retribution, office of, 217
Spirit code, 180n13, 180–81, 185, 189,
  203–6, 219–21, 222, 227–29
Spirit Code of Nüqing, The, 173,
  180n13, 204
Spirit medium, 209, 217
Spirit money, 164, 172, 181, 183–84,
  188; use today, 167n9; specifications
  of, 193. *See also* Currency, facsimile
  money
Stage, model of, 178–79, 188
State Affairs, Department of, 118
Status to contract, 7
Statute of limitations, 98
Stein, Sir Aurel, 20
Stove gods, 219
Su Bai, 173n11
Subsoil rights, 225–26
Subterranean bureaucracy, 172–73,
  181–82
Sudatta, 53
Sudo Yoshiyuki, 4
Suggested Policies for Local
  Administration, 89
Suits, those who encourage, 90, 97,
  192. *See also* Courts for the dead;
  Courts for the living
Sulaiman, 8–9, 222–23
Surface rights, 152, 158, 225–26
Survey, Land. *See* Land survey

Taiping rebels (Han dynasty), 154
Taishang hundong chiwen Nüqing
  zhaoshu tianlü, 219
Taishang zhuguo jiumin zongzhen
  biyao. See *Secret Essentials*
Taiwan, 157
Taizong, Tang, 194, 218
Taizu, Song, 174
'Tale of Li Wa, The,' 6
Tale of Lord Yuan of Mount Lu, The,
  51
Tang Code, 17–19, 115, 204, 228; land
  sales, 30–32; failure to pay debts, 35,
  59; livestock sales, 39, 55, 85–86,
  143–44; slave sales, 41–42, 50, 51–52;
  government intervention in disputes,
  43, 223; divorce, 64, 101; eventual
  failure to enforce, 76
Tang Dynasty, 17, 18, 29, 60
Tang Lin, 192–94
Tang Quenei, 99
Tang Taizong's Entry into the
  Underworld, A Record of, 194–96
Tangerine orchard, 118–19
Tanguts, 138–40
Tao Gu, 150–51, 159
Tao Hongjing, 156, 190
Tao Mei, 167–69
Tax on contracts, 40, 75–77, 78; rate of,
  80, 86–87, 92, 118–19, 144–45; time
  limit for payment of, 86, 117;
  division between central and local
  governments, 91, 117; evasion of,
  111–12; office of, 116; procedures for
  paying, 119, 137–38, 144–45
Temple of Agriculture, 226
Ten kings, 195
Textbooks, language, 3, 114, 140–45
Textiles, 162, 179, 209–10
Thirty-eight generals, 241
Tian, Lady, 185
Tiancao. See Heavenly section
Tiandi. *See* Celestial Emperor
Tianxin. *See* Celestial Heart Daoism
Tibetan language, 67
Tibetan occupation of Dunhuang, 54
Timing of payment, 222–25
Toilet gods, 219
Tomb contracts, 3, 13, 149–51;
  materials for, 150–51, 160–64, 175,
  177; prices in, 151–53; earliest
  examples, 151–54; government
  financing of, 159, 164–65; *Earth*
  Patterns, described in, 160–73, 177,
  180–84; enforcement mechanisms of,
  172; mirror images of, 185–88; and

Tomb contracts (*contd*)
cypress figures, 196–98, 203; similarities to this-worldly contracts, 222–23; dated *82*, 153; dated *955*, 170–71; dated *1033*, 167–69; dated *1199*, 184; dated *1233*, 184; dated *1454*, 185, 225; dated *1568*, 185–88
Tomb gods, 179, 183, 184
Tomb land, 81, 89n2, 94, 108, 110, 215–16
Tulufan. *See* Turfan
Tun-huang and Turfan Documents Concerning Social and Economic History, xi–xii
Turfan, Xinjiang, 223, 229; contracts from, 3; geography, 19–20; preservation of materials at, 20, 23, 159; daily life in, 21; Gaochang Kingdom, 21–22; history of, 24, 45, 139
Turks, 38
Turtle, fresh-water, 87
Twelve harvest altars, 240

Uighurs, 139
Underworld courts. *See* Courts for the dead
Unsanctioned gods, 219

Van Gulik, R. H., 89n3
Vegetarian feasts, 192
Vernacular Chinese, 129, 142
Vietnam, 19, 72

Waley, Arthur, 49
Walls and moats, god of, 218
Waln, Nora, 226
Wang Chong, 152
Wang Chucun, 159
Wang Qi, 156
Wang Yi, 213
Wang Zhu, 174–75
Water Margin, 7, 135–36
Weaving and dyeing service, 162
Well gods, 219
Weng Fu, 103, 106–7
Wet nurses. *See* Milknurses
White contracts. *See* Contracts, stamped and unstamped
Wide-Ranging Notes from the Forest of Life, 127–29
Widow Along. *See* Along, Widow
Widows, 93, 105–7, 135
Wine, 25, 122, 124, 153, 183, 210–14, 216, 229
Witnesses, 10, 89, 94, 102, 137; as

signatories, 24, 25, 26, 56, 59, 63, 67, 68, 69, 71, 116, 126, 131–32, 137, 139–40, 141; terms for, 33; divine, 152; as signatories to tomb contracts, 153, 166, 172, 185, 225; in underworld courts, 193, 211–14
Women: use of contracts, 12; painting of, 21; as witnesses, 56, 58; as sellers, 63, 116, 137; Widow Along, 68–74; sales of, 83, 103, 217, 224; kidnapping of, 87, 90; in business, 90; literacy of, 97, 134; property rights of, 106, 132; Dou E, 135, 216–17; divorced, 136; use of tomb contracts, 160–63, 185; tomb of Buddhist, 178; use of cypress figures, 196–98, 200–202; seeking posthumous divorce, 208. *See also* Widows; Concubines; Divorce; Dowry; Engagements
Wood, 151
Wood covenant, 197
Writing. *See* Backward writing; Handwriting, analysis of; Literacy
Wronged Creditor, The, 217–18
Wrongful burial, 179, 204, 222, 227
Wrongful sale, 103–7, 137, 179, 222, 227
Wuxing, 174
Wuyi King, 196, 240, 241n4

Xia, Registrar, 210–14, 229
Xiao Hong, 25
Xie Household, 93–95
Xinjiang. *See* Turfan
Xiong family, seventeenth woman of, 196–98
Xiwangmu. *See* Queen Mother of the West
Xiyouji, 140
Xu Mi, 190, 227

Yama, 189, 194, 195
Yamamoto Tatsuro, xi, 4
Yan Shigu, 203
Yang Xi, 156, 190
Yangzhou Boy, 129–31
Yanluo, 189, 193, 218, 229
Ye Changchi, 242n5
Yellow Emperor, 152, 180–83
Yellow River, 226
Yellow Springs, 174
Yi family, eighth daughter of, 200–202
Yijianzhi. See *Record of the Listener, The*
Yingying, 101
Yingyuan zonglu, 184–85

Yitian, liangzhu, 225–26
Yiyuji. See *Collection of Difficult Cases, The*
Yu Wenbao, 92
Yuan Cai, 90, 91–92
Yuan Dianzhang. See *Yuan Institutions*
Yuan Dynasty. *See* Mongols
Yuan Haowen, 217
Yuan Institutions, 116
Yuan Zhen, 57
Yuanjia zhaizhu, 217–18
Yuanqu xuan, 129
Yulanpen Sutra, The, 38

Zangjing, 180
Zanglu, 174, 180
Zhang Daoling, 154
Zhang Jiangu, 240–41, 242n5
Zhang Shanyou, 218
Zhang Wujia, 159, 165
Zhao Gongming, 156
Zhejiang, 95; Lake Shanglin, 58; Quxian, 87; Hangzhou, 87, 98;

Chuzhou, 106; Juzhou, 106; Lishui, 122; Ningbo, 206, 210–15
Zheng First-Victory, 121–24, 127, 138, 225
Zheng Tingyu, 217–18
Zheng Xuan, 8
Zhengshen. See Sanctioned deities
Zheyu guijian. See *Mirror for Deciding Lawsuits, The*
Zhiyuan xinge, 228
Zhong Sicheng, 129
Zhou Bida, 165, 175, 188, 226
Zhou Kuan, 185
Zhou Mi, 151, 159
Zhouli. See *Rites of Zhou, The*
Zhouxian tigang. See *Suggested Policies for Local Administration*
Zhu Xi, 93
Zhuangzi, 154
Zodiac. See Animals of zodiac
Zuo Chongxi, 33–39, 229
Zuo Qiuming, 39
Zuoyi zizhen. See *Self-Admonitions*